VICTORIAN ARCHITECTURE

"We are just now far enough away from the Victorian Age to appreciate its merits as well as its faults," writes John Betjeman in his introduction. "Some of our finest architecture was built by the Victorians, and we must rid ourselves of prejudices about date and style in order to sift the good Victorian architecture from the bad jerry-building of those days."

These essays, including contributions from Nikolaus Pevsner, H. S. Goodhart-Rendel, E. M. Dodd, Paul Thompson, and several others, are a very informative and entertaining move in that direction. Some are concerned with the general aspects of Victorian architecture—homes, public buildings, and country houses. Others are about individual architects of note—Sir Joseph Paxton, who was responsible for the famous Crystal Palace . . . Philip Webb, to whom is paid the compliment that he could "consider a stable from the point of view of the horse" . . . Charles Robert Cockerell, who is called the Grand Old Man of English Architecture . . . Sir Charles Barry, designer of the Houses of Parliament . . . and C. F. A. Voysey, who "like Frank Lloyd Wright, had no respect for his self-appointed successors and not a little resentment at their claims."

"Though many of the contributors are members of the Victorian Society," wrote the

Also by Peter Ferriday
LORD GRIMTHORPE

VICTORIAN ARCHITECTURE

edited by
PETER FERRIDAY

with an introduction by
JOHN BETJEMAN

and contributions by
NIKOLAUS PEVSNER
FRANK JENKINS
H. S. GOODHART-RENDEL
E. M. DODD
PETER FLEETWOOD-HESKETH
ALEXANDRA GORDON CLARK
ROBERT FURNEAUX JORDAN
PAUL THOMPSON
DAVID COLE
CHARLES HANDLEY-READ
JOSEPH KINNARD
JOHN BRANDON-JONES
HALSEY RICARDO

J. B. LIPPINCOTT COMPANY
PHILADELPHIA & NEW YORK

1964

1. Architecture, Victorian

CONTENTS

ILLUSTRATIONS

LIST OF ILLUSTRATIONS

LIST OF ILLUSTRATIONS

LIST OF ILLUSTRATIONS

LIST OF ILLUSTRATIONS

ILLUSTRATIONS IN TEXT

Mukhang kvarta si Theresa M. Evangelista!

ACKNOWLEDGMENTS

The editor wishes to thank the executors of the late H. S. Goodhart-Rendel's estate for permission to reprint three of his essays, and Sir Harry Ricardo, F.R.S., and the *Architectural Review* for permission to reprint Halsey Ricardo's essay.

INTRODUCTION

JOHN BETJEMAN

ENGLISH ARCHITECTURE in the Victorian Age (1837–1901) made two notable contributions to the architecture of the world. One was the introduction of cast-iron and sheet glass into building construction, which resulted in the Crystal Palace and its precursor the London Coal Exchange (1846–9) and many railway termini with glass roofs and cast-iron columns. The other was the small detached house built of local material and in the style of earlier buildings in its district. It was designed for the middle classes, for artistic people of moderate income. The origin of the small house of this kind is, as Henry-Russel Hitchcock has shown, the parsonage houses built by such men as Butterfield and Street. It flowered into garden suburbs, such as that laid out by Norman Shaw among the orchards of Chiswick at Bedford Park in 1876. Many an Earthly Paradise with Morris fabrics and papers and Kate Greenaway and Walter Crane colour schemes was built elsewhere in the world after this experiment. Soon The Studio was making English domestic architecture famous with designs by Voysey and Baillie Scott of the English School and George Walton and Mackintosh of the Scottish.

We are now just far enough away from the Victorian Age to appreciate its merits as well as its faults. It is worth recalling how slow this process is, of admiring the work of our forbears. In the 'thirties we were permitted by the purists to admire civil engineering of the last century provided no architect was connected with it. The late H. S. Goodhart-Rendel, whom Sir Kenneth Clark rightly describes as 'the father of us all', was almost the only man who saw merits in Victorian buildings which were not engineering only. Few can ever appreciate the work of their immediate forbears. For instance, today no one would dare to extol neo-Georgian which has become a term of abuse among the pundits just as the word 'Victorian' was derogatory in the 1920s and '30s. Victorian was associated in the minds of architects who had been brought up in the arts and crafts tradition of the 1900s with hard and unsympathetic imitation of gothic and vulgar things like conservatories, stations and hotels which were not considered within the realms of art at all.

Even the neo-Georgian of the Ernest Newton and Reginald Blomfield school rarely appreciated any classic buildings later than Wren. Symptomatic of this is the fact that until not long before the beginning of the last war the Royal Commission on Historic Monuments admitted no buildings into its publications built later than 1714.

Because of this narrow outlook, many masterpieces later than 1714 like George Dance junior's Newgate, Rennie's Waterloo Bridge and almost all

15

the works by Sir John Soane were destroyed. Georgian terraces with stucco façades like those of Brighton, Cheltenham and Regent's Park were threatened because stucco was considered false, insincere and 'debased', a favourite word with pundits. There were even plans to rebuild Carlton House Terrace in Portland stone. The frustration of this scheme was one of the reasons for the formation of the Georgian Group, which did not come into being until 1937.

It has taken twenty years since then to form the Victorian Society, many of whose members have contributed to this book. German bombing destroyed much of our architecture in towns, but ruthless speculation in property and brutal traffic schemes by road engineers have destroyed much more. We have come to regard all our heritage from the past as expendable. But it is not. Some of our finest architecture was built by the Victorians, and we must rid ourselves of prejudices about date and style in order to sift the good Victorian architecture from the bad jerry-building of those days. The present healthy and natural reaction in favour of the Victorians has its minor disadvantages. One is over-enthusiastic and uncritical of all things Victorian provided they are highly decorated. This may be called the 'wax fruitery' approach. The other is preoccupation with styles and dates and obscure names and much writing of unreadable theses on pages spotty with foot and notes disease.

A book like this collection made by Peter Ferriday is timely and essential, for it is both a stimulant and a corrective and it puts the age into proportion. I would advise those who are fairly new to the complex subject of Victorian architecture and building (they are two separate things) to start this book in the middle by reading Mr Furneaux Jordan's essay. His inspiring account of Sir Joseph Paxton catches the atmosphere of the time when we were top nation and Britannia ruled the waves. From there you may read back to the violent medievalism of Pugin and the cool classicism of Cockerell and forward to the men who came out of the offices of Street and Sir Gilbert Scott. Thereafter, the full flavour of Goodhart-Rendel's observant wit can be enjoyed, together with the other essays on Victorian architecture in general such as those by Dr Pevsner and Frank Jenkins.

In conclusion, I would like to express the hope that Mr Ferriday will collect another book of essays on Victorian architects who are as equally deserving of appreciation as those included here. For instance, J. L. Pearson, William White, J. Brooks, Alfred Waterhouse, G. F. Bodley, G. G. Scott Jr., Comper, Temple Moore and on into the Edwardian period of Baillie Scott and George Walton, Rickards and Mewes and Davis. In the end, though, it is not just by reading books and looking at pictures but by visiting the buildings themselves, that we are able to sift the good from the bad.

VICTORIAN
PROLEGOMENA

NIKOLAUS PEVSNER

As FAR AS the knowledge and appreciation of architecture goes, the Victorian Age is the most neglected of all ages. The situation is strikingly contrary to that in literature, music and painting – perhaps for good reasons. That will have to be considered later. For the time being the fact remains that the layman, including most architects and most architectural historians, just has not got the information available to pass any worth-while judgments on Victorian architecture.

Where up to now can this information be obtained? More material in the form of buildings exists than for any century before, but less literature or at least scholarly literature. Henry-Russel Hitchcock's *Architecture: Nineteenth and Twentieth Centuries* in the Pelican History of Art was a boon. It came out less than five years ago and was the summing-up of all that the most expert of experts on the Victorian Age in architecture knows. It provides an uncountable number of facts and safe guidance on the symptoms of changes of style. Professor Hitchcock's two-volume book on *Early Victorian Architecture*, three years older, naturally went much more into detail and comes as near to the ideal textbook as one can hope to. The late H. S. Goodhart-Rendel, whose knowledge of Victorian buildings and their soi-disant and real architects was unmatched in England and whose literary style is always a delight, died without having written the book we had hoped for. His *English Architecture since the Regency*, of 1953, is nothing like as valuable and entertaining as his various short papers published in divers places. Add to this Basil Clarke's *Church Builders of the Nineteenth Century*, pioneer work of 1938, and you have all that is neither merely a popular summing-up nor deals only with special aspects of special personalities. But even there, though we have a brilliant book on railway stations (Carroll Meeks: *The Railroad Station*, 1956), we have none on other building types, and there are no twentieth-century biographies of Barry, of Scott, of Street, of Butterfield, of Burges, of Brooks, of Bodley, of Pearson. It is a disgrace.

This book will fill some gaps, but it will fill them provisionally, and as regards this introductory essay in particular, its object is solely to draw attention to four characteristics of Victorian architecture which seem to me significant and which have not perhaps so far been sufficiently ventilated. They are concerned

21

with scale, with types of buildings, with Victorian historicism, and with aesthetic quality.

Scale first. The scale of Victorian buildings is so much larger than that of any current architecture before that it leads to a devaluation of scale and ought to lead to a reconsideration of what scale does to one's judgments on architectural values in the centuries before the nineteenth. The position, stated in its simplest form, is this. You see a very large, tall, circular structure against the horizon. If you think it is a keep, of a larger diameter even than Coucy, you are thrilled and rush towards it. If you know that it is a gasometer you take no notice. The reason is, of course, that there are hundreds of gasometers on this scale all over the country, but a keep on the same scale would be unique. Neither argument has, strictly speaking, anything to do with aesthetics, with architectural values. A gasometer might have them – cooling towers for instance usually do – and most keeps have none. The case may induce us to separate in our architectural appreciation of buildings of the past aesthetics more carefully from scale, and to consider why it is that scale impresses us at the Ypres Cloth Hall or the Seville tobacco factory or indeed at Versailles. The answer is that rarity is connected with it and effort. In the nineteenth century, larger population and industrial and transport improvements reduced the effort and so rarity no longer applies. Versailles is 1,900 feet long, the mental hospital at Charenton, outside Paris (by Gilbert, 1838), about 1,350 feet. The mental hospital at Bracebridge in Lincolnshire (1849) is 780 feet long, Sir Titus Salt's mill at Saltaire (1852–3) 550 feet – as against the 440 feet of the Cloth Hall at Ypres. The Amsterdam Town Hall, now the royal palace, with its 260 by 200 feet is so much the biggest and proudest of town halls that it knocks us over. But it comes as an anticlimax to realize that the Vienna Town Hall of the 1870s, just one of quite a number of major Victorian town halls, is 450 by 360 feet in size. And so it goes on to the Pentagon at Washington, built between the wars and providing 600,000 square feet of office space and accommodation for a staff of 28,500.

It was larger populations in the first place which needed larger premises. Why populations rose so spectacularly in the nineteenth century is not easily explained. Hygiene has a good deal to do with it, i.e. a lower mortality especially among babies. The figures of the growth of towns are familiar. A very few will suffice. London 1801–1901, 959,000 to $4\frac{1}{2}$ million; New York 125,000 in 1820, $3\frac{1}{2}$ million in 1900; Paris 1800, c. 650,000, 1900 over $2\frac{1}{2}$ million; Berlin 190,000 to 1,900,000; and then Manchester 1801–41 from 102,000 to 353,000, Birmingham from 73,000 to 183,000. Leeds and Sheffield both doubled their population between 1801 and 1831. And so on. As regards the architectural scene, what matters is of course less the doubling and trebling than the actual number of people involved, the housing, the workplaces, the transport for the 3½ million new Londoners, the 2 million new Parisians, the 1¾ million new Berliners.

Laymen today would assume that here was a challenge to the architects. In the event it was not, and we shall have to see why. The housing estates needed were a novel type of job. It would be absurd to compare them with the planned West End housing of Georgian London and the crescents and squares of other towns – all designed for well-to-do lessees. Nor can they be compared with the sixteenth-century Fuggerei, or Nyboder, the naval housing of Copenhagen of the seventeenth and eighteenth centuries, or model villages of Georgian England. Once more, scale alone forbids that. Noel Park at Wood Green was designed to consist of *c*. 2,600 houses. It was designed by Rowland Plumbe (1838–1919), and who knows him? The Peabody Estates of flats for the poor were designed by Henry Alfred Darbishire (1839–1908), and who knows him? The sad fact is that the architects whom one knows, those for instance who were mentioned earlier on as in need of biographies, took no interest in working-class housing nor indeed in any of the other types of building which the Victorian Age had to create or to develop from elementary pre-Victorian origins.

Architects up to the eighteenth century were the providers of churches, of palaces and of wealthy town and country houses. To this one can add the occasional town hall, hospital, theatre, university building (the Sheldonian in Oxford, the Senate House in Cambridge), and government office building (Kent's Treasury in Whitehall, then Somerset House – and of course the Uffizi in Florence which, begun in 1550, have always been *uffizi*). Now you get houses of parliament and law courts, you get schools and universities, museums and libraries, you get hotels and jails, market halls, railway stations, exhibition buildings, and exchanges and banks and shops and stores, and factories and office buildings. In fact a survey of Victorian architecture might best be made by types of buildings rather than biographically or chronologically. Most of these types posed their special planning problems. In those that had existed before 1800 they had not been recognized. Libraries are a particularly characteristic example, where the separation of reading-rooms from stack-rooms came only in the early nineteenth century. In universities science laboratories made their claims. The Victorian hotel is fundamentally different from the Georgian inn, even if this had an assembly room attached, and so on. And in addition there are the completely new types, the market halls, railway stations and exhibition buildings, the office buildings, stores and factories. Once again it is remarkable how limited the interest of the more distinguished architects in these new types was. True, Cockerell designed banks, E. M. Barry hotels, Sir George Gilbert Scott the St Pancras hotel, Waterhouse St Paul's School, but these are the exceptions. The career of the successful architect remained devoted to churches, major private houses and major public buildings, and even there emphatically more to façades and the grander interiors than to planning.

As one looks at the plans of Victorian government offices or hospitals, one is struck time and again by the imposition of schemes of symmetry dictated by aesthetic rather than functional considerations. Now the Georgian architect had also been a provider of façades and grand interiors. So in this respect the Victorian architect did not change, although, owing to the Industrial Revolution, the Victorian Age changed drastically, and though Victorian architecture in other respects changed equally drastically,

To the layman what characterizes Victorian architecture more than anything else is the imitation of past styles. The nineteenth century is the century of historicism. Admittedly, already the Georgian style had not been in sole command. The Gothic Revival in England can now be traced back as far as James I, has quite a say in Wren's and even more Hawksmoor's *œuvres*, and became a real fashion at the time of Horace Walpole. As early as *c.* 1713 Hawksmoor had offered to All Souls College a Baroque and a Gothic façade to choose from for one and the same building.[1] Neo-Egyptian comes from Piranesi and flourished under Napoleon. Neo-Renaissance is at least heralded in Ledoux and others of his generation, i.e. round arches on detached columns and round-arched windows, and complete in Klenze's Leuchtenberg Palace at Munich in 1816 and Barry's Travellers' Club in 1829. Smirke and Pattison went neo-Norman at Eastnor about 1810 and Brancepeth about 1817. Schinkel's and Gärtner's *Rundbogenstil*, part Early Christian, part Italian Romanesque, goes back to just before 1830, there is a very little neo-Byzantine in France, when Huyot had returned from the Near East in 1817, and even the neo-Northern-Renaissance, i.e. neo-François I in France, neo-Elizabethan in England, takes us back to before Queen Victoria's accession – see the Elizabethan house in the one plate of Richard Payne Knight's *The Landscape*, of 1794, and then, in reality, for instance Mamhead in Devon, by Salvin, of 1828.

But in spite of all this, historicism remains the hall-mark of the years between the 1830s and the early twentieth century. The sequence of styles imitated in Britain is something like this: Grecian declined after 1840. Gothic turned from fancy details to archaeologically accurate details about that date, remained

[1] The same was done by Wilkins for Tree Court, Trinity College, Cambridge, in 1823, by Schinkel for the Werdersche Kirche in Berlin (classical or Early Christian with English Gothic connotations) about 1825, by Soane for the Commissioners' Churches (even including Norman) in 1825, by Pennethorne for the University of London Offices in 1866–70 and of course by Scott – willy-nilly – for the Government Offices in 1856. Scott in fact writes in his *Personal and Professional Recollections* (1879, p. 176): 'It is a pity that we have not two professorships in the Academy – the one for classic, the other for gothic architecture.'

unchallenged for churches, but also captured the public buildings – from the Houses of Parliament (designed in 1835) to Street's Law Courts, begun in 1871, Waterhouse's Manchester Town Hall begun in 1869 (and for instance Schmidt's Vienna Town Hall of 1872–83), and beyond. But after 1870 Gothic for such purposes was outmoded. It only came back in an Arts and Crafts fancy version about 1900. The *Rundbogenstil* has many varieties. Neo-Norman was specially favoured for churches in the 'forties, although very occasionally it appears earlier.[1] It disappeared soon. Waterhouse's neo-Romanesque Natural History Museum is an exception for its date. The neo-Renaissance falls into the palazzo style, carrying on from the Travellers' Club and culminating about 1860 in city buildings as well as clubs, and the villa style, picturesque and asymmetrical, and also at its height in the 1840s (Mount Felix, by Barry, at Walton-on-Thames 1835–9, Osborne, 1845–6). The Elizabethan comes to the fore in the 1830s and goes on unabated to the end of the century, though turning soberer after 1870 or 1880. Elizabethan was a permitted option, side by side with Gothic, in the competition for the Houses of Parliament. Barry, the architect of the Houses of Parliament, used it with gusto at Highclere in 1837, even if not with quite the braggadocio of Salvin at Harlaxton (Plate VI) in 1834. French Renaissance motifs, especially pavilion roofs, were added to the apparatus too (P. C. Hardwick's Paddington Hotel, 1850–2; Knowles's Grosvenor Hotel at Victoria, 1860–1; Knowles's Clapham Common North, 1860). The fashion was stimulated by the completion of the Louvre begun in 1852.

The preference for the various forms of the so-called Northern Renaissance is a sign of the way the Victorian style went, independent of what styles of the past were imitated. The tendency was towards ever richer surfaces, a higher relief, a more animated skyline. Hence the Reform Club (1837) has more depth in its façade than the Travellers' Club, and Bridgewater House (1847) (Plate XLVI) than the Reform club. Hence the same Barry, at the end, built Cliveden (1851) (Plate XLV) in imitation of the Genoese Cinquecento villa rather than the Roman palazzo. Elizabethan allowed for more drama and more licence than any of the versions of the Renaissance. When it becomes Late Victorian, fashions turn daintier and more refined. So in the field of the French Renaissance the robust Second Empire version was replaced by free versions of the style of the Loire châteaux. Aston Webb excelled in it (*see* the Birmingham Law Courts, of 1887, etc., and the Victoria and Albert Museum, of 1891, etc., and, of course, Collcutt's Imperial Institute (Plate XXXI), of 1877–93, and so on to the Russell Hotel, of 1898, and Harrods, of 1901). With this tendency towards ever busier

[1] Old Wolverton, Bucks, by Hakewill, 1815; Calverton, Bucks, 1818; Teignmouth, St Michael, by Paty, 1823; Leamington, Christ Church, by Robinson, 1825.

and livelier surfaces, within the Mediterranean styles Baroque was bound to replace Renaissance. In England it started early, but only in interiors. Benjamin Dean Wyatt is the reprobate who already indulged a Louis XV in the second half of the 1820s (Lancaster House, Londonderry House, Crockford's Club, Apsley House). But for major work the time was ripe only after the Renaissance had had its innings. On the Continent the climax is of course represented by the Paris Opera, of 1861, etc., the Brussels Law Courts, of 1866, etc., and Ludwig II's Herrenchiemsee, of 1878, etc.[1] In Britain there is less, rather details going wild than whole buildings. And where there are whole buildings, they turn to the Wren of Greenwich for inspiration, not to Italy. The Leeds Town Hall (Plate XXVIII) is the grandest early example (Cuthbert Brodrick, 1855, etc.); the climax came only at the end of the Victorian Age, with Brydon's Government Offices, of 1898, etc., and the Old Bailey (by Mountford, 1900–7). In fact the Imperial-Edwardian-Palladian-Baroque evolved straight out of it and, in a chastened version, may still today be demanded by certain die-hard clients.

This survey will have demonstrated that the order of the styles imitated is unmistakable. But none, once it had been taken up, disappeared entirely. More and more styles were available. The choice made by an architect and his client was not always dictated by what styles were specially *en vogue*, but also by another quality which we must now examine. It is not fashionable to say so today but it remains true all the same that all works of architecture, apart from appealing aesthetically, appeal associationally or evocatively. Boullée in his unpublished treatise had been the first to emphasize this fact in France,[2] Richard Payne Knight in England. The nineteenth-century architect designed his façade to evoke certain associations, and who can say that this is a less consistent and realistic attitude to design than that of functionalism. A school today is designed so that its appearance assures us of its well-functioning. Hamilton's magnificent Greek Doric High School, at Edinburgh, evokes Academe, Barry's King Edward's, at Birmingham, evoked the learning of the cloisters and the early col-

---

[1] The change of taste from Renaissance to Baroque can be illustrated by quotations from the great Jacob Burckhardt's *Cicerone*, of 1855, and then a letter (to Alioth) of 1875. In the *Cicerone* he more or less apologizes for devoting 'some attention to this mass' of material and then goes on to 'repulsive means', 'morbid life', 'rightly notorious'. In the letter of 1875 he writes: 'My respect for the Barocco is growing *from hour to hour* and I am inclined to consider it the real end and principal result of live architecture.' Twelve years later Cornelius Gurlitt brought out his *Geschichte des Barockstils in Italien*, the first comprehensive and more objective account of Italian Baroque, and in 1888 Wölfflin his *Renaissance und Barock* where at last the Baroque was appreciated as a 'vital force' and sympathetically analysed – in spite of the fact that Wölfflin was by his own nature entirely a man of the High Renaissance. The quotations are taken from J. Jahn: *Der Barock und die deutsche Kunstwissenschaft* in Omagui lui George Oprescu (Bucharest, 1962), pp. 313–15.

[2] 'Les images, que [nos édifices] offrent à nos sens, devraient exciter en nous des sentiments analogues a l'usage auquel ces édifices sont consacrés.' (H. Rosenau: *Boullée's Treatise on Architecture*, 1953, p. 26.)

leges. Banks are palazzi to remind us of the princely merchants of Florence, town halls Late Gothic to conjure up thoughts of Bruges and the Hanseatic League.

The justification of Hardwick's glorious Euston Propylaea which was no more originally than a screen in front of an insignificant station is this. The achievement of a railway from London to Birmingham was rightly considered an overwhelming achievement of the human intellect. To express this, only the style which is evocative of the greatest human achievements ever could be suitable. The attitude is romantic, but that is neither for nor against it. The case of St Pancras is different from that of Euston. Here, at a greater distance from the decades when Romantic thought and feeling were almost alive, the style selected is without evocative meaning. It is High Victorian-Franco-Early-English. Scott considered this the best of all styles, and that alone explains his choice. Different again is the case of King's Cross. Lewis Cubitt, its architect, as against Hardwick and Scott, was a minor man, and hence he was less hidebound by styles. His attitude to a railway station is functional and nothing conceals this in the façade, except perhaps the Italianate little clock turret. What was needed? A train-shed to have arrivals and departures under cover. The arching could not be done in a single span. So two wood and glass vaults were provided, and this – and nothing else – the façade tells us. Then there are *portes-cochères* needed for coaches and vans to stop, and they also were provided. That is all. The attitude is perfectly straightforward, and that to the mid-nineteenth century meant un-architectural. Fergusson in 1862 compares King's Cross unfavourably with the more ornate though basically equally functional Gare de l'Est in Paris which, he writes, 'from its higher degree of ornamentation ... becomes really an object of Architectural Art'. Lewis Cubitt's is fundamentally the same attitude as Paxton's when he designed the Crystal Palace three years before. A man had to be an outsider to be so radical in his thought and its application.

Now the iron-and-glass aspect of the nineteenth century is so well known – from Professor Giedion's *Space, Time and Architecture*, and, I presume, my own *Pioneers of Modern Design* – that I can leave it aside here. The stages are these. Iron framing had already come in with late-eighteenth-century factory buildings, iron and glass vaulting with such pieces as the dome of the Halle au blé, of 1811, façades with exposed iron framing for office buildings and warehouses before the middle of the century. But few were the architects who were ready to come to terms with iron. Nothing could be more telling than the fact that Scott wrote in 1858: 'Metallic construction is the great development of our age',[1] and

[1] *Remarks on Secular and Domestic Architecture, Present and Future* (1858), p. 109.

yet in 1868 hid with his Gothic terminal hotel the engineer Barlow's train-shed which, with its 243 feet had the widest span ever up to that time achieved by man. The most memorable exception in England is again a small architect, Bunning, whose Coal Exchange in London of 1846–9 was internally entirely of visible metallic construction; in France a greater architect, Labrouste, whose Bibliothèque St Geneviève, of 1843–50, also proudly displays its iron. Both buildings betray nothing of this externally. Bunning's exterior is of a debased Italianate kind, Labrouste's of a noble, restrained Cinquecento style. In France, thanks to Labrouste and then Viollet-le-Duc, reputable architects were readier to use iron – the Boileaus, for instance, for the rib-vaulting of churches – than in England. For Victorian England it can be stated that iron and glass remained the domain of the engineer, stone and brick the domain of the architect.

The split between engineer and architect as such is a nineteenth-century event, too. It is marked at its very beginning by the foundation in Paris, immediately after the revolution had destroyed the old system of academies, of the École Polytechnique and the École des Beaux-Arts. The splendid English suspension bridges of the early nineteenth century are by engineers, Telford and Brunel. In the eighteenth century an architect like Robert Mylne had still built bridges as well as mansions.

So much and no more of this aspect of Victorian building. If it has been brought in at all, the reason is largely a caveat. Books like Professor Giedion's and my own tend to create the impression with unwary readers that those technological and functional innovations of the nineteenth century which herald the twentieth and can be regarded as its prehistory are what matters most in Victorian architecture. But that is not so. Victorian architecture must be considered and judged by its most Victorian not its pre-twentieth-century qualities. It will not do to paint a picture of the Victorian style leaving out all the most monumental buildings and all the most successful architects.

The Victorian Style. Does a Victorian style exist at all, independent of, or visible through, the imitated styles of the past? Certain architects were worried about all that historicism, few had a consistent answer, and those who had it did not follow it. To start with a German triplet for a change, Heinrich Hübsch, a representative of the *Rundbogenstil*, actually wrote a book in 1828, called *In what style should we build?* Semper, in 1834, characterized the state of affairs like this:

> The disciple of the arts runs through the world, fills his herbarium full of tracings of all kinds and goes home a happy man, hoping cheerfully that a commission will not keep him waiting long for a Valhalla à la Parthenon,

a basilica à la Monreale, a boudoir à la Pompei, a palace à la Pitti, a Byzantine church or a bazaar in a Turkish taste.[1]

Schinkel, in his old age, at least pointed out the direction in which a solution may lie, even if only very generally and philosophically:

Why should we always only build after the style of another period? If it is meritorious to preserve the purity of every style, it is a greater merit to conceive a pure style in general terms, which is not in opposition to the best that each other period has done. Only lack of courage and a confusion of ideas ... without consideration of general conditions ... and of progress ... can restrain us from such an enterprise.[2]

Hübsch is very much more specific. He writes that the new style 'must proceed not from a past, but from the present state of nature and resources', i.e. 'from our ordinary materials, from the present point of technological experience, from the shelter needed in our climate'. Hübsch's summing-up is that the new style must 'move freely in the present' and solve the various new tasks 'in the modern way'.[3] There we get quite near to the most progressive thinkers of the mid-century in France and England. Viollet-le-Duc in the tenth of his *Entretiens*, delivered, according to Dr Middleton's unpublished research, in 1863, calls the buildings of the nineteenth century 'des corps dépourvus d'âme, restes d'une civilisation effacée', and exclaims: Is the nineteenth century condemned 'à finir sans avoir possédé une architecture, à elle? Ne transmettra-t-elle à la postérité que des pastiches?' Not, if we decide to be 'vrai selon le programme, vrai selon les procédés de construction'[4] and off he is in praise of the engineer, the locomotive and the structural use of iron. Similar voices in England, first Pugin, then Matthew Digby Wyatt and even, as we have seen, Sir George Gilbert Scott, I have collected in another place.[5]

Here I will only refer to a few little known ones, and first to Charles Fowler, specialist in Grecian market halls, who already in 1835, i.e. even before Pugin, wrote that 'the present enlightened period in architecture is woefully distinguished as having no character of its own nor any pretension beyond that of adopting the various styles that have prevailed in all ages ... ' 'Originality without the affectation of novelty' can only result from 'suitableness to the occasion and the beauties growing out of the arrangement as applied to convenience,

[1] *Vorläufige Bemerkungen über bemalte Architektur und Plastik bei den Alten* (1834), p. vii.
[2] Quoted from A. Grisebach: *Carl Friedrich Schinkel* (1924), p. 130.
[3] Quoted from W. Herrmann, *Deutsche Baukunst des 19. und 20. Jahrhunderts*, i, *Von 1770 bis 1840* (1932), pp. 62 and 64.
[4] i, 1863, pp. 449–51.
[5] *Matthew Digby Wyatt* (1950) and *High Victorian Design* (1951).

locality, etc.'[1] Then, secondly, Thomas Harris and his little known *Victorian Architecture*, published in 1860: 'The works of past ages, whether Egyptian, Greek, Roman, Italian or Gothic ... ever will charm the admiration and respect of every thoughtful mind ... ; but a reproduction of any of these ... will not suffice; no remodelling or adapting will ever do, but ... an indigenous style of our own.' And a little later he adds: 'This is an age of new creations; steam, power and electric communication are entirely new revolutionizing influences. So must it be in Architecture.'[2] And thirdly – an odd witness – Cardinal Wiseman in an equally little-known publication of 1864; *Judging from the Past and the Present*; *On the Prospects for Good Architecture in London* writes that to find the promising work one ought to go to commercial buildings and that the equivalent of Roman palaces and aqueducts are warehouses and railways.[3]

At the other extreme stood Ruskin insisting hysterically: 'A day never passes without our hearing our English architects called to be original and to invent a new style. We want a new style of architecture. It does not matter one marble splinter whether we have new or old architecture. The forms of architecture already known are good enough for us and far better than any of us.'[4] And so he recommends to one's surprise 'the Pisan Romanesque, the early Gothic of West Italy, the Venetian Gothic and the English earliest decorated'. And between the extremes remained those who were satisfied with what went on, and who praised it as eclecticism. Scott is extremely interesting on this topic. He asks:[5] 'Are we to invent a spick-and-span new style? Is it morally possible to invent such a style?' and assures us that 'if we had a distinctive style of our own day worthy of the greatness of our age', he would be ready to follow it. But he comes to the conclusion that we have not and cannot have one, because 'the peculiar characteristic of the present day ... is that we are acquainted with the history of art'. That explains historicism. And now for eclecticism. Here Scott distinguishes two kinds: the eclecticism 'of expressing the liberty of the same architect choosing for each building just what style he may fancy', which he calls 'manifestly vicious', and the other 'of borrowing from all we know of art, elements wherewith to enrich, amplify, and render more perfect that style which we have laid down as our nucleus and groundwork', which he calls 'a principle of the greatest value' – his groundwork being of course Gothic. Robert Kerr (1823–1904), later Professor of Construction at King's College, London, puts the same more succinctly in his early and entertaining *Newleafe Discourses*, published in 1846:

[1] *Architectural Magazine*, II, 1835, p. 382.
[2] See *The Architectural Review*, CXII, 1942 (D. Harbron) and CXIII, 1943 (P. F. R. Donner).
[3] Quoted from John Steegman: *Consort of Taste* (1950), p. 287.
[4] *The Seven Lamps of Architecture*, Libr. Ed. VIII, p. 258.
[5] *Remarks*, loc. cit., pp. 191, 204 and 263–66.

'Why has not our age a style of its own like all other ages? Our age, let it be answered, has a very notable style of its own, and a very novel one, the style of this miscellaneous connoisseurship of ours, of instinct superseded by learning.'[1]

These quotations must be enough. They show the confusion of nineteenth-century architects, the vain hankering after an original style of some, the satisfaction with eclecticism of others. What we, from our twentieth-century platform, have to try now is to scrutinize the qualities that make a Victorian building Victorian. Eclecticism is not the best term, historicism is more precise and more non-committal. Eclecticism is of course the term applied to the Bolognese school of painters in the seventeenth century, and what it meant then was to create a style out of the best of Raphael, Michelangelo, Correggio and the Venetians. The procedure applies to the Bolognese; it does not apply to the Victorians.

Here two attitudes exist side by side and must be distinguished. The first is to allocate different styles to different buildings – on the strength of the evocative arguments or other arguments. John Foulston in his *The Public Buildings erected in the West of England* (1838) writes of his Ker Street, Devonport, that it occurred to him that 'a happy result might be obtained ... if a series of edifices exhibiting the various features of the architectural world were erected in conjunction and skilfully grouped'.[2] So Greek Doric, Indian and Egyptian stand cheek by jowl – dead-serious and no longer as irresponsible, as Sir William Chambers had mixed Classical, Chinese and Moorish at Kew Gardens. Associationally more logical and of course not placed in proximity to each other are Barry's Houses of Parliament on the one and Travellers' Club on the other side.

The other Victorian attitude to what is called eclecticism comes closer at first sight to the Bolognese. It is to mix elements of various styles in one and the same building. The Victorians had a word for this. Ralph N. Wornum in his summing up of lessons of the exhibition of 1851 says that the design 'designated ... by the vague term Renaissance' may contain ' the classical orders and ornaments combined with conventional Byzantine scroll-work, Moorish tracery and interlacings, scrolled shields, fiddle-shapes, and strap-work, and natural imitations of animal or vegetable forms of every description', and in the end calls this style 'the Mixed Style'.[3]

---

[1] *The Newleafe Discourses*, 1846.

[2] But Foulston's conscience was not entirely clear. In the preamble, called Address, he writes: 'As objections may be made to the introduction of pure Grecian, Egyptian, or Oriental Architecture, in modern English buildings, which neither emulate the character, nor serve the purpose of a Parthenon, a Memnonium, or Indian Temple,' he begs to intimate, that he had only followed the example of other architects, in the hope that the precedents they have afforded might warrant him in making similar experiments.

[3] *The Exhibition as a Lesson in Taste* (1851).

VICTORIAN ARCHITECTURE

With these provisos, what qualities can we now at last and ultimately list as Victorian? The first is superficiality in a literal sense, i.e. a concentration of the architect on the façades at the expense of the plan which, at least in major buildings remains axial, i.e. faithful to the classical ideals of the preceding age. So a Victorian style cannot be analysed in terms of space – which is an innovation and an indictment. But in terms of façades it can, and here the principal characteristic is overcrowding, the fervent urge of applying decoration wherever possible and however much possible. This urge comes from the deep conviction that things themselves are ugly, and that, as Ruskin preached, the beauty of a building lies in its decoration, in the impression on it of 'certain characters venerable or beautiful, but otherwise unnecessary'.[1] Hence the Georgian street was regarded as rock bottom. Disraeli in *Tancred* calls it 'insipid and tame'. Scott writes of Gower Street as 'utterly intolerable' and of 'abject insipidity', because of 'prescribed flatness',[2] and even Morris agreed though with an interesting qualification, when, in cursing the present and describing its iniquity he ends by saying that 'one is beginning to think with regret of the days of Gower Street'.[3] But this qualification is Late Victorian against Scott's High Victorian, and Late Victorian will require a paragraph to itself presently.

As against this sameness the Victorian façade has variety, it avoids symmetry, if not always in the whole, at least in the detail. So the Victorian façade is a picturesque façade. It is also self-confident to a degree our architects today must envy intensely. The way Waterhouse's tower of Caius College, Cambridge, rises at the north end of King's Parade and next to the Senate House, the way the new black-and-white shop and office building of the small west-country town is invariably bigger than the originals between which it stands, Barry's tower in the middle – or rather of course not in the middle – of the Georgian Bowood, the High Victorian Gothic chancel all polished granite and thickly carved naturalistic foliage capitals, added to a modest medieval nave, the conversion by jolly Italian or Italianate decorators of the interiors of such houses as Alnwick Castle or Longleat – there are endless examples, and they can be taken from all fields of Victorian architectural activities.

Or to be precise from all but two. The two exceptions are these. First the Gothic purists, such noble architects as Bodley and Pearson, and also, as far as they are church architects, Scott and mature Street. They are of course historicists too, in so far as they express themselves in a style not created by their own age. But they do not consider themselves any longer at liberty to choose from

---

[1] *The Seven Lamps*, Libr. Ed. viii, p. 28.
[2] *Remarks on Secular and Domestic Architecture, Past and Future* (1858), pp. 171 and 174.
[3] *Collected Works*, xxiii, p. 148.

several styles. To them Gothic is almost not a choice, it is their nature, their second nature, and they use Gothic forms not only accurately but also with perfect ease and a strong sense of responsibility. They look down on the flimsiness and ignorance of the pre-archaeological Gothic, as Pugin looked down on his own beginnings and Scott on his. And they hand down the torch of Pugin to Morris, to Philip Webb, to the Arts and Crafts.

This takes us to the second and, internationally speaking, even more important exception: the so-called Domestic Revival of the Late Victorian decades, the houses by Philip Webb and Norman Shaw and those who followed them to make England the pattern country for all others in the field of elegant and snug living. Webb's Red House for William Morris, dating from as early as 1859, is the first herald; the style is complete twelve years later, when Shaw, more supple and attractive, established himself as the unchallenged leader. With him – and with Morris's designs – qualities of sensitivity, daintiness, subtly calculated picturesqueness of composition reappear, in total contrast to the robustness and coarseness of the preceding Victorian style.

What we have called the Victorian style thus turns out to be the Early and High Victorian style only, starting in fact with the drapes and colossal tobacco leaves of the Brighton Pavilion as early as 1820 and being in full blossom with the Louis XV interiors of 1825, etc. by Benjamin Dean Wyatt. That Norman Shaw, that the garden suburb of Bedford Park, which he designed, that even Voysey are Victorian, we all tend to forget, and yet, of the sixty-five years of the Queen's reign, very nearly half is the age of Morris, Shaw and the Arts and Crafts. Of course it cannot really be called an age, for Morris's and Shaw's reforms were without effect before 1900 in any but the domestic field. Official architecture, as we have seen, remained Baroque on the Continent and Wrenaissance in England, even if this Wrenaissance was handled with more circumspection and discrimination than the Mixed Renaissance and Baroque had been in the 'sixties and 'seventies.

Aesthetic judgments come in here all the time and indeed cannot be avoided. History of architecture can never be written without them. The very selection of what to present as examples of a style and what to leave out implies them, and no worth-while analysis of a paradigmatic building will be found to be without them. As a rule they will be positive, but negative criticism also forms part of the historian's responsibility, not negative by measuring a building against the criteria valid today, but against those valid in its own day, i.e. against the best of its own style.

Now if one accepts that, one will find a situation in Victorian architecture which is without precedent. The alarming fact is this. The majority of Victorian

33

buildings are aesthetically indefensible. Not all by any means, as the layman is still inclined to think, but the majority. To illustrate how this is meant it might be as well to point out a few typical buildings of about 1860. The first is by Thomas Harris whom we have met as an architect theoretically in sympathy with the glass and iron functionalism. But in these premises at No. 26 South Audley Street (Plate IV) (no longer in existence) a vague general Gothicism is combined with basket arches of the windows on the main floor, and curly iron railings. Yellow and red brick are mixed freely and in strange schemes. Above the basket arches are blank, sunk three-quarter circles, and a steep, pointed, blank arch appears between them, jarring yet without force to maintain itself. Similarly the one window in the mezzanine below, in spite of its Gothic colonnettes and the slit windows to its left and right, has not the force to make its point in competition with the plate-glass of the shop on the ground floor and the large windows and balcony on the main floor. The downfall of the exactly contemporary Overstone Hall, Northamptonshire (Plate II), by W. Milford Teulon, brother of the better-known S. S. Teulon, has the same cause; the lack of tension between windows of different sizes and shapes, most of them Jacobean, but some with slightly Gothicizing motifs, and the multitude of details in no way pulled together. The third illustration, Bassett Keeling's St George's, Campden Hill (Plate III), only one or two years later, shows something more robust, but equally disorganized, even if what was only irritating in the other two examples is here more aggressive.

Now these three examples require some provisos. Firstly it may be objected that their choice is not fair. This is true to a certain extent, and it has already been admitted that the qualities of much of the Late Victorian Domestic Revival and the qualities of certain church architecture in the same years and before, and indeed much else, ought to be treated as positively as those of other ages. Is then the seeming aesthetic breakdown of the Victorian Age no more than the result of the survival of so much more than of any age before? Hardly. More buildings, more bad buildings, but not quite so many. Rather it might be said that so individual, so frantically un-uniform a style will throw up more aesthetic failures than a staid pattern-book style like the Georgian. This is an argument of importance. It is incidentally also an argument of topical interest at the moment of Ronchamp and Chandigarh. Everyone wants to be different from everyone else, but only the few can afford to be.

Secondly, is one perhaps still blind to positive values in the perversity of Teulon and Keeling? Is it perhaps no more than an *outré* form of that 'character', of that 'reality' which the age itself appreciated in Butterfield, which Eastlake called 'somewhat stern' and, putting the words into the mouths of future judges, 'eccentric', sometimes 'ill-judged', often 'daring' but never 'commonplace or mean'.[1] No objective decision can here be reached. The judgment must remain personal, and it may be more positive with the Victorian *cognoscenti* of a younger generation than my own.

Even so, half an hour's walk along Oxford Street is enough to confirm beyond question the breakdown of aesthetic values which we are concerned with. So now the question is why it happened, and the answer, which can here only be outlined, is social changes underlying the aesthetic changes.

The first of them concerns clients. The Industrial Revolution had brought to the top a new class of clients, men whose money came from industry and commerce, self-made men without a chance of the education of the Georgian gentleman and without the leisure to acquire it later in life. Admittedly, in Britain the nobility remained clients on a large scale, too, and admittedly, merchants had been clients as early as the fourteenth and fifteenth centuries, and manufacturers – especially brewers – had been clients (and good clients) at the time of George III. Yet the change of class and of capacity to appreciate remains a fact. What this new class wanted was spectacular effects, partly because only the grosser differences were noticed, and partly because prosperity had to be hammered home with a bang.

Secondly, from another angle, historic styles could be more easily appreciated than subtleties of proportion and detail, because the one was a matter of facts which could be learned, the other a matter of sensibility. The growth of interest in history and hence of archaeological knowledge was a concomitant of the Romantic fascination with the distance in time (and also in space) anyway. More styles were available, more styles were re-used, and their recognition was a game that appealed to an age so fond of facts.

Facts, not feelings; science and technology, not the arts. To take art seriously would have been considered effeminate; the history of painting in the nineteenth century, the history which runs from Blake to the Impressionists and beyond, proves that. These painters demanded a new vision, spiritually or pictorially, and so they were left aside or ridiculed. It is an evident parallel to what happened in architecture that in painting, too, not the aesthetic values but extraneous values were sought, values appealing to the intellect. Successful painting was painting telling a story.

But which came first? The turn of the public from the artist, or the turn of the artist from the public? Whichever the answer, the nineteenth century is the century of the final break between artist and society. The break had been made earlier, with the conception of the growing Romantic Movement that the

[1] *A History of the Gothic Revival* (1872), p. 263.

artist is a high priest, not a provider of an aesthetic commodity in demand. Blake marks this moment in painting. In architecture it is marked by Ledoux and his group, designers of buildings of monstrous size for vaguely defined virtuous purposes and sometimes of shapes in demonstrative contradiction to their practical functions. The nineteenth century at its start took on the unwelcome artist and the architect building for architecture's sake. Both types became the exemplars of the century.

But whereas the artist, whether Millet or Renoir or Gauguin, stayed proudly independent and starved, refusing to produce what the prospective patrons wanted, the architect could not do so. No architect ever can. Where there is no patron, there is no building. Hence two things happened in the nineteenth century. You could either become an architect and compromise, or you could be rather an artist or an engineer. The uncompromising artist-architect only reappeared towards the end of the century. The change is marked at its most violent by the architecture of Gaudí, as uncompromising as the painting of Gauguin, and at its mildest in Norman Shaw's and his friends' *Architecture, a Profession or an Art*, which came out in 1892 and pleaded for architecture being 'on precisely the same footing as painting and sculpture'.

In the light of these social and cultural ambiguities it may now be found easier to see how the lack of unity between façade and plan in Victorian buildings came about, how the lack of unity between the theory and performance of distinguished Victorian architects – especially their plea for iron and glass and their refusal to use it – and how the prevalence of historicism and ultimately the breakdown of aesthetic values.

THE VICTORIAN
ARCHITECTURAL
PROFESSION

FRANK JENKINS

At first sight the architectural scene of Victorian times seems dominated by what has become known rather journalistically as the 'Battle of the Styles' – that championship of various forms of architectural expression, often bitter and frequently expressed in language as ebullient as the architecture itself, which poured from Pugin and Ruskin, from the *Ecclesiologist*, from Garbett and Fergusson, Lord Palmerston, the press and Parliament. But parallel with this colourful and at times exciting feud, another battle, less spectacular but equally bitter – the battle of architectural professionalism – was being waged for the acceptance of the architect, not only as an artist and technician but as a professional man, secure and respected in the Victorian social hierarchy.

At Victoria's accession the nucleus of the modern profession existed, but it was new-born and weak; at the close of her reign the concept of the architect as a figure socially and professionally equatable with the lawyer and medical practitioner was generally accepted. While Victoria's reign did not witness the actual birth of the modern profession, it saw its growing pains and its steady and at times stormy rise to maturity in the present century. It saw, as well as the establishment and acceptance of the architect as a professional man, the clarification of his duties and the formulation of organized formal training for his work.

But to appreciate fully these developments, it is first necessary to look back to the second half of the eighteenth century. By the 1780s a number of signs of architectural professionalism were already evident. The confusion which had characterized the English architectural scene forty years earlier with regard to the composition of the profession and the training and general conduct of architects, was slowly giving way to a more ordered state of affairs, still far removed from the modern situation, but nevertheless very different from that of the first half of the century. Practitioners, at least those of standing, had begun to work to something approaching a common code of conduct, and training by serving articles with an established practitioner had become accepted as the best means of preparation for a career in architecture. In addition, there was a new consciousness among architects of the dignity of their calling and of their social responsibilities, perhaps most clearly exemplified in Sir John Soane, but seen too in practitioners like Chambers and James Paine.

89

Soane – born, it should be remembered, just after the turn of the mid-eighteenth century – was very different in his outlook from architects such as Gibbs or Campbell. The latter were still within the Renaissance tradition of the artist-architect – not only in their approach to design and the organization of building work, but also in their relations with and their attitudes to their employers. Soane represents a new type – the prototype in many respects of the Victorian professional man.

As early as 1788 he defined an architect as 'the intermediate agent between the employer, whose honour and interest he is to study, and the mechanic whose right he is to defend', thus stating what was to become one of the basic tenets of architectural professionalism – the complete impartiality of the architect, and his dual and equal responsibility to both parties involved in a building contract. Although such ideology was incompatible with the then current practice of the architect himself acting as contractor, it indicated very clearly the way in which the profession was to develop.

At the same time there were signs of a growing uniformity among architects with regard to such matters as their terms of employment and fees. For instance, in the 'seventies, in a dispute with the Earl of Thanet over travelling expenses, Chambers supported his claim on the grounds that it was in accordance with the general custom of the profession, and obtained a statement from James Paine in corroboration of this. In 1794, Joseph Bonomi issued as a printed leaflet his *Terms of Employment,* which listed charges for various professional services, and these accorded with those of most of his contemporaries. Already, in 1791, the first professional association of architects, the Architects' Club, had come into being – a convivial group, including all the leading practitioners of the time, which met once a month for dinner in London at the Thatched House Tavern. Other instances illustrating the development of architectural professionalism could be cited, but perhaps the position at the close of the eighteenth century is most clearly – and simply – seen in the change from 'patron' to 'client' to describe an architect's employer, the architect, at least theoretically, no longer seeking patronage as his predecessors had done, but being himself sought after by his clients.

The reasons for these developments are not hard to find. Essentially they were reflections of the social effects of the Industrial Revolution. The landowner, who had been the English architect's mainstay in the first half of the eighteenth century, was now being joined by others – industrialists and men of commerce. New types of building were coming into being and the emergent middle class was making its voice heard in architectural matters through the medium of the building committee. Theatre shareholders, prison boards, the committees for new public buildings, all became important clients, and their influence on the development of professionalism was considerable. Dealing with an individual patron, informed of at least the rudiments of architecture and *au fait* with the latest canons of taste, was very different from working under the direction of a committee of business and professional men, possibly divided among themselves, almost certainly uninformed architecturally, and primarily concerned with financial issues. To the architect in the latter situation, the advantages of belonging to a definite professional group and of a clearly defined professional status are clear.

At the same time there were important and far-reaching changes in the building industry, as a new figure, the general contractor, began to displace the individual master-tradesman, who traditionally had held first place in the industry. By the 1830s, encouraged particularly by the tremendous opportunities afforded by speculative housing, the general contractor had assumed a dominating position. His interest in building was first and foremost financial. Essentially a business man, he employed on a permanent basis workmen in all the necessary trades, competing for building contracts with others operating in a similar way.

Thus at Victoria's accession the architecturally informed individual patron had been displaced as the prime source of employment for the architect by industrial and commercial clients, often in the collective form of a building committee; the master-tradesman had given way to the general contractor as leader of the building industry; and to meet these changed circumstances new attitudes had developed in the architect. The last found expression in the regulations of the Institute of British Architects, founded in 1834, which rigidly defined the relations of its members not only with other architects but with clients and builders.

The Institute was founded for 'facilitating the acquirement of architectural knowledge, for the promotion of the different branches of science connected with it, and for establishing a uniformity and respectability of practice in the profession'. The last aim was to become the Institute's paramount objective, and for the remainder of the century it provided firm and single-minded leadership to the developing profession.

Although in 1835 its membership amounted only to eighty-two, by the end of the century this had grown to well over fifteen hundred. Its history was one of steady expansion, marked by dogged determination, often against considerable difficulties. In 1837 it received a charter of incorporation and six years later was honoured by the presence of the Prince Consort at one of its meetings. In 1866, by Victoria's command, it became the Royal Institute of British

Architects. Its membership included most of the more eminent Victorian practitioners and its publications maintained remarkably high standards of writing and scholarship. Among the presidents were such distinguished Victorians as Professor C. R. Cockerell, Sir George Gilbert Scott, G. E. Street, and Alfred Waterhouse.

Despite this, the Institute's membership represented only a fraction of the total architectural population of the country – in 1841, only nine per cent. While members accepted a rigorous code of professional ethics, practitioners outside the Institute's ranks were at liberty to make whatever charges they liked for their services, to compete with other architects by cutting fees to secure commissions, and to indulge in profitable alliances with builders and speculators.

In the provinces there was, it is true, a number of other professional bodies, which like the R.I.B.A. were concerned with raising and standardizing the conduct of architects, but until late in the century there remained considerable confusion among the public as to the architect's duties and status as well as widespread suspicion of his professional claims. In the 'forties, Richard Brown considered it necessary to point out the difference between the architect and 'the mere builder', and as late as 1870 *The Times* referred disparagingly to the R.I.B.A. as a 'highly respectable trades union'. A decade later, an anonymous writer in the *British Quarterly Review* expressed himself in no uncertain terms on the subject of architectural professionalism:

> Modern professionalism is an organized contrivance to impress the public with the notion that 'professors', a self-constituted class, have a mysterious claim for pay immensely greater than the simple workman's wages ... A draughtsman is not born again when he is called an 'architect'; and the deluding prefix of 'profession' is a mere vulgarity, intended by that class of business agents to assert some vain superiority to trade.

Nor were the champions of professionalism helped by the general composition of the profession. While there were practitioners like the gentlemanly and learned Professor Cockerell, a travelled and erudite scholar as well as the designer of a number of important buildings, there were many more who approached nearer to Martin Chuzzlewit's master in their knowledge and capacity. The Pecksniffs of the profession provided a considerable obstacle to its progress and favour with the public, and some of the practices in which they could indulge were discussed by a writer in the *Monthly Magazine* during 1884. These were in addition to the relatively harmless ones mentioned by Dickens – of rent collection and the 'pocketing of premiums' from the unwitting parents of intending architects – and included the deception of their employers, 'either by ignorance or knavery ... by making very pretty and attractive drawings, and reporting that the expense of carrying these into execution will be about half or two-thirds of what it actually turns out to be', and that of 'exacting from the builder a commission for all works done under their direction; and, if these be refused, informing the builder that his services are no longer required.'

Furthermore, the storms of criticism which centred around almost every important architectural competition – those for the Houses of Parliament, the Royal Exchange, and the London Law Courts among them – did little to enhance the architect in the eyes of the public.

The system of selecting designs on a competitive basis, particularly for important public buildings, has much to recommend it, and it became extremely popular during the last century. Unfortunately, unless carefully controlled, architectural competitions are readily open to abuse, and so unsavoury did the position become in Victorian times that many established practitioners refrained from taking part in them. A major criticism was that they were almost invariably assessed by laymen who could, as the Competitions Committee of the Institute of British Architects reported in 1838, 'select a design without suspecting in the slightest degree that they may have been captivated by the meretricious allurements of the artist, and that they may have admitted the accessories of pictorial representation to have the weight of argument and reason'.

Canvassing by competitors was by no means unknown and in fact seems to have been the general rule. Even such a pillar of the profession as Sir George Gilbert Scott admitted that he had not been blameless in this regard in his younger days when, with his partner Moffatt, he was carrying out work for the workhouse unions. In addition, it not infrequently happened that the successful competitor was not appointed to undertake the work, which instead was handed over direct to the builder or some other architect.

This almost became the case with Liverpool's St George's Hall, for which a competition was announced in 1839. Of the seventy-five entries, that by the young H. L. Elmes was awarded the first premium. The following year another competition was held – this time for Assize Courts at Liverpool – and once more Elmes was successful. The City Council then proposed to unite the two buildings, and instructed their surveyor to prepare plans to this effect. For his refusal to do so, posterity owes him a debt, and thanks to his integrity, ultimately Elmes was asked to prepare a new scheme. Regrettably the attitude of the surveyor was an exceptional one.

Over the century, however, the position gradually improved and this provides a gauge of the growing recognition of the professional status of the architect and the increasing stability of the profession as a body. The question of competitions was one of the first to which the Institute of British Architects gave its attention, publishing in 1838 a full and forcefully-worded report. In 1872 the R.I.B.A. gave definite instructions for the conduct of competitions, recommending that the first premiums in all cases should be half per cent of the total estimated cost of the work competed for and that all the premiums should together total one per cent of the estimate; and in 1880 recommended that in all competitions at least one of the assessors should be an architect. In 1903, the Institute laid down that members who took part in competitions which did not conform to its requirements could be adjudged guilty of unprofessional conduct and expelled from its ranks. It remained for the Registration Acts of the 1930s to bring the whole profession into line on this matter.

Besides developments in the purely professional aspects of his work, the nineteenth century saw a growing complexity in the technical questions with which the architect had to contend. New types of building, new materials, increasingly involved building legislation, together with a growing emphasis on the economics of building and the dangers of a highly competitive building industry had profound effects on his methods of practice.

An instance is found in the Victorian working drawing, an infinitely more detailed document than its eighteenth-century equivalent; and another in the specification of materials and workmanship, in earlier times generally a simple description incorporated in the contract agreement itself, but now a very full and often elaborate statement. The architectural encyclopedist, Gwilt, indicated the value of the latter:

> The importance of an accurate specification or description of the materials and work to be used and performed in the execution of a building, is almost as great as the preparations of the designs for it. The frequent cost of works above the estimated sum, and its freedom from extra charges on winding up the accounts, will mainly depend on the clearness, fullness and accuracy of the specification.

The scope of contemporary practice is seen too in the growth of other professions, dealing with particular aspects of building work which had lain previously within the general province of the architect.

In 1818 the Institution of Civil Engineers had come into being, receiving its Royal Charter a decade later, and throughout the century the civil engineer, whose roots as far as this country is concerned lie in the mid-eighteenth century, was carrying out a growing volume of work. At first architects seem to have been able to hold their own in structural and technological matters, maintaining an informed interest in and contributing to developments in these areas. John Foulston, for instance, a relatively minor provincial practitioner of the Regency, produced a remarkably adventurous design in iron for the interior and roof of his Theatre Royal at Plymouth; Charles Fowler, joint honorary secretary of the Institute of British Architects on its foundation, designed a daring cast-iron structure for Hungerford Fish Market (indeed, too daring, for it subsequently collapsed) and there were many similar instances. As the century progressed, however, a gulf seems to have grown between 'structural science' and 'building art'. In 1862, W. H. Leeds admitted that 'Mathematics have, perhaps, been too much neglected by some of the Architects of this country. The consequence has been the establishment of a new branch of art whose professors are called Civil Engineers'. In the second half of the century, architects tended to regard the engineer as a dangerous rival rather than as a collaborator, and Leeds continued – 'As Art is open to all, we would not quarrel with these gentlemen ... if they would be content with practising strictly in their vocation ... it would surely not be asking too much of them to submit to the advice and correction of those who have made the art of design the principal study of their lives'.

The sort of position which a rising and self-conscious profession found distinctly embarrassing can be seen in the Brunel-Wyatt partnership at Paddington. Matthew Digby Wyatt was a distinguished architect and a respected figure in the profession, but the engineer left no doubt as to what he considered their respective roles to be. 'I am going to design in a great hurry and, I believe, to build a station after my own fancy', he wrote to Wyatt. '... It is at Paddington ... [and] almost, of necessity, becomes an engineering work, but to be honest, even if it were not, it is a branch of architecture of which I am fond, and, of course, believe myself fully competent for; but for detail of ornamentation I neither have time nor knowledge ... '

Victoria's reign saw also the emergence of another professional figure, the quantity surveyor. With the development of highly competitive 'lump-sum' tendering for building projects resulting from the rise of the general contractor, it became necessary to provide as firm as possible a basis for pricing by the competing builders. To this end the practice came about of using detailed abstracts, measured and calculated from the architect's working drawings, from which the builder could work out his tender in the knowledge that his competitors were basing their prices on the same detailed information. The bill of quantities in this form was apparently first used by Sir Robert Smirke about 1830, and initially architects prepared their own bills. Gradually, however, the practice came about of employing an independent surveyor, and by the end of the century the quantity surveyor was established in his own right as an important and necessary *aide* to the architect.

In view of the conditions of practice which these developments indicated, it is not surprising that increasing attention was given to the training of architects. Throughout Victorian times the system of articled pupilage, generally for a period of five years, remained the accepted method of training. Premiums ranged from two to five hundred pounds or more, and the environment afforded by different offices was equally varied – from the 'cold, cheerless and unvarying round of duty' in the elder Pugin's menage to the enthusiastic and friendly, even jolly, atmosphere of George Edmund Street's office, where the pupils vented their high spirits in Gregorian chant and which celebrated the major Christian festivals with office holidays. It became clear, however, that by itself the pupilage system could not provide training adequate for contemporary conditions. As early as 1831 one of the aims of the Architectural Society had been the establishment of a 'British School of Architecture, with the advantages of a Library, Museum, Professorships and Periodical Exhibitions', but this was not realized and, despite complaints of the paucity of the facilities available to architectural students in this country, particularly when compared with those in France, it was not until 1840 that a positive move was made. In that year classes commenced at King's College, London, under William Hosking, on the 'Arts of Construction in connection with Civil Engineering and Architecture' – the structural emphasis being not without significance at this date. The following year saw the appointment of T. L. Donaldson as Professor of Architecture at University College, London. Here he devised a comparatively ambitious course, under the headings of 'Architecture as an Art' and 'Architecture as a Science', intended to augment the training articled pupils received in their offices and provide them with 'a fund of knowledge which the hurry of subsequent practical life forbids their ever acquiring'. A more important event occurred in 1847 when the Architectural Association came into being, entirely through the energy and enthusiasm of a group of young men who were themselves articled pupils and thus fully aware of the difficulties and weaknesses of the system. In its early days the Association provided an excellent example of the Victorian ideal of self-help, for the students literally taught one another – by the discussion and criticism of designs which they had prepared on their own initiative.

THE VICTORIAN ARCHITECTURAL PROFESSION

By 1870 the Royal Academy, which as far as architectural training was concerned had remained virtually dormant since its foundation, was roused sufficiently to reorganize its facilities and appoint R. Phené Spiers, a product of the French École des Beaux-Arts, as Master of Architecture. Interest in training continued to grow. In 1891 the Architectural Association, now under the presidency of Leonard Stokes, set up a new course, still part-time but more ambitious and more directly related to professional needs than previous ones, and the following year saw the establishment of a full-time, three-year course at King's College, London. At the same time there was interest and action in the provinces. In 1894 a Chair of Architecture was founded at University College, Liverpool, and six years later an honours course instituted for the degree of Bachelor of Arts in Architecture. At this point a new phase opens in architectural training, but Victoria's reign saw one of the most important chapters of its history – the rise of architecture from the category of a trade to that of an academic discipline.

Developments in training, although very largely brought about to meet the needs of a profession facing unprecedented demands in practice, were also intimately related to the issue of professional status, which crystallized into the concept of a profession closed to all save those who possessed clear evidence as to their abilities. By the mid-century a number of practitioners were of the opinion that examinations should be set up in order to distinguish 'qualified' architects from others, and in 1855 a positive proposal was made by the Architectural Association that such examinations should be organized by the Institute of British Architects and a diploma, in the manner of the French Diplome d'Architect, awarded to successful candidates. Examinations on these lines were instituted on a purely voluntary basis in 1863, and in 1882 it was decided to make the successful completion of these a requirement for election as an Associate of the Institute.

The next step was to widen the field of action and work for legislation requiring statutory registration, based upon compulsory examinations, for all who wished to practise as architects. Dissatisfied with the progress made in this direction by the Institute, a new body – the Society of Architects – came into being in 1884 with registration as its expressed aim. Throughout the 'eighties and 'nineties a number of Bills were introduced in Parliament, but none reached the statute-book, due largely to the opposition of kindred professions like the civil engineers, but also to that of the R.I.B.A. which, while obviously in favour of the principle of statutory registration, felt that the time had not yet come for its application.

In its reluctance to support the aims of the Society of Architects, the Institute indicated its awareness that the profession was by no means united on this question. In fact by the 'nineties it was clearly and dramatically divided. Registration implied compulsory examinations in architecture for all who wished to practise, and while few would have argued against examination in subjects like building construction and sanitation, the question of architectural design was a very different one.

During the promotion of a registration bill in 1891 matters came to a head. Above seventy eminent signatures, a memorial protesting against attempts to make architecture a closed profession was presented to the R.I.B.A. and later published in *The Times*. As well as most of the leading architects of the day, the signatories included distinguished figures like Alma-Tadema, Burne-Jones, Walter Crane, Holman Hunt, and William Morris. In their own words, they believed that a student's 'artistic qualifications (which really make the Architect)' could not be brought 'to the test of examination, and that a diploma of architecture obtained by such means would be a fallacious distinction, equally useless as a guide to the public and misleading as an object for the efforts of the student'.

The following year the memorialists' case, expanded into a series of lively and entertaining essays, was published as *Architecture: a Profession or an Art*; but the question posed by this title was one which had confronted architects throughout Victoria's reign. While there was the *profession* of architecture, for which qualification by examination was clearly desirable, there was also the *art* of architecture. It was here that the main difficulty lay. When, for instance, in 1855 the Vice-President of the Institute of British Architects had accepted the proposal of the Architectural Association that examinations should be set up, he had done so on the understanding that they would be confined to 'practical' subjects only and would not trespass into the realm of 'design' – for at that time the problems likely to arise on a 'Gothic' student being confronted by a 'Classical' examiner were very real!

Towards the end of the century, a president of the Institute defined the architect as 'artist, constructor and man of affairs'. As we have seen, social and economic conditions had caused great emphasis to be placed on the last of these attributes and indeed had brought into being the concept of a closed profession. At the same time the architect found himself in the full flood of the Romantic movement, with its insistence on the ideas of personal genius and artistic individuality, the latter virtually equatable with artistic integrity. He was caught, to use Barrington Kaye's phrase, in the 'dilemma of artistic autonomy'; he was torn as it were between a Romantic dream and the realities of a commercial society.

THE VICTORIAN ARCHITECTURAL PROFESSION

Throughout the century the conflict is illustrated in numerous architectural drawings – superb and highly-idealized water-colour perspectives frequently possessing greater aesthetic merit than the projected buildings they represented – for which their authors were severely criticized, to the point in many instances of being accused of flagrant dishonesty. It seems likely, however, that a great many of these drawings should be regarded not so much as dishonest attempts to win the confidence of unwitting clients, but rather as the yearnings of artists – Romantic artists – frustrated by the environment in which they found themselves. While the realization of such drawings in building materials must have been a bitter disappointment to clients, the extraordinary fact remains that in many cases the Victorians came so near to achieving their dreams, that before a black mantle of soot changed the scene, Venice became so nearly reincarnate in the palazzo warehouses of Manchester, and Tennyson's Camelot, despite the heart-breaking difficulties with which Street had to contend, so close to reality in the Law Courts in the Strand.

But the dreams of the Romantic artist – or even of William Morris's honest craftsman – were transitory; ultimately the facts had to be accepted as they existed. Pugin's New Jerusalem could not be reconciled with Victorian material progress, with the mill and the mine, the factory and the counting-house. It was the age of the 'man of affairs', and eventually the champions of the closed profession won the day. Statutory registration of architects was finally achieved by the Act of 1938; nevertheless it was a Victorian victory rather than a twentieth-century one, for by the end of Victoria's reign the battle was virtually over.

THE
COUNTRY HOUSE
OF THE 19th CENTURY

H. S. GOODHART-RENDEL

[A lecture given at the Victoria and Albert Museum in 1957.]

IN THIS discourse it is my business to pick up the story of British house-building at the close of the eighteenth century and bring it a century forward. Obviously, this can only be done rather summarily. As a whole, nineteenth-century building, like nineteenth-century expenditure of all kinds, was in England extraordinarily profuse, and whereas in the preceding century it had been unlikely that a country house of any importance should not be delineated and described in one or other of the publications illustrating such places, count-less Victorian houses of great size and pretension are unknown to any public outside their neighbourhood, and have probably always been so. In recent years the mortality among them, consequent upon social change, has been enormous, and yet, in spite of that, very many remain, not probably in residential use but serving rather awkwardly some other purpose. The only thing that makes it possible in any degree to give a fair account of so overwhelming a mass of mater-ial is the tendency that material itself has to fall into distinct categories not too large to handle. First of all there are the houses built by the landowning class, whether as replacements of family homes grown decrepit or as new establish-ments for cadet branches; there are palatial houses built for undeniable grandees; there are solid, capacious houses that scorn all architectural niceties. All these have their predecessors in the eighteenth century, and, although changed in character, do not within that character exhibit any very bewildering variety. There appear, however, as the nineteenth century goes on, very numerous houses of a kind that in the eighteenth century were comparatively rare, houses of great cost and display built by what in a country neighbourhood would be called 'new people', people who had acquired land because its ownership was the accepted badge of respectability, but who had no hope of making a park out of it for several lifetimes, and whose often enormous houses probably needed in their own eyes no other setting than what they would call 'handsome grounds'. The story is told of one of these, built as early as the reign of William IV, that its owner, unrecognized by the society in which he was proposing to settle, instruc-ted his architect to provide in his great new house one more room of every separ-ate kind that could be found in the recently rebuilt ducal mansion in the next parish. No doubt a story of this kind is certain to be invented even when it is not true, but it would not be invented if experience did not make it credible. In the eighteenth century there had not very often been a Duke of Chandos to make display ridiculous; display was a natural prerogative of established wealth and position. The new wealth of the nineteenth century, however, could command it without any support or privilege, with the consequence that after a period of indecisive competition magnificence was handed over disdainfully by the aristocracy to any one who thought it worth paying for. In a survey of country house building during the Whig domination of the eighteenth century, we shall note great general conformity with accepted models, and much evidence of a general reluctance to innovation. Towards the end of the period imitation castles certainly became immoderately popular as an alternative to Burlingtonian mansions, but they were still mostly very much like one another, and not at all like any real remains of antiquity.

In the early years of our nineteenth century, castles grew rankly and were of a wilder kind than had been of late. Mansions planned formally and trimmed regularly with battlements and towers continued to be designed by Sir Robert Smirke and academic architects of his school, but the fashion for them was rapidly giving way to that of buildings irregularly grouped, and in which the conveniences of modern life were coaxed into shapes that externally suggested no rule beyond an imaginary one of military necessity. John Nash's castles were much admired specimens of this new type, although it must always have been obvious that the irregularity of their grouping was contrived to secure picturesque effect rather than security in defence. Belvoir Castle by James Wyatt, far grander than anything undertaken by Nash, shows the type in its most splendid realization, crowning its hill with an impressive composition of various buildings each arranged to set the other one off scenically, but equally puzzling to any garrison that might attempt to hold it under siege. A later and very remarkable example, Penrhyn Castle, finished only when Queen Victoria was already on the throne, does display the semblance of a dominating keep, and is perhaps the least improbable example of the hybrid style that we have. Sir Jeffrey Wyatville's enormous works at Windsor Castle conform essentially to the same standards, and certainly led the taste of nobility in their direction. Wyatville's fantasy here, however, is raised upon a foundation of historic reality. His blocks of buildings all either elaborate or replace works that owed their position to original necessity, before the notion had been born that the picturesque could be the object of conscious human endeavour.

Penrhyn Castle is the masterpiece of its architect, Thomas Hopper, who was a discovery of George IV when he was Prince Regent. Windsor owes nothing to him, but his enormously elaborate Gothic conservatory in the old Carlton House was a nine-days' wonder in its time. As is rightly said in the dictionary of the

Architectural Publication Society, Hopper's authorship of this work led him 'to so large a practice among the nobility and gentry that probably no other architect of about the same period, except James Wyatt, was so extensively employed in erecting new and in enlarging old mansions'. When Penrhyn was finishing, however, the sun of Hopper's day was setting, and younger men with more novel ideas were pushing to take his place. When in the year 1847 John Guest, the great ironmaster, with his ambitious and brilliant wife, Lady Charlotte, prepared to rebuild Canford, in Dorset (Plate IX), the house they had just bought from Lord de Mauley, Hopper was the architect they sent for, partly perhaps because Guest's ironworks had not been far from Penrhyn. We read in Lady Charlotte's diary that later in the year, 'We find it will be impossible to go on with Hopper. He has not the slightest taste in Gothic decoration.' And, a month later, that Guest called upon Barry and arranged for him to undertake finishing Canford. 'We have quite given up Hopper whose taste is hopeless. Barry talks of coming down in Christmas week.' Canford was never a castle. Barry, in the end, gave it a great tower, but that was Barry's way. Until it became a public school its name always was Canford Manor, and, when the Guests bought it, it was a typical specimen of what the nineteenth century believed to be 'manorial Gothic', built between 1826 and 1836 from the designs of Edward Blore. Much of Blore's work remains by the side of Barry's enormous extensions, although touched up in parts to bring it into harmony with them. Blore's discoverer was Sir Walter Scott, who made him his first architect at Abbotsford, and his skill in drawing Gothic design recommended him for much employment in cathedrals, churches, and the older universities. When Barry was beginning to pull about his work at Canford, Blore, deserting Gothic of necessity, was giving to Buckingham Palace the front to the Mall that I and my contemporaries can remember, and the loss of which I am not afraid to say that I regret. Although the number of country houses recorded as having been designed by him is not very large, what there are are so perfectly typical of early nineteenth-century manorial architecture in England that to see one of them is to see all the essentials of its class. Steep roofs and chimneys of the kind loosely called Tudor are to this manorial style what towers and battlements are to the castellated. Windows are mullioned and transomed, for the most part without any arched heads or tracery, gables are frequent both in main roofs and in dormers, and oriel windows with flat roofs are sparingly introduced. Pointed arches mostly probably of the flattened, Tudor variety will occur in doorways, but nowhere else. Should the architect's fancy lead him away from Tudor into Elizabethan or Jacobean, the arches will be round and the gable parapets may possibly take curvilinear forms. The walls will be faced with stonework or with brickwork, the architectural dressings being of stone in either case. This verbal description may sound very little different from what would be a verbal description of a stone house of the sixteenth century in the Cotswolds, or of a brick house of the same date in Berkshire or Hampshire. What then is it that gives the undeniable different look to the Victorian manor, when we compare it with the model it goes so far in imitating? Most obvious at first may seem the colour and texture of the materials, architects of a century or more ago not having learnt that any tint or surface could be allowed to vary any more than was absolutely unavoidable from strict uniformity. Such a superficial distinction, however, does not really tell us much. You can take an old manor house and denaturalize it by roofing it with machine-made tiles, or very thin and even slates, by replacing its hand-wrought stonework by stone machine-dressed with the aid of carborundum, by putting a single plate of glass into every light of its mullioned and transomed windows, but its new Victorian skin will not make it Victorian. Victorianism resides not in the skin but in the bones. Compared with the old house the newer one, both as a whole and in its details, looks too tall, too pulled up, too restricted, too pinched. Everything from the mass of the building in general to its skimpy, Tudorish chimneys in particular seems to have grown up rankly without any opportunity for amplitude. Now of this, if it be a leading fault in the first would-be revivals of our manorial architecture, we can find an easy explanation in the conventions of the style to which manorial architecture had given way. In Georgian houses of any importance, sitting-rooms were at least fifteen feet high, and a room measuring only ten or eleven feet from the floor would have been regarded as fit only for servants. Casement windows would have been regarded as barely fit even for them, but they had lingered on in basements and attics with an effect that might there have been tolerated, although certainly not condoned.

In England it was held to be incontrovertible that the great benefit to mankind, the sliding sash-window, had thrown back all other forms of window into a barbaric past, and its upright shape, not only convenient but required by all post-Renaissance styles of architecture, was regarded so much as normal that nobody felt it to be an injustice that any window broader than usual should incur a double window tax. No doubt neither of these reasons for the pinching and upstretching of traditional proportions was a compelling one, but they seem to have been quite forceful enough to keep Blore and his contemporaries from any re-creation of manorial Gothic that could be permanently acceptable.

To illustrate what I have just been saying I have not found available any illustration of an appropriate example by Blore, but will borrow one from the earlier work of an architect with whom much of this lecture will be concerned.

Anthony Salvin's house called Scotney Castle, in Kent (Plate VII) wonderfully experienced for the work of a young man, does, nevertheless, show its pre-Victorian date by a slight primness and attenuation foreign to the true nature of its adopted style.

Worsley Hall was Blore's largest house, and, I think, justifies the place I am according to him here – that of a competent practitioner in a kind of building not logical or consistent enough to be considered a style in its own right. When Nicholas Hawksmoor modified Gothic forms to serve new purposes, his originality had made those forms his own. I doubt if Blore ever did anything original in his life. He could draw old Gothic buildings very accurately as well as very prettily, and he had early learnt the habits and customs of the nobility and gentry sufficiently well to be able to plan very adroitly for their convenience. When Regency or early Victorian convenience could not be made very easily to accord with the traditional practice of manorial architecture, he spent no sleepless nights searching for a new adjustment. He just built the houses his employer wanted, making them as manorial as circumstances would allow. I do not myself consider that the conventional castellated, or the conventional manorial trapping of the early-nineteenth-century houses are necessarily less pleasing than the Adamish or Regency-style trappings against which the newer fashions were in revolt. This is really to say that I think on the whole the century's house-building did not begin very well; exceptional houses were exceptionally good, but in a general account such as this there is no place for exceptions. To find house-building pulling its weight in amassing architectural riches proportionately with the amassing of other kinds of riches for which the nineteenth century was so conspicuous, we must skip over the century's first three decades and plunge into the great days of the young Barry and the young Salvin.

Of these two, Barry, with the recent success of his two Italianizing club-houses in Pall Mall to his credit, not to mention his victory in the competition for the new Houses of Parliament, has been regarded by historians as far the more important, I think only because the information about him and his works has been more readily accessible to the general public than that about those of a man who did not need, who indeed positively eschewed publicity. In England, not as in France, the domestic architects in whom the aristocracy had chiefly placed its confidence had not often been members of the Royal Academy, nor in the habit of regularly sending their drawings to exhibitions or allowing them to be published in the press. Salvin and Devey exhibited at the Royal Academy only in their early youth; William Burn, I think, never, and yet even in the shortest balanced account of the nineteenth-century vicissitudes of great houses, the mention of no other names would be as inescapable as that of theirs. Charles

Barry, on the other hand, moved always in the public eye. His delight in splendour whenever it could be obtained, and when it could not, in showiness of the most uninhibited kind made him the perfect servant of grandees whose grandeur industrial wealth had suddenly reinforced, and the palaces he concocted for a few patrons of this kind have been commonly accredited with an influence that they were, in fact, not numerous enough to exert.

The Duke of Sutherland, who loved to spend his great riches upon building, gave Barry three tremendous opportunities: the remodelling of Stafford House (now called Lancaster House), certainly the most important house in London after Buckingham Palace; the rebuilding of Cliveden (Plate XLV) as a vast Italian palace towering over spectacular terraces, on one of the most beautiful reaches of the Thames; and the rebuilding of Trentham Hall in Staffordshire, a house still larger, again with architectural gardens of vast extent and elaboration. A fourth great undertaking for the same patron was Dunrobin Castle, in Scotland, but here Barry's control was not complete, his designs were carried out none too faithfully by Scottish agents. At Stafford House and at Trentham Hall there was architecture anterior in date to Barry's that had to be accommodated and retained, but at Cliveden the house as it stands may be regarded as entirely Barry's own. Its peculiar characteristic, the monotony of its façades, deliberately chosen in order to enhance the majestic length and height of the great block whose surface they are, is one I have never seen imitated by any of Barry's contemporaries; nor do I think that the now destroyed Trentham Hall offered anything which an architectural historian could establish as the certain source of anything else. Barry's only positive innovation in domestic architecture, whether of town or country, was his substitution of an Italian repertoire of forms for the Grecian repertoire commonly used in his youth, even by him himself. This change of architectural idiom, this adoption of a style not familiar in this country, brought fame to the modest little building in which it was first apparent, the Travellers' Club in Pall Mall, begun in the year 1829. Very soon after Barry displayed his new style again in the only entirely new country house besides Cliveden that I believe him ever to have designed. This is the elegant villa, now the Xavierian Seminary, above Queen's Park in Brighton, a villa intended to act as a decoy duck to other villa builders who somehow or other never arrived. Both the Travellers' Club and the Xavierian Seminary showed that Barry during his student years in Italy memorized wisely the forms he could import with profit into his own country, and, one suspects, took hints from the adjacent country of France as to how they could be re-used most acceptably. The Duke of Sutherland did everything for Barry that a rich patron could. Barry, by his independence in style, and also by his very great skill in planning, did a great deal for himself. Nevertheless, his fame as a domestic architect rests more than anything else upon his ingenuity in dolling up ordinary old houses into an appearance of extraordinary magnificence. The best-known example of this is his conversion of the modest Georgian Highclere House into the far from modest neo-Elizabethan Highclere Castle; here, by facing the external walls and adding a tower at each corner, he at least doubled the apparent size of the house without materially adding to its extent. At Harewood House, in Yorkshire, additions in height to the side wings, together with the provision of high balustrades hiding the roofs and supporting a multitude of urns, have given an air of palatial grandeur to what before Barry's attack upon it was a great house of a perfectly ordinary kind. Transformations, ambitious and always extremely ingenious, were affected by Barry at Walton House, in Surrey, at Gawthorpe Hall, in Lancashire, and, although by little else than the addition of wings, to Duncombe Park, in Yorkshire. In every case the transformed edifice qualifies for the epithet 'striking', which would certainly not have been applied to it before transformation. I am afraid, however, that we must admit that in every case also, what I may perhaps call the authenticity of the old work has vanished. The natural material of the original design has been picked apart and reapplied to uses for which it was not originally designed, and in what has been added little attention has been paid to quality of detail so long as a general rich appearance has been obtained.

Of all great architects, which description, I think, must undoubtedly include Sir Charles Barry, because of his never-failing skill in planning, and his large grasp of large conceptions, I know of none so insensitive as he to excellence in the character of ornament. His opinion is well known that ornament could not be excessive provided it were good in itself, and in his greatest work, the Houses of Parliament, the assistance of ornamental designers of the first order – Pugin not being the only one of them – guaranteed him against any defect of quality. Possibly Lady Charlotte Guest was justified in supposing that elsewhere than at Westminster his taste in Gothic decoration would prove superior to that of the discarded Thomas Hopper. Nevertheless, I do not believe that in Barry's London clubs, or in all the domestic decoration he carried out for his grand employers from the date of Walton House to that of Bridgewater House, there is any carved, modelled or painted detail approaching the excellence of what would have been required by his contemporaries, Cockerell or Pennethorne, in England, or their many equal confrères in France. Barry's architectural gardens, with which he surrounded his houses whenever he could, were consistent with them in magnificence, and also in the ingenious, but rather questionable means by which that magnificence was achieved. Bedding-out plants, mostly having little beauty beyond that of strong and uniform colour when seen in the mass, were combined with red and blue gravels, with yellow sand, and sometimes, I believe, even with broken glass, in enormous carpet-like mosaics of extremely elaborate design. Statues and vases punctuated profusely the general pattern, and elaborate balustrades edged the great terraces and flights of steps into which all sloping ground was converted. Seen from the windows of the house it surrounds, a garden by Barry is impressive, but as a place for walking in it has little to recommend it. Very little in Barry's work, either horticultural or architectural, repays close inspection. The imposing garden vases may prove to be not in bronze but in cast iron coarsely painted, the noble and symmetrical aloes which appear to be growing in them may also be actually made of painted metal, the fountains and balustrades may be formed not out of marble or of stone but rather of scabby Roman cement, and the Italian details throughout, although very often recognizably copied from some Classical model, are sadly likely to be coarse and perfunctory in execution. In Barry's Travellers' Club, he had introduced into England a small *cortile*, or architectural courtyard; and in the Reform Club, which he built afterwards, as well as in Bridgewater House, which he built later still, he made a central top-lighted hall out of such a *cortile* by throwing a glass roof across it. I shall have something to say later of the central top-lighted hall's being one of the most distinct introductions into country house-building made by the Victorian Age, and it may perhaps have been Barry's example that brought them into favour.

If I gladly turn from the splendid, but as I think rather vulgar, achievements of Sir Charles Barry to the works of his more widely-esteemed rival, Anthony Salvin (I speak, of course, of their comparative fame in domestic architecture only), it may seem that I am swallowing camels in Harlaxton Manor and Moreby Hall, which makes it rather ridiculous that Cliveden and Highclere should disagree with me. Harlaxton (Plate VI) certainly was built with an intention of display as great as that which underlay the building of Cliveden, and from a man much less secure socially than the Duke of Sutherland. Moreby Hall was also, I believe, the production of a family not having deep roots in its neighbourhood. Yet these two vast and sumptuous houses – I judge of Moreby only by its contemporary repute, never having seen it myself – were completed by Anthony Salvin before his thirtieth birthday, and entrenched him in far securer favour with great landowners than was ever won by the conjurer, Barry. Anthony Salvin was a Salvin of Croxdale, a family whose arms Fox-Davies acknowledges as dating from the reign of King Edward I. His father was a general in the army, and his first cousin and brother-in-law, William Andrews Nesfield, an amateur painter who became the most successful landscape gardener of his time, had begun life as a soldier serving under Wellington in the Peninsula. Although the first two of his great houses have nothing military in their architecture, Salvin's deep interest when a boy in the remains of Brancepeth Castle is supposed to have decided him in his vocation, and he did not have to be in practice for many years before he established his position as the highest authority in the kingdom on medieval castles and their fortification. If we wish to find him building his conceptions as an architect as freely as he might have painted his conceptions as a painter, we must look at the astonishing Peckforton Castle (Plate VIII), which he built for the romantically-minded Mr John (afterwards Lord) Tollemache, the Anglo-Saxon names of whose progeny form so notable a curiosity of the English peerage. Here, crowning a hill over against the other hill on which stand the conspicuous remains of the great Beeston Castle, Salvin was able to build a new castle, which was not, if I may make play with adverbs, 'as though' but 'as'. Here is no Victorian mansion with wine-cellars, barred like dungeons, with a drawbridge that won't draw up giving access to a handsome front door decorated at the top with a portcullis that won't come down, with convenient water-closets in turrets lighted by arrow slits, and with a frowning keep at the top of which are the servants' bedrooms. Here, on the contrary, is a seemingly medieval castle, pictorially quite wonderful, in which, if every part is not put precisely to the use which its form suggests, any incongruity is completely concealed from the spectator.

Anthony Salvin's most important work is usually supposed to be his reconstitution of the Duke of Northumberland's tremendous castle at Alnwick: where although he was obliged by his patron to confine his control over the interior decorations to the supervision merely of work done in the Renaissance style by Signor Canina, on the outside he was unreservedly given his fling. Yet nowhere at Alnwick nor even in such work as he did at Windsor is the purity and severity of his taste displayed as it is at Peckforton, and if only the building of such a place in the nineteenth century could be regarded as a reasonable proceeding, and not a romantic whim, it would be by Peckforton that one would wish Salvin's powers to be judged. During the fifty odd years between the date of Salvin's first important house and his last, Lord Leconfield's very dignified mansion in Chesterfield Gardens, which the older among us may well remember, his architectural production was very large, and his reputation unrivalled with the English ruling class, although little realized by the press and the general public.

When he died in the year 1881, his nephew, William Eden Nesfield, supplied *The Builder* with a list of his uncle's works, the length of which must have astonished the readers of that journal. Mingled with the names of castles and famous houses are the names of not a few churches, none of which, I am afraid, is among the happier of his productions. At the very beginning of the Tractarian Revival, Salvin was the chosen architect of the Cambridge Camden Society, restoring at its behest the round church at Cambridge, designing for Alexander Beresford Hope the alterations he paid for in the Master's Lodge at Trinity College, proposing a rebuilding of St Peter's Church, and making drawings for a church to be built at Alexandria. He was the architect young Beresford Hope and his friends were most likely to have heard of at home. Indeed, his was the church at Kilndown, next to Bedgebury Park, the house Beresford Hope's stepfather, Marshall Beresford, had bought when he married his mother, when Alexander was twelve years old. Younger architects of the true Tractarian faith soon showed the young members of the Cambridge Camden Society that Salvin would never do, and although in their eyes his chief defect was probably in strict churchmanship, I am afraid that aesthetic grievances against him would have been well founded. In church architecture Salvin's striking powers of composition and of massive grandeur found little scope. That he could design beautiful, and in its way, original Gothic detail can be seen in the richer parts of his castellated architecture, such as a staircase to the Waterloo Gallery at Windsor Castle, but, for some reason or other, in Salvin's churches there is little detail beyond stereotype, and an only too frequent awkwardness of proportion. In short, the preferred architect of English aristocracy, this man who thought as his employers thought, and designed for them as they would have designed for themselves, if they had had the necessary professional skill, was no exceptionally gifted artist. When visiting any of the great houses that are left to us, one can ask 'What did Salvin do here?' knowing that the answer is very unlikely to be 'Nothing'. Having learnt, however, what was his work one feels in no hurry to look at it. It may, no doubt, be grandly fantastical as at Harlaxton; solemnly impressive as at Peckforton; proudly reticent like the neo-Classical entrance-hall and porch that he added to the back of Petworth House; but it may also, even in so grand an undertaking as Thoresby, built regardless of expense in the very heart of the Dukeries, be merely good, amiable opportunism, mere courteous conformity with the taste of the time. To any informed historian of architecture, Salvin's work and influence must in its age have almost unique significance, but to any fastidious critic he cannot appear always as a friend. There is no evidence that he regarded himself either as a dedicated artist or as one likely to amuse, or be amused, by those whose art was their life. He seems to have been a most attractive man, honourably and unpretentiously exploiting the talents that secured his livelihood without pretending to anything more. His knowledge was great of ancient and modern fortification, and where in a work of his a military flavour was justified, we may expect designing both expressive and powerful without disappointment. When considering Salvin's non-military work it is wise to keep one's expectations in check. It might perhaps be said that his most valuable contribution to nineteenth-century English architecture, viewed historically, was the steadying moderation of his practice, which the high station of most of his employers led many to accept, who might otherwise have preferred extravagance. Among architects of the eighteenth century the same could be said of James Paine and of John Carr.

What Anthony Salvin was in England William Burn was in Scotland, and more. As an artist not more but less, no doubt, but almost without a rival as the architect in whom, when domestic building was afoot, the great families would put their trust. Not only did he never exhibit publicly, but he never allowed any design that he had made to be illustrated in the press, and when he died in the year 1870 many readers of his obituary notices may never have heard of him before. When, a year or two ago, a large collection of his drawings and notes came before the Library Committee of the Royal Institute of British Architects, with a view to the selection from it of what the Library would wish to retain, there was a sad contrast between the amount of what was available and the amount of what could be desired. All Burn's house designing, however, without as far as I know any exception, supports the reputation to which he owed his exceptionally large practice, that of being adroit and judicious beyond all rivalry in planning for domestic convenience. Beside his innumerable works in his native country, he built large houses in England and in Ireland; the best-known English one being the Duke of Buccleuch's Montague House, in Whitehall Gardens, which has lately disappeared to make room for the new Government buildings there. This, although not standing in the country, was quite typical enough to be fairly cited as representing the general style of Burn's domestic architecture. It was of simple and regular external form, with a simple and convenient plan that co-existed with, rather than gave rise to, the simple and conventional architecture of the exterior. High roofs gave this a French flavour; in the English country-side the flavour would probably have been Elizabethan, in Scotland almost certainly Scottish Baronial.

Burn had been a pupil of Sir Robert Smirke, and, I am afraid, seems to have been afflicted by some of his master's artistic debility. When quite young he had given Edinburgh a conspicuous ornament in the Episcopal Church of St John at the west end of Princes Street, a pretty piece of conventional Late Gothic, and in one or two neo-Classical houses that were probably early works of his Regency virtues survive. Burn's chief interest for us, however, must be in the extent and success of his employment, and in the direction he gave in house planning away from the grandeur and the Romantic picturesque towards modesty and good sense.

In the almost impossibly concise survey I am attempting of English country-house architecture during the nineteenth century, William Burn must appear not only in his own right as the chosen designer of those in power, but in the context of the story to which it is quite time that we should turn our attention – the story of the domestic architecture provided for those whose power was still in the forging, for the newly rich who wished to bring their families into the country, and hoped some day to enrol them in the County. Into William Burn's office came Norman Shaw, there to meet William Eden Nesfield, whose engagement with Burn in preference to one with his uncle, Anthony Salvin, I am at loss to explain. It was from William Burn's office, in the year 1853, that Nesfield did in the end, move into Salvin's office, taking Norman Shaw with him. Nine years afterwards in 1862, when Shaw, never very long in one place, had passed through the office of George Edmund Street with great artistic profit to himself, he recaptured Nesfield and set out with him on the enormous architectural adventure that resulted in the emancipation of British domestic architecture from its aristocratic domination.

Nesfield soon proved an unsuitable partner, leaving Shaw and building on his own account some houses of remarkably idiosyncratic design. Of these Cloverley Hall, in Shropshire (Plate XV), follows approximately what we shall shortly see to have been the initiative of George Devey, but with internal details of unusual and peculiar charm. Kinmel Park (Plate XXII), on the other hand, a house built of stone of two colours in a style more usually associated with brick, reflects seignorial airs from across the Channel. This house is as strange and *sui generis* as Boughton or Petworth were in another age. It is recorded here as a beautiful rarity, having had few if any imitators.

While the unchallenged paymasters of Hopper, of Burn, of Blore, of Salvin, and of Barry were still calling the tune, the less grand architects of less grand folk danced obediently in the set measures. Most rich newcomers to country life had enough sense to refrain from building competitive castles, but few, if any wished their new houses to be in aggressive variance with what was considered appropriate by the hereditary lords of the soil. In the first two-thirds of the nineteenth century there were built in England a great many houses, by new arrivals in their neighbourhood, in which types of design were established that are reasonably independent of tradition and authority. Some keep Victorian novelty at a distance, continuing the tradition of James Wyatt, in a rather sketchy and irresolute way: others – and these were the pick of their period – cultivated the fruitful notion of a top-lighted central hall, whose-ever that might have been, and achieved new compactness of plan very favourable to early experiments in central heating, of which the only practical disadvantage was the insufficient privacy of the bedrooms, approached from galleries overhanging the hall below.

The redoubtable Sir Edmund Beckett, afterwards Lord Grimthorpe, who in his own estimation knew so much more about architecture than those who had made it their profession, sums up in his work *A Book on Building* the recommendation that procured so great a popularity for this type of plan. 'All other possible plans,' he states, 'have none of the advantage of compactness which you may get from a house with rooms all round a hall lighted by a lantern from the top.' It cannot, he thinks, be charged with wasting room in the upper floor, as 'the only wasted space is the area of the well contained within the stairs and gallery, since there must be passages of some kind to the rooms, and a gallery may save a second wall to form that passage: so that unless the hall is very large it does not follow that this is a wasteful plan as to either space or cost of building in a moderately large house, and it is certainly a very convenient one if the rooms are judiciously arranged round the hall, as it gives people the smallest possible distances to travel like an army moving upon inside lines as they call it.' All of us can probably remember many houses, neo-Classical and neo-Gothic of this type, which, if the large skylight did not leak, was generally approved until the strange Edwardian fashion came in of sitting not in one's sitting-rooms but in the hall outside them. A central hall in Edwardian times, with a stream of housemaids issuing with slop-pails from the bedrooms after breakfast on to a gallery in full view from below, left much to be desired as a sitting-room, however invitingly it might be furnished with sofas, screens, palm trees, and perhaps a grand piano. For this and for other reasons that we need not now discuss, the beginning of the present century found the central hall obsolete. An example of it at its best is the house Leonardslee, begun in 1853 from the designs of Thomas Leverton Donaldson. Donaldson was an authority upon the architecture of Classical antiquity, and in the central hall of this house used columns and pilasters of yellow scagliola, the Order of the lower storey being that of the Erectheum and that of the Choragic monument of Lysicrates. The exterior of the house is not neo-Grecian but neo-Italian, suiting well the beautiful local stone of which the walls are built – a stone in which Grecian mouldings designed for marble would have been quite unrealizable. Houses of the size and kind of Leonardslee, houses not pretending to be stately but displaying modest sumptuousness of an age that set great store by solidity, durability, and comfort, and was well able to pay for them – such houses arose in great numbers all over England during the first sixty years of the last century, and, although comprising few masterpieces of architecture, form an essential part of the visible England that we love and venerate. For architecture more intense, more adventurous we must look not at them nor always at the grand works of palace- and of castle-builders, but at the smaller works, more often parsonages and schoolhouses than anything else, in which Augustus Pugin's compound of medieval sentiment and constructional rationalism bore fruit in a new form of domestic architecture in which England was not to follow but to lead. Pugin had little if any direct influence upon the country-house building of his time; he built for a few enthusiasts whom none but fellow-enthusiasts would wish to imitate. Pugin's principles, however, his 'True Principles', as he was not afraid to call them in the title of his best-known book, put the whole of English domestic architecture since before the Renaissance in the wrong. It was wrong to give a regular external shape to a building irregularly divided internally, and this had been the governing ambition of Renaissance architecture from its early days until its defeat by Romanticism. It is wrong to impose upon a building an irregular shape designed primarily to produce a picturesque effect, and the advisability of doing this had been the chief article in the Romantic creed. Pugin's 'True Principles' were so nearly akin to the doctrine that has since been labelled 'functionalism' that we need not pause here to consider the trifling matters in which they differ from it. His prejudices in favour of medieval ways in life and thought led him as an architect to the use of a medieval language of form, but never does the language shape the notion, always the notion the language; and Pugin's notion of a building was that building's essential nature. It may even be said that he held the architect's function to be that of inducing a building to design itself with his careful but never forcible guidance.

While the years between 1800 and 1860 were still near enough for their architecture to be regarded as merely old-fashioned, and devoid of merit, it was usual to say that a complete reform of the art was brought about by the labours chiefly of Philip Webb, of Norman Shaw, and of Ernest George, and that these three men, with others like them but less known, recaptured long-forgotten artistic virtues and owed nothing in theory or in practice to the earlier Victorian architects whom they succeeded. We now see that the facts are not nearly as simple as that – that the house that Philip Webb built for William Morris (Plate XCI), once supposed to be a primary source, can be traced as flowing from the simplified Gothic used by Webb's master, George Edmund Street, in the rectory houses and schools, that the so-called 'Queen Anne' flavour supposed to be Norman Shaw's most original introduction had been anticipated by some early Victorians long before his day, and that what seemed unusual in Sir Ernest George's design was simply transported from the streets and canals of Flanders. Nevertheless, the simplifications in Street's work which Philip Webb made his *point de départ* had been produced by working on the principles of Pugin, and with Webb the

Puginic principle of allowing a house to design itself was extended into allowing materials and handicraft a great deal of say in the uses to which they were put. Shaw and George, on the other hand, were more inclined to keep materials and handicraft in servitude, and themselves were most likely, being extremely expert draughtsmen, to be controlled by the pencil and the brush. Ernest George's pretty little pictures of what he and his employers hoped that their houses would look like were famous in their day, and, although a great deal of his fame has evaporated now that we have the actual houses to judge him by, he did for a time occupy a position almost analagous with that of Hopper, Burn, Blore, or Salvin in the importance and social influence of clientele. Norman Shaw, an artist of far more durable reputation, built great houses for industrialists and shipowners, and smaller houses for artists and artistic amateurs, in which domestic agreeableness and convenience of a detailed kind seldom attempted before were reconciled with external appearances more like improvisations than the deliberate compositions, whether formal or picturesque, that had hitherto been expected of architecture. It was not Norman Shaw, however, who was the first to disappoint deliberately that expectation, it was George Devey who in the year 1856 began for Sir Walter James the remarkable recasting of Betteshanger House (Plate XIII), near Dover. What the original house, then twenty-seven years old, was like I do not know, but its recast form according to a drawing of it by Devey's biographer, Mr Walter Godfrey, is astonishing for its date. It is mature Devey, almost as mature as the later house, Goldings, in Hertfordshire (Plate XVIII), which I have chosen as my first Devey exhibit. Comparison of it with such a house as at Stoke Rochford shows not only what I have ventured to call a difference between improvisation and composition, but also the rejection by Devey of any obligation to mark his architecture decisively as being of its own time. William Burn when designing Stoke Rochford obviously intended to build not an Elizabethan mansion but a Victorian mansion in the Elizabethan style. George Devey at Betteshanger would obviously not have been offended if the house were mistaken for a real Jacobean one, and he was supposed merely to have restored and adapted it. In the *Dictionary of National Biography*, a notice of Devey, one of the three most influential domestic architects in England of the nineteenth century, consists of only fifteen lines. He was 'principally known', its writer remarks, 'by the successful manner in which he added to and altered many of the English mansions. Among these may be mentioned those of the Duke of Argyll, Lord Granville, Lord Rosebery, Lord Wolverton, Lord Revelstoke, Lord Kenmare, and others. He died at Hastings in November 1896.' Anyone at all familiar with the larger country houses of England will know the measure of this understatement. To know those houses is to become extremely familiar with the signs of Devey's authorship, with those little personal peculiarities in mouldings, in materials, and in ornament, which he allowed to mingle with his most faithful and sympathetic adoption of the architectural flavour suggested in each work by its occasion. At Melbury House, in Dorset, he built at the end of a gallery added by Anthony Salvin a large towering wing in the local Gothic style, which groups with the old house most successfully. At Sudbury Hall, in Derbyshire, he built an almost detached wing of pavilion form that carries on to perfection the architectural peculiarity of the old house without degrading it by any exact imitation. Of his houses altogether new, the design of St Albans Court, near Nonington, in Kent, has always seemed to me one of the most agreeable. Adderley Hall, in Shropshire, and Longwood, in Hampshire, near Winchester are also of great repute, and I much regret my never having had the opportunity of seeing them.

Devey's first ambition had been to be a painter in water-colours, and he had worked in that medium under the instruction of John Sell Cotman. We first hear of him as an architect in the year 1851, when he was thirty-one years old, and working for Lord de L'Isle at Penshurst, not only on the house and garden, but also on building new cottages, which, as Mr Godfrey has written, have since 'been repeatedly photographed as actual buildings of Elizabethan times, and they are in every way worthy of this unconscious compliment'. That it may be doubted whether this altogether is a compliment indicates, I think, the only disparagement that could be made of Devey's achievement as a whole. Salvin's and Burn's houses are intended to proclaim architecturally a standard of convenience of which Elizabethans knew nothing, and the houses Norman Shaw built, whether for plutocrats or for his artist friends, show a deliberate heightening and emphasizing of picturesque qualities that when they have been possessed by old buildings had arrived only by happy accident. Devey never wished either to sophisticate or to dramatize the forms that he re-used so lovingly; consequently, there are in his vast output, as there are in ancient architecture, dull buildings as well as interesting ones, failures in proportion as well as successes. Looking back on his work, what impresses one chiefly in it is its perfect adaptation to the needs and tastes of those who paid for it, and there is abundant record of the strength of the reciprocal friendship that sprang up between him and his employers. One of these recorded his affection for him and admiration of his talents by fixing upon a wall of the house they had altered together a bronze bas-relief portrait of the architect with a touching inscription in Latin beneath it. I remember being told by the widow of another, a man of whom architectural tastes would not have been predicted, that she had never seen her husband happier than when expecting Devey as their sole guest for a Saturday-to-Monday of planning.

Devey died before I was born, but Sir Ernest George was still fully in practice when I began to look about me at contemporary architecture. I was not encouraged to admire his work by those whose opinion I then allowed to guide mine, and it may be that I absorbed a prejudice against it that still distorts my view. George's professional success during a long career was very great, and one certainly found his name well known among the people who would have employed Devey or Salvin, but would, if they had heard of them, have regarded Philip Webb as fantastic and Norman Shaw as catering more suitably for *nouveaux riches*. The admirable notice of his life in the *Dictionary of National Biography*, written by Mr Darcy Braddell, tells us that George's clientele ' ... was drawn from the most highly placed and the richest in the land. Young men scrambled to get into the office of "George and Peto", which soon began to be known all over the kingdom as a fashionable training ground.' Among those who got in were Sir Edwin Lutyens, Sir Herbert Baker, and Sir Guy Dawber. Alas, soon after the year 1906 (to quote again from Mr Braddell) 'the Liberal party came into power and the democratic legislation with which it heralded its advent meant the ruin of this side of George's practice.' The day of this particular kind of building with which this discourse is concerned had passed. What little lingered for a while was mostly entrusted to Sir Edwin Lutyens.

Sir Ernest George was certainly a very skilful draughtsman, making line sketches washed in sepia that seemed to portray delightful old houses, the ancient character so well established in silhouette and massing that the eye took for granted a similar character in architectural detail and texture of materials, even though actually there was only the vaguest indication of what those would be. The charm of these sketches became legendary, although rival architects might disagreeably suggest that the task of providing their happily-imagined exteriors with convenient and constructible plans for every floor would often cause a good deal of trouble in the master's office. The trouble of getting them built in appropriately pretty materials seems also to have often proved to much for the George executive, although in this respect his office was less remiss than Norman Shaw's. Shiplake Court (Plate XVII), on the Thames, a house of only modest size, has always seemed to me one of George's most pleasant productions, pleasantly planned, pleasantly massed, and pleasant in external colour and texture.

Comparison of this or of any other of George's houses with a house by Philip Webb would contrast a low aim with a high one; but might sometimes award to the lower ambition a nearer degree of attainment. Personally I feel that in Webb's laboriously sincere designs one constantly sees what he means, but not so constantly finds it clearly expressed. In any case, his houses are so few and only so indirectly influential that despite their intrinsic interest we cannot let them delay us now.

Before this discourse can be ended there is, I think, an inescapable obligation which also, I hope, will be found a pleasure; that of inspecting illustrations of characteristic houses designed by the scenic magician, Norman Shaw. The first I have chosen is a view of the entrance front of Cragside, built on a rocky slope in Northumberland for the successful engineer, Lord Armstrong. This seems to me one of the most dramatic compositions in all architecture, and is certainly one in which Shaw's idiosyncrasy is most completely displayed. His other large Northumberland house called Chesters, designed long after Cragside, shows no diminution in vigour, but, in my opinion, a lamentable coarsening of sense – one could guess from it that he was soon going to design the Piccadilly Hotel. The third is what I believe to be Shaw's only mansion built for a territorial grandee – Bryanston, in Dorset (Plate XIX), replacing a house by Wyatt, and now used as a school. It seems to me difficult to imagine its ever having been a private house – its palatial character (as also, for the matter of that, the character of the smaller Chesters) is so much more municipal than domestic – but, despite discords in scale, its architecture is powerful and less vulgar than Barry's display-pieces, to which in some respects it forms a latter-day parallel.

Mr Braddell's opinion that it was democratic legislation that killed Sir Ernest George's aristocratic practice, with the passing of power to the Liberals, might very well have been enlarged by me into a peroration of a discourse that I fear may already have become too long. I would not use it, however, because, although it has been my aim to tell the true rather than the usually accredited history of English house-building, I should have committed an absurdity in excluding from my survey the remarkable designs of Norman Shaw.

Of a great many other things I now regret the exclusion – of the handful of great houses designed for reckless owners by Samuel Teulon, of the less alarming but depressingly tamer mansions by Messrs Wyatt and Brandon, of the excellent and distinguished contributions of Henry Clutton and of the extraordinarily complete Victorian Gothic of Waterhouse's Eaton Hall (Plate XVI).

But about all these we can learn as much as we choose elsewhere in the accounts of what has generally been supposed to be the main course of country-house architecture in England. My purpose has been to chart where the main course really flowed, ignoring as tributary much that has often been regarded as of the parent flood. I have hoped to supply a footnote to history over which perhaps too confident history may stumble. The dismissal of George Devey in that paragraph in the *Dictionary of National Biography* is not the sort of thing that should occur again.

THE
VICTORIAN HOME

H. S. GOODHART-RENDEL

[A lecture given at the Geffrye Museum in 1948.]

An art historian must never forget that for distances less than one hundred years his critical vision is likely to be out of focus. The outlines of early Victorian achievement are just beginning to clear, and those who, like myself, have long felt tenderly towards the period must be no less prepared to review it than must those who have made it the theme of mockery. So, with strong predilections for it, I feel bound to confess its loss of Regency virtues and its lack of strong compensating merits. Great artists worked in its idiom and produced some great art, but the idiom in itself was too confused and lawless to have the power of keeping mediocre artists within the bounds of respectability. And, as in all periods of swollen production, mediocre artists were in the majority. The old ideas of neatness and of fashion were broken, fragments of them flying all over the place in the form of shininess, novelty, and cheap ostentation. The idea of comfort too often was misdirected into the pursuit of elaboration and futile ingenuity. And, above all, sentimentality, which in Regency days at its worst was merely silly, became a force that at its very best could only be excused as infantile.

The level of craftsmanship was still high; the new machinery, clanking and whirring night and day, had not yet been taught to scamp its work for its owner's profit. A countless number of new consumers was fed every moment with articles for which it had both the desire and the money to pay. The desire for them was constantly whetted by an increase in the articles themselves, not of usefulness but of ornament. Now, nothing is more natural to man than a love of ornament, and nothing can lead him better towards the mental and moral improvement that comes with the power of aesthetic discrimination. But, if the ornament be aesthetically worthless it will lead him nowhere, and very likely in the end make him sick. Unfortunately in the rush of mid-Victorian money-making the traditional principles of ornamentation had been mislaid and nobody knew quite where to find them. The race of learned and noble patrons was extinct; the Regency fashionables had been exiled by outraged, and possibly envious, Virtue; the Royal Academy was concentrating its energies upon painting narrative pictures for the masses, and there was really nobody but Prince Albert to turn to.

This virtuous and benevolent man was as sure as a serious German could be that all ornament was desirable that could confer upon the deserving lower orders a sense of prosperity and if possible convey to them a moral message. The noblest beauty was that which while ministering to material well-being also brought refinement to the mind. High art would do this most effectively, by 'high art' being understood that which included representations of the human figure. Mere floral ornament, however, was not to be despised, and if a cast-iron doorscraper could not always display Tritons and nereids, it could always at least be garlanded with ferns and convolvulus. The Prince's great exhibition in Hyde Park has been too often described for any description of it to be necessary here. The only jarring note in its concert of profuse naturalistic ornament was the Medieval Court, containing church furniture arranged by Pugin; and in this court were contained the exhibits that of everything shown in the huge building were, perhaps, the most significant aesthetically.

In one kind of furniture, in one kind of decoration, and above all in one kind of architecture both ecclesiastical and domestic, there had been at work throughout the 1840s a new influence of the greatest importance. At first sight it appeared, as genuine artistic reforms generally do appear, to be essentially reactionary. It appeared, indeed, as a revival of medieval design and craftsmanship, as a rejection of most of what was being loudly trumpeted as modern improvement, as a plunge – perhaps – from rational daylight into monkish obscurity. It was, in fact, an attempt at the recovery of first principles in arts in which principles of any kind had almost faded from view. In its application to ecclesiastical uses the movement acquired its greatest momentum, its warmest adherence and its most deeply suspected reputation. It was regarded by the many as a manifesto of Puseyism, as in much of its production it certainly was. But in parsonages and schoolhouses, and occasionally in houses having no ecclesiastical connection whatever, it was breaking new architectural ground, or at any rate turning up ground that had long lain fallow. It was indeed, to requote and adapt James Malton's words, 'perpetuating on Principle what had lately been the effect of Chance'.

The 'old English mansions' that were being built by rich Early Victorians were often Gothic enough in the forms of their details, but the adaptation of these details to modern shapes and masses was guided solely by their architects' preconceptions of the picturesque. To Pugin, father of the new movement, the contrived picturesque was anathema. It was certain, in one way or another, to violate his 'two great rules for design: 1st that there should be no features about a building which are not necessary for convenience, construction, or propriety; 2nd, that all ornament should consist of enrichment of the essential construction of the building'.

Houses built by Pugin and his disciples are therefore easily distinguishable from those built by Gothicists outside his fold. They are Gothic inside as well as out, and are planned with no regard to bilateral symmetry on the one hand nor to scenic irregularity on the other. They are seldom faced with ashlar masonry and never with any superficial imitation of it, walling of brick, flint, or rough stone being normally preferred as more natural and less pretentious. Those that are not parsonages, convents, or houses for schoolmasters look to us rather as if they were. Not very many were built before the year 1850, but enough to lay the foundations for an enormous output of them later in the century.

The Puginists were in earnest, and were employed by earnest people who, for the most part, made some effort to decorate and furnish their houses in accordance with their architecture. The ordinary householder of the time, however, whether gentle or simple, left the greatest as well as the least matters of house equipment to his wife. To have shown any strong interest in them himself would have been thought to be disagreeably effeminate. His wife, in turn, chose tables and chairs, papers and materials, as she chose her gowns and bonnets, from the limited collections put forward as truly fashionable in the shops with which she dealt. Fashion ruled, as it had during the Regency; but now the fashions were dictated not by the purchasers but by the trade. Dictated not only to the undiscriminating middle class from which by now far greater number of purchasers were drawn, but dictated also to those the beauty of whose inherited treasures should have taught to judge for themselves. There is something very discouraging to contemplate in the failure of the Victorian aristocracy to resist the fierce commercialization in their time of arts and crafts that their ancestors had proudly protected.

An early specimen of the 'old English mansion' style untouched by Puginism is Mamhead, designed by Anthony Salvin, which in the year 1828 heralded in Devonshire a way of building that within ten years or so was to prevail throughout the land. If we leap twenty-one years and inspect Aldermaston House, in Berkshire (Plate XII), built in the year 1849 after the Puginic leaven had worked, the contrast is great. Classical regularity, only slightly dissembled at Mamhead, is completely flouted at Aldermaston, a particularly symptomatic example, seeing that its architect, Philip Charles Hardwick, was no exclusive Puginist but rather a man who fell in with the prevailing moods. The style of Mamhead is faintly reflected in numberless small houses built before the fiftieth year of our century, among which those in Lonsdale Square, Islington, have a particular interest on account of their authorship. Their design is a boyish work of Richard Cromwell Carpenter, the Puginist apostle of the Anglicans, who, later in his short life, fixed the master's style upon public schools so firmly that it took a whole generation to shake it off. The residential parts of his design of Lancing College show the style to great advantage, as also do many small houses and very many parsonages built at about the same time. The interiors of such houses are generally rather dark and rather too full of stained and varnished woodwork to be easily decorated and furnished. They have, however, more claims to be regarded as serious works of architecture than have most houses of other kinds that are contemporary with them,

Rich merchants and tradesmen, however, when they could not build as splendidly as at Aldermaston, were hardly likely to relish Puginism in its humbler manifestations. Italian of a nondescript kind suited them far better, with large plate-glass windows, a handsome *porte-cochère* and a noble conservatory. The external architecture of houses of this kind is so familiar to all of us that I shall cite no particular example of it, but the internal decoration has so generally been altered out of all knowledge, that an untouched specimen is rare. Photographs, however, record for us in detail the rooms hinted at in the backgrounds of John Leech's drawings and show us the result of Edwin's manly indifference and Angelina's reckless shopping when they prepared their family nest.

The Great Exhibition was a great success. It made every householder long to have a bigger and better conservatory. It advertised our national wealth and opened to us new markets. It made many people desire things they had never desired before and showed manufacturers how to supply them cheaply. It increased enormously the quantity of available art. But, as I am afraid ought to have been expected, it left the quality of the art exactly where it had been before.

The only effect of the Exhibition that I have been able to trace in English homes was the sudden advent of usually very large exhibits that father had bought and room had to be found for somewhere. The artificial stone fountain would be all right in the garden of course, but hardly the bog-oak sideboard. A good many of such enormous pieces of furniture survive in our older houses today, I suppose because once they have been got in it has proved extremely difficult to get them out.

If the Exhibition was a cause, and not merely a symptom, of our national prosperity, it may be held indirectly responsible for the great increase in size and cost noticeable afterwards in houses built by the upper and upper middle classes. Old houses, also, were greatly enlarged, and very often veneered all over with new architectural magnificence. Sir Charles Barry was veneerer-in-chief to the nobility, and a designer of gardens in the grandest of grand manners. At Harewood House, in Yorkshire (Plate XLIV), he worked up the delicate details of a design by Carr and Adam into what was virtually a new design, splendid but far from delicate. This he set upon a new and equally splendid terrace. Highclere in Hampshire he recased entirely in a manner that is recorded to have given him especial satisfaction. It is impossible to deny the ingenuity with which these operations were performed, nor the skill in planning and architectural composition displayed by Barry in all that gave adequate scope to his powers. It also, I fear, cannot be denied that the magnificence he aimed at and achieved was always a parvenu magnificence, whether provided by him for parvenus or for those who ought to have known better. This, I think, was less his and his employers' fault than the fault of their age.

The 'old English mansion' style, during the first twenty-five years of its prevalence had undergone a change to which attention must now be called. When it sprang first from the side of the castellated style, it preserved the Gothic marks of its origin, although in its houses Gothic was apt to change on the threshold to a conventional Classicism within. Gradually, however, in its details there set in a neo-Elizabethanism, an imitation of bastard Renaissance that was found to be as easily applicable to ceilings, staircases, and chimney-pieces as it was to parapets, gables and doorways. It thus acquired some consistency, at the expense of a complete rift with Puginism, to which all post-Gothic forms were 'debased' and utterly reprehensible. Puginists continued to build rectories and schoolmasters' houses with great vigour, and were imitated generally very badly, by architects (of no settled convictions) who found no other models available for houses of the smaller kind that they could be sure were thoroughly up to date. Squires built cottages by the village-full, generally now in a style more bracing than sentimental, in a style nearer to that of the adjacent Puginic schoolhouse than in that of the ornamental dairy in the park.

Let us, now that we are approaching the grand climacteric of the century, leave architecture alone for a moment or two, and examine mid-Victorian homes as settings for domestic life. To begin with the smallest of them, what were the squire's new cottages like inside?

The smallest of them would contain a living-room, a scullery, and two bedrooms, the general run having a parlour and third bedroom in addition. These rooms would all be not quite so big as our present notions require, and might be arranged less conveniently than is customary today. For example, the only way of reaching one bedroom was often by passing through another, and the front door would often open directly into the parlour without any second, internal door behind it. On the other hand, there would be what seldom are provided now, an ample larder, big enough to hold a pig; some roof space, easy to reach, for the storage of apples; and occasionally an oven for baking at home. There were probably no taps, water being got by a bucket from a well and from the water-butt for washing. There was no drainage, the sink emptying into a bucket, and a privy being situated in the backyard or in the garden.

Internally the finish was neat, the woodwork being painted by the landlord, and the walls papered either by him or by the tenant. The furniture would be homely, with, as its most massive pieces, a very large bed and an imposing dresser. The window of the chief room, whether that were living-room or parlour, would be filled up by pot plants and lace curtains. In the chief room, also, the fire-place would almost always be surmounted by a looking-glass in a maplewood or gilded frame.

In the towns the 'fourth-rate' house had no more rooms than had the country cottage, but was built by a speculator for a slightly superior class of occupier. It might contain an internal tap, but probably would not contain a water-closet. In parts of the town where streets were made high above ground level the fourth-rate house would have a basement, although this disagreeable feature was usually reserved for houses of a higher rating. Internally it would be furnished very much as the country cottage was furnished, but probably with a grander 'front room' as its parlour.

Houses for small retired tradesmen, or for those small tradesmen not retired who did not live over their shops, were generally eight-roomed, semi-detached, and arranged on four floors, one of which was more or less a basement. They were commonly called 'villas' and were planned to suit the convenience of the builders rather than that of their occupants.

On each floor there were two rooms, or two rooms and a large closet hardly meriting the name it usually bore of 'dressing-room'; there was water, hot and cold, laid on in the basement and perhaps on the first floor a cold tap. There would be a water-closet on the first floor, sometimes with its only window opening into the staircase. There would never be a bathroom. The rooms on the ground floor would have handsome cornices and chimney-pieces and there would be pretty coloured borders to the glass doors in the hall.

The country equivalent of the villa was the small farmhouse or parsonage, in both of which the tenant usually had the security of a freehold without the fact. Such houses as a rule were planned as agreeably as villas were disagreeably, the chief peculiarity of each kind being that the farm-house kitchen and its dependent offices were large and adapted to the use of a family keeping at most one servant, and the parsonage possessed an extra sitting-room for study and parochial business. In both, bathrooms were practically unknown, but there might be hot water upstairs. There would be a water-closet on the bedroom floor for the ladies and an earth-closet out of doors for the gentlemen.

Of grander houses I cannot speak in detail now, but will point out in passing the prevalence in them of glass-roofed halls in two storeys with a gallery at half-height giving access to the better bedrooms. I believe that the Victorian love for a hall of this kind was inspired by its capability of keeping the whole house warm. Even without central heating, which in primitive forms was already becoming popular, such a hall will send well-warmed air up to the bedrooms, and its provision enables the planner to dispense with long outlying passages, which in Victorian winters seem always to have been icily cold.

Of houses in flats I have nothing to say, because in England with very few exceptions there were none. What there were consisted of a few blocks of workmen's dwellings built by benevolent societies, and some luxurious apartments built speculatively in Victoria Street, Westminster. The first were thankfully occupied by the poor, for whom they were intended; into the second the rich refused to go at any price until, gradually, the more adventurous thinkers among them determined upon the hazardous experiment of living without front doors of their own.

Early Victorian houses in all their different kinds seem to me to have proved reasonably good machines in which to live the life of their time, with one exception – that of the pinched and basemented suburban villa. *That* was a bad machine for any purpose except making money for its manufacturer, a purpose it served so effectively that it was manufactured in enormous numbers during a long period. Nobody wanted to live in such a thing, but most people of the middle class had to. It stood for home to thousands of people whose tastes were revolted by it and whose lives it needlessly complicated by its insensate inconvenience.

How much better than such a place would be a little country parsonage designed by one of the good post-Pugin architects, above all one designed by George Edmund Street! When William Morris began his famous house at Bexley Heath (Plate XCI) in the year 1859, his architect was Philip Webb, who had been Street's chief draughtsman when Morris was a pupil in the office. Being young they both knew much better than their master; being anything but strict Anglican churchmen they probably found the slightly monastic flavour in Street's domestic architecture rather distasteful. But Street is at the bottom of all that is most successful in Webb's earliest way of building, of the broad unbroken surfaces, of the long peaceful roof lines, of the skilful concentration of emphasis at some one significant point.

VICTORIAN ARCHITECTURE

This is a very different way in which to talk about architecture from that in which I have talked hitherto. I have said nothing about any conscious use of unbroken surfaces, any skilful localized emphasis, in the designs of cottages, villas and mansions that we have been considering. I have said nothing, because for the most part there was not any. We are now talking about something new, something of great moment. We are talking of a time at which the architecture of small houses shook off the paralysis of stylism and was brought back into contact with the real – and no longer only with the fancied – needs of its day.

Cottages ornés had been all very well for honeymoons and as the kind of holiday retreat that a Frenchman rich enough to have one calls his *maison de campagne*. But with its ubiquitous French windows, and creepered verandas such a house was apt to prove rather too draughty in winter and 'earwiggy' in summer for a family's only home. But why should that only home not combine the easy informality of the real cottage not *orné* with all the conveniences and prettinesses of Victorian civilization, with the ingenious planning, the improved modern fittings, the neat ornamental finish that had hitherto been reserved for houses of a better class? There was no reason why not, except that nobody seemed to have thought of it.

Somebody thought of it in the late 1860s – William Eden Nesfield perhaps, or Edward Godwin perhaps, or Richard Norman Shaw – I have never been able to fix the occasion of the cottage-villa's very first arrival. The first parade of such buildings in any force was in 1876 at Bedford Park, near Chiswick (Plate LXXXIII), where Jonathan Carr's enterprise in building a whole suburb with the new look attracted much attention and an eager throng of buyers. Here were cheap little seven-roomed and eight-roomed houses, not produced by the simple formula of a four-storeyed box divided on each storey into front and back, but flexibly and ingeniously planned with pretty irregular exteriors. Unqualified approval of the suburb was not universal; we find a responsible writer as late as in the year 1893 saying no more of it than that 'as it is well furnished with trees and gardens, the effect of it is pleasing, if a little theatrical'. But the general public took it to its heart, and since its building, every suburb making any pretence to pleasantness has owed its fundamental character to the example set at Bedford Park.

By the time Bedford Park came to be built it was no longer thought effeminate in a man or peculiar in a woman to take pleasure in beautiful domestic surroundings. To take such pleasure marked you as an *aesthete*, which though not a fashionable thing to be was not necessarily a disreputable one. **W. S.** Gilbert, who in his comic opera, *Patience*, derided aesthetes, nevertheless built for himself an elaborately tasteful house in South Kensington. On the other hand, Sir John Millais, anxious, one guesses, to do nothing detrimental to the fashionable position he had won, built for himself a house that flaunts almost every characteristic that the aesthetes regarded as Philistine.

Not that the new cottage-villas were bought only by aesthetes; their appeal to buyers, if not always to critics, was universal. Those bought by aesthetes were decorated and furnished very, very carefully indeed, but their appointments also were likely to be copied in many respects by the Philistines next door. Let us enter in imagination one in which the aestheticism is not extreme. The front door, not oak-grained as it would have been formerly, is painted sage-green or white with a shining brass handle. Inside it no cast-iron hall-stand receives our hat and stick; instead we find an oriental china tube for umbrellas (the Philistines may have a decorated drain-pipe) and a row of pegs and hooks behind a curtain of Liberty cretonne. In the hall hangs a simple Benson oil-lamp of copper and opalescent glass; the staircase has a dado of Indian matting, and over the dining- and drawing-room doors railed shelves support some jugs and vases of Royal Doulton stoneware. In the drawing-room we find one or two chairs and little tables of eighteenth-century date mingled with other chairs and a cabinet, all of ebonized wood but of light design. They may very likely be the Anglo-Japanese ones designed by the architect of the house, Edward Godwin. Above a dado of blue paper geometrically patterned, a paper of paler blue covers the remainder of the walls, its pattern consisting of an open arrangement of bamboo leafage. The window curtains are of gold corduroy. The colour of the woodwork generally is that of the ground of the wall-paper except that on the door panels are painted birds and apple blossom in their natural colours on a gold ground. On the overmantel are displayed a great many pieces of blue-and-white china, and over the doors in this room are blue-and-white plates. To the brass-lever bell handles on either side of the fire-place are attached painted Japanese fans. Hanging on the walls are etchings, china plates and *kakemonos*.

I should like to spend longer in this charming little house, describing to you all its rooms. But I have said enough to give you its flavour, a flavour that in course of time permeated upwards and downwards through the whole of our domestic architecture. Norman Shaw, who designed most, though not the first, of the Bedford Park houses, became the domestic architect-in-chief of merchant princes and supplied them by the gross with the gables and balconies that in suburbia he doled out in dozens. Benevolent parsons building workmen's dwellings with the advice of Miss Octavia Hill, regarded at least one or two of each as necessary for their tenants' self-respect. Even cottages built by country landlords began to approximate to the styles of the cottage-villa; their windows became larger, their outlines more varied.

I have described the style which I have typified in Bedford Park without yet mentioning the name it was known by. It was called 'Queen Anne'. Why it was so called has never been satisfactorily explained. The real style of Queen Anne's day had been echoed much more faithfully in such Victorian buildings as Wellington College and the Royal Naval School at New Cross, the last built as early as 1843, to which the works of the newer style bore no resemblance at all. Once, however, that the so-called 'Queen Anne' style was completely established its sobriquet was dropped. It became not so much a nameable style as just the way in which all houses except some grand ones were built. It was really a new and living vernacular in which all the elements of old cottage architecture – half-timbering, weather-tiling protecting upper storeys, catslide roofs, ingle-nooks, and the rest – were combined with a few details of more mature Classicality than the Elizabethan. Some of it survives in a state of deep degradation in the quite recent domestic architecture that lines our arterial roads.

The last change that I have to record in the architecture of the English home during the nineteenth century occurred very near to that century's close. It took the form of a retreat from flexible planning, of a return to bilateral symmetry. Norman Shaw again had more to do with this than had anyone else. My description of this great man as a supplier of gables and balconies by the gross to merchant princes (and, of course, to other men of wealth) needs every sort of qualification when we consider the grandest of his houses such as Cragside and Flete in which the 'Queen Anne' characteristics are all kept indoors. On the outside these houses are magnificent compositions of elements that are more Gothic than anything else, but have a personal flavour that prevents exact classification. And then quite suddenly, after all this, he builds a house like Bryanston! His change of mind is also enacted in a single street in London – in Queen's Gate, Kensington. Remark there the contrast between No. 180 (Plate LXXXI) built by him in 1885 and No. 170 (Plate LXXXIV) built by him in 1888. At last a 'Queen Anne' style had arrived which that monarch could have recognized.

Now, formal mask-architecture of the windows-all-in-a-row-with-the-door-in-the-middle variety may be all very well in houses large enough or simply enough planned for all the important windows to serve important purposes; nature, in the form of unimportant windows, and soil-pipes, being relieved round the corner. It is all very ill when it causes small rooms to get large windows where they do not want them and no windows where they do. Architects from the time of Queen Anne to the Regency proved that in little houses simply planned it could be *just* managed by discreet resort to the use of sham windows to fill inevitable breaks in the pattern. Even so, with the walls tamed and in good order, chimneys were apt to shoot out of the roof in the most ill-disciplined way. Late Victorian architects were inhibited by convention from using sham windows, and were compelled by heightened standards of comfort to plan more complicatedly than before. I do not see how they can have hoped to fit their convenient little living machines into cases of unbroken regularity. Norman Shaw had too much sense to try, reserving regularity for grander occasions, but in this discrimination his disciples deserted him.

In consequence, at the close of the century, houses of the cottage-villa size were sharply divided into two classes. In one class the Bedford Park idiom survived, modified by M. H. Baillie Scott and by Charles Annesley Voysey, who made changes in it that were thought at the time to be of great moment. Perhaps Baillie Scott's innovations really were important; in his plans he eliminated customary partitions, valuing spaciousness above privacy, and led the way to much that has since been done in this direction. Voysey brought into the style a quality for which the only exact word that I can find is a French one, *mièvrerie*, which can perhaps be loosely rendered as 'only-little-me-ishness'. His houses were mostly very long, very low, with very small windows, very large chimneys – very artily artless altogether.

In the second class were houses with near-eighteenth-century exteriors and interiors in which unlike those of the eighteenth century no window or fireplace ever seemed to come either in the middle of any wall or where anybody would want to have it. The sentiment that inspired them was not very different from that underlying a curiously bogus play of the period entitled *Quality Street*. Victorian domestic architecture was losing confidence in itself. So was Victorian decorating and furnishing, which came to rely less and less upon the contemporary manufacturer and more and more upon the antique dealer.

VICTORIAN
PUBLIC BUILDINGS

—◆❋◆—

H. S. GOODHART-RENDEL

[The text of a lecture given at the Victoria and Albert Museum in 1952.]

IT is probably safe still to say that most public buildings in Great Britain date from the Victorian age, in spite of the many that have been built since. Of those built before, the number is small, although the quality is often excellent. From the seventeenth century remain some guild-halls and market-houses, from the eighteenth some town halls approaching in a small way the functions and forms of the London Mansion House, and from the latest days of Georgianism more of the same kind of thing, together with a few important public buildings and a great many prisons and workhouses. But the municipal offices, the corn exchanges, the post offices, the fire-stations, the libraries, the baths, have all come since – as it is obvious that they must have done, their uses not having formerly been regarded as calling for provision from the public purse.

The variety of these must prevent anything better than a catalogue from being given in a single lecture, unless the scope of that be narrowed. I propose, therefore, to consider chiefly, some typical examples, keeping in mind the character owed by them to their origin in public rather than in private enterprise. In this they are differentiated strongly from the buildings considered in other chapters in this book, and also from most of their pre-Georgian predecessors, those having generally been provided by landowners or other benefactors in towns with which they were concerned. Those, therefore, reflect – as, for example, do the town halls at Doncaster and Newark – the educated taste of their day. In buildings provided for their own use by mayors and corporations no such reflection was probable.

For in Victorian England educated patronage of the arts was to be found only in a class of society from which mayors and corporations were not recruited. The Lord Mayor's Show in London itself was no inspiring civic pageant, but a display of vulgar splendour that with journalists was a standing joke. Not that the barbarism of burgesses was anything new. In the preceding century, the Mansion House with its pretentious portico, its clumsy proportions and crowded ornament, must have seemed ridiculously inelegant to any dilettante accustomed to debate architectural deportment with Lord Burlington, and although in the years between its building and the birth of Queen Victoria aldermen may have become more sophisticated and dilettanti less exigent, the gulf between their architectural standards was little diminished.

Victorian architects, also, were not, as a rule, men having the education that would empower them to ennoble the plebeian requirements of plebeian employers. Freed from the superintendence of cultivated patrons, they probably saw little harm in the crudities with which their employers were content, nor any betrayal of their art in supplying them. Many of them would not have claimed any art they could betray, being avowedly no more than professional men, apt to the conduct of building operations, but in matters of design tradesmen rather than manufacturers. In all ages and countries such architects have been numerous, but in fortunate ages and countries they have been counterbalanced by others who have apprehended the nature of the art of architecture, who have regarded the aesthetic interplay between line and line, between form and form, as being in their proper province no less than it is in the proper province of the painter or the sculptor. In Victorian England the counterbalance was but partial – the tradesman-architect was the rule, the artist-architect the exception.

This, indeed, is not all the story: the design of the tradesman's goods had to be made by somebody somewhere, and even if made in the tradesman's own office would often be the work of some anonymous artist in his employ. Again, the tradesman might himself be an artist, even though it was as a tradesman that he gained opportunities for his art's display. Art as a means towards beauty was little in demand. Mayors, corporations, and vestries, invited designs for what they wished to build with little more thought of architecture than when they invited tenders for building it. For the Birmingham town hall they accepted a design and tender made by the same person, influenced probably less by the magnificence of the former than by the cheapness of the latter; and, although as the century went on the repetition of such procedure became improbable, it was long before the usual invitations of designs became regularized into a competition in which architectural considerations were weighed by a capable assessor. Even when the appointment of an assessor had become obligatory if members of the Royal Institute of British Architects were to be allowed by their Society to compete, he had at first no authority. He decided which designs deserved premiums, and in this his decision was respected; but his employers acted without reference to him, as often as not, in deciding which design was to be built.

In the highest class of public buildings, those built by the Government for national purposes, popular sentiment demanded architecture worthy of the occasion without having any very clear notion of what such architecture should be. The competitions by means of which the designs of these were selected were usually open to all architects, even to those of other nations, but were usually announced in a manner that tempted few entrants from abroad, and conducted in a manner liable to be questioned at home. Nevertheless, the results that we owe to them are indisputably much better than any likely to have been obtained by the arbitrary choice of a Minister or a Department. What is now called 'Offical Architecture', architecture provided by Departmental staffs without any reference to public choice or use of external ability, was extremely limited in scope during the early years of the century and was never thought by Liberal Victorians to be wholly respectable in principle. During the whole of our period it was scarcely respectable at all in quality, with the exception of that directly due to Sir James Pennethorne, the first salaried architect of the Board of Works, a stepson of John Nash, and a designer of great ability. At its worst, in the unskilfully planned and exuberantly ornamental post offices it provided in our larger provincial towns, its irresponsibility and reckless extravagance were continually commented upon in the press, but only very slowly reduced.

The competition for the design of the Houses of Parliament, although held two years before Queen Victoria's accession, rings up the curtain on the most creditable architectural performance of her reign. Not the Houses themselves; they – though creditable enough – are the prologue only to the long drama of exploratory adventure played by Augustus Pugin and his followers. At the end of the Regency, British architecture, under a confusion of leadership, had lost its way. The principle, imposed upon Europe by the Renaissance, of what may be called façade-architecture – architecture in which the subdivisions of a building must be masked by an overlying arbitrary pattern – had been shaken by the demands of the fashionable 'picturesque' that this pattern should be seemingly irregular. Complying with this demand, many architects were falling into the practice of using pattern-making methods to make no pattern at all, were conceiving symmetrical compositions in the first place and then knocking them about until no one part matched another. In the Gothic of Wyatt and of Nash the hand of an experienced designer steadies in some degree the indecision and vacillation inevitable in architecture so made: in the Gothic of most of his contemporaries, and in the other supposedly free styles into which they were escaping from neo-Classicism – notably the Tuscan villa style and the Elizabethan – the discarded rules were replaced by a complete anarchy.

To architecture thus disorientated Pugin gave a new direction, less powerfully, perhaps, by practice than by precept. The *True Principles of Gothic* – and to him of all – *Architecture* which he had enunciated in his book so entitled, showed incontrovertibly that façade architecture and the picturesque are naturally incompatible. The picturesque cannot be attained by contrivance, it must occur in Art as it occurs in Nature as the result of deep unseen processes, and in architecture as the result of logical opportunism, of turning materials to the best ac-

89

count, of supplying necessaries in the best way, of using labour with the best economy. Build well what is good and beauty will be born.

For nearly three centuries before Pugin had preached his gospel, the architectural manner in which necessaries had been supplied and materials and labour used had been governed by preconceptions of appearance. A façade had to fit the building to which it was applied, more or less, and had to be constructible and stable when constructed – but it had above all to be a façade, obeying laws to which these considerations were subservient. Now that those laws were becoming suspect, and new ones seemed indiscoverable, it was welcome news to architects to learn that none was needed, that the obligation of a façade was a groundless superstition, that buildings might look exactly what they were and yet be beautiful. In ancient Gothic building this conjunction had been achieved so conspicuously that it was almost inescapable that those who sought to recapture it should attempt to tread in medieval footsteps.

Revived Gothic, hitherto a tired art's fantasy, now burst upon romantic minds as the architecture of Nature, the architecture of Truth, the architecture of Hope. To architects not primarily interested in Nature, Truth, or Hope it appeared to be the architecture in which new requirements of convenience and economy could be met with much less subterfuge and embarrassment than in that whose means had been shaped to ends now obsolete. To those charged with obtaining designs for the Houses of Parliament it contained, in its Tudor variety, one of the only two styles national enough for the occasion. That the other style permitted by them – the Elizabethan – should in its ornamental detail be national to Germany rather than England seems to have been overlooked. The internationalism of the so-called Classic style, the style normal through Europe, made it ineligible.

Among the competitive designs submitted for the building one is known to have been the work of Pugin, embodying all his theory, although submitted as his own by another architect whose name would be more likely to secure public confidence. This was not the winning design by Sir Charles Barry, in the execution of which Pugin was afterwards to take so large a part. In Barry's design as it was when first accepted Pugin could find little to approve beyond the style. 'Gothic details on a Classic body,' he said sadly, and truly, as we must allow. But we are unlikely to share his regret at an inconsistency that has combined so much dignified arrangement with so much sparkling and delightful surface decoration. The Houses of Parliament (Plates XLI, XLII, XLIII) struck no blow for Pugin's cause, but they prepared a sympathetic reception for the manner in which that cause was afterwards to be presented.

It had been presented already, and popularly espoused in fields of architecture other than that of public buildings. In churches, country houses, and schools, fantastic Gothic was everywhere losing ground to enthusiastic Gothic; façade-making was being discarded, natural grouping taking the place of conventional arrangements, methods of construction being no longer concealed but proclaimed. On the domestic and commercial architecture of towns the new theory made little effect until later, and on the architecture of public buildings still less. Jails, which were very commonly castellated already, may have become more romantic in silhouette, but their irregularity remained fantastic for the most part rather than functional. At Bristol a guild-hall was built in 1844, which, although far clumsier in detail and arrangement, resembles essentially the Houses of Parliament in the manner of its compromise between Gothic and Classic. This is the earliest English neo-Gothic town hall of which I have found any record, and, if any others were built before the 'sixties of the century they were inconspicuous and uninfluential. I should be very much surprised to learn of any in whose design Pugin's True Principles had been regarded, although in matters of detail they might mimic his practice.

Admitting such exceptions, it may be said that the architectural nature of Early Victorian public buildings of every kind was universally neo-Classical, and, when we examine them, the bearing will be perceived of what has been said earlier in this discourse concerning the character and proficiency of most British architects of the period. The town halls, the assize courts, the corn exchanges, the markets are tradesman's work, honourable tradesman's work very often, but seldom approaching, even at their best, the artistic level of mere routine work in contemporary France. They were as good as could be expected in a country having no effective teaching academy, and no general educational system that could foster in the prosperous commercial classes, to which architects and their civic patrons almost wholly belonged, any true mental culture. In the technique of neo-Classical design most architects were self-taught, if taught at all, and, should a commission for a town hall involve them in a struggle with the Corinthian order, they but seldom emerged victorious. Smirke and his followers, in the preceding age, had reduced the versatility of neo-Classical design until its process became little more than the application of a formula, and except in the hands of a very few men, all elasticity had been lost.

Supreme among these men, supreme among those to whom neo-Classicism supplied a living architectural language, stood Charles Robert Cockerell, and by his side must be placed the coarser-fibred Barry, a designer insensitive to delicacy, but capable of mastering all difficulties in his art and suffusing ordinary conceptions with extraordinary grandeur. No great public enterprise was confided to Cockerell, his magnificent project for the Royal Exchange (Plate XXXVI) having been rejected in favour of the vulgar design of the building we see today. This was the work of Sir William Tite, one of the only Victorian architects recorded to have made a fortune, presumably by means other than architectural, the extent of his practice not having been exceptionally large. Its Corinthian portico is as good as any other of its date in England, and larger than most. The body to which the portico is attached is uneventfully Corinthian also, with, between its pilasters, characteristically Victorian windows, most of the lower ones serving originally for shops. The central courtyard, now covered in by a glass roof, may have looked well enough when open to the sky. Architecturally it is neither attractive nor offensive. Sir William has supplied the goods ordered, and has done so with strict commercial integrity and none of the unpredictability that might have been feared in a transaction with an artist.

The opportunity lost at the Royal Exchange was never recaptured. No great public building has Cockerell for its sole author, although his share was large in the completion of one of the noblest. St George's Hall, at Liverpool (Plate XXXII), a splendid monument judged not only by English but by European standards, was designed by a young architect, Harvey Lonsdale Elmes, whose health gave way when the building was scarcely begun. The completion of it was entrusted to Cockerell, and to him are due the remarkable interiors of the two halls (for what is called 'St George's Hall' is really two) and the sculptural adornment of the exterior (Plate XL). In the design of decoration as ornate as that of these interiors taste plays a large part, and Cockerell's taste here has not been that of many critics, who have found his rich orchestration of colour and form oppressive. Personally I find it inspiring and beautiful. Any just critic, whether he respond to it or not, must acknowledge the decoration to be the work of a master, of an artist completely enfranchised, as was none of his compatriots at the time, from the thraldom of our national inexperience. Contemporary French architects would not just have had to be polite about it, they would have found in it something to consider seriously. I expect they did.

Sir Charles Barry, a medievalist of necessity when designing the Houses of Parliament, has left only three complete public buildings in the neo-Classical manner more natural to him, and of these the Manchester Athenaeum and the Manchester Institute of Fine Arts are pre-Victorian both in date and character. The third, the town hall at Halifax, was designed less than a year before his death in 1860, and executed by his son Edward, not without some modification of his father's intentions. Whatever their virtues neither the earlier buildings nor the later one show the Barry most admired, the Barry of the Travellers' and the Reform club-houses, of Cliveden, and of Bridgewater House. The Manchester buildings are one of Grecian the other of Italian severity; the Halifax town hall is of the most voluptuous Renaissance, more French than Italian, but not that of which either of those countries would willingly acknowledge paternity. Barry, however, when he broke in pieces Sir John Soane's building for the Board of Works, in Whitehall, and put it together again in a façade of strangely different form, created what was virtually a new design in a style half-way between the prudence of his youth and the temerity of his age. So well pleased was he with the result that throughout the whole of his tremendous unexecuted design for Government Offices stretching from the Mall to Birdcage Walk he continued the ordonnance he had established in this fragment. Comparison of this ordonnance with that of Cockerell's contemporary Taylor Institute and Ashmolean Museum, at Oxford (Plate XXXVII), displays clearly the contrast between one man's work and the other's. In both there appears an ambition for more energy, more variety, than would have satisfied architects of the preceding generation. In Barry's ordonnance this is sought by the not unfamiliar expedient of emphasizing verticality by breaking horizontal lines that might conflict with it: he has re-used Soane's columns (he was always great at using things up), but has deprived them of the continuous base beneath and the continuous entablature above them, hoisting them upon high buttress-like piers and surmounting them with fragments of an entablature broken forward from the wall behind. Blocks at either end, containing an additional storey, and a row of high vases outlined against the sky, sustain the excitement; and Soane's simple rustication and window dressings give place to others richer and more emphatic.

Barry's son, Alfred, recording these operations, claims that they 'have given one more striking building to London', and with this claim we shall probably agree. Nobody need mind looking at it, but nobody would want to look at it long. It is entirely without subtlety; all of its merits can be seen and enjoyed at a glance, none of its defects disappoints any aroused expectation. Cockerell's building at Oxford, with which a comparison has been suggested, is not a public building within the scope of this lecture, and therefore cannot appropriately here be analysed. The most hasty inspection of it will reveal however, the greater profundity of its beauty than any dreamt of by Barry, the finer virtuosity in its designer than any to which his rival could aspire. Such profundity, such virtuosity, would be presumed in the land of Labrouste, of Hittorff, of Duc, but in Barry's day they were beyond the normal range of the British imagination. Cockerell could command them, but public authorities did not please to command Cockerell.

Yet Barry, with all his insensitiveness to refinements of architectural expression, was a great architect, great in his planning, great in his pre-vision of great procurable effects. His qualities were those to make him in architectural matters not only the model but the mentor of his age, and his position such that as mentor he was frequently and fruitfully consulted. As assessor in the competition held in 1852 for the design of the Leeds town hall (Plate XXVIII) he recommended the design of a young untried man, Cuthbert Brodrick, who produced in the event what seems certainly the most respectable English building in its epoch and of its kind. Its plan as first submitted was of unusual excellence in its general distribution, but in its details faulty. In execution most of these faults were corrected. Its style is what a more Grecian age would have called Corinthian pseudo-peripteral, which is to say that whatever parts of the outside walls are intended for inspection are either recessed behind Corinthian columns or carved with Corinthian pilasters: and – whether at Barry's suggestion or through a development of Brodrick's taste in the direction of the master's – the flat roof effloresced while building into one large and four small towers together with a prodigious number of terminal vases, few of which were originally contemplated. These plume-like finials, and the thick coat of black that now encrusts the stonework, give to the building the sombre grandeur of a magnificent hearse; it is pictorially extremely impressive, although damping to any mood of festivity. The interior of the great hall, as many can remember it, appeared very good, owing to the complete harmony of its form and colour, but a singularly inept and ill-judged redecoration has since revealed a mediocrity in the quality of its architectural detail that discounts some of the virtue of its noble lines and proportions. Young Brodrick was obviously unusually experienced for his age, but his experience cannot have been gained among masterpieces. In middle life he retired from practice to spend a quarter of a century in Paris and its environs, amusing himself with landscape painting. It is sad to reflect how much greater might have been his achievement could Paris have been the school of his youth rather than the retreat of his age.

When Brodrick won the Leeds competition he was in practice in his native city of Hull, and it was with difficulty that Barry induced the Leeds Corporation to employ any but a Leeds architect. Sixteen years later the Bolton Corporation wanted a town hall like that of Leeds, but offered to Brodrick, now a Leeds man, only a half-share with a Bolton architect in its designing. Brodrick refused and the Bolton people had recourse to a competition into which Brodrick entered, securing the second premium. The first premium was awarded to, and the building subsequently carried out by, another Leeds architect, William Hill, who knew enough of the antecedents of the competition to imitate as closely as was honourable the general character of the former design by his fellow-contestant. The resulting building is as original as it has any need to be, and, although smaller than its prototype, is no less satisfactory. Years later still, Hill was employed to repeat it with very few external variations at Portsmouth (Plate XXX). So one thing leads to another!

I have read that there is another town hall more or less of the Leeds pattern at Morley, in Derbyshire, but I have never seen it. I can hardly think there are any more, because by the time other towns became rich enough for them their type was out of fashion. Corinthianism had gone to sleep to be awakened only by the coming of King Edward VII. The small town hall at Todmorden, in Lancashire, certainly has an exceedingly handsome Corinthian peristyle, but this is an exceptional building given to the town by the benevolent manufacturer who was its principal landlord. The ordinary neo-Classical town halls of the time were modest enough, judged even by the Todmorden standard, attempting at most something special in the way of an entrance, as, at Cardiff, or a tower, as at Burslem.

For the Pugin leaven was working, and architects who used their minds at all were only giving half of them to the continuance of neo-Classical practices in which they seldom excelled. Churches and schools had gone Gothic almost without exception, and in country houses other styles had become rare. Gilbert Scott, the leader of the architectural traders, had received an afflatus, thenceforth holding himself supernaturally charged with the duty of stocking only Gothic goods, whatever the purpose for which they might be required. 'The old and the new worlds', he wrote, 'were severed by the most marked line of separation which Providence has ever drawn between different periods of history – the destruction of the Roman Empire, and with it the arts and civilization of the ancient world.' To ignore this dispensation was impious, and had resulted in the buildings of the 'vernacular classic style' with which he found himself surrounded. Of these, he states, 'I am just now hard at work, in more than one instance, in transforming their outside and their inside into my own style, and flatter myself that no one will ever regret the change'.

When Scott wrote these words, not very much solid ground had been won in the campaign that Pugin had inaugurated. The Gothicism of schools, churches and country houses rested largely on the shifting sands of fashion and national sentiment and was seldom rooted in the True Principles of the master. The Westminster Hospital, whose front stood at right-angles with that of the Abbey, had been built in fantastic Gothic before Pugin's voice was heard, and in 1857 Scott had been allowed to put up a range of houses in enthusiastic Gothic opposite to it. Such doings were all very well at Westminster, but elsewhere 'vernacular classic' had been little challenged. Pugin's friend and biographer, Benjamin Ferrey, had designed a Gothic county hospital as early as 1839, the

Bristol Guildhall had followed in 1844, but the normal practice of the time was typified in the new residential quarters of London and other large towns, where a Gothic church, parsonage and school were run up simultaneously with surrounding neo-Classical terraces and shops. Scott, indeed, sorely complained that advocacy of the revival of Gothic seemed to debar a man 'from exercising his talents in designing the great secular buildings of the day, as if he had committed a misdemeanour depriving him of the honours of his professional standing'. No great secular building had yet come his way.

> Let wealth and commerce, laws and learning die,
> But leave us still our old nobility.

Everybody laughed at those lines, misinterpreting 'nobility' as signifying a caste rather than a virtue. But their author, the philanthropic idealist Lord John Manners, was First Commissioner of Works in the year 1858, and this for opponents of the Gothic Revival was no laughing matter. Gothic was slighted by public authorities and commerce, but that which people thought Lord John had meant by the 'old nobility' had taken it up; and in days when most true Britons regarded questions of Art as trivial enough to be appropriately decided by the aristocracy, such championship promised victory. Lord John, in what proved a brief tenure of office, made two brave decisions. Leaving competition winners to console themselves with their premiums, he commissioned the unsuccessful Alfred Stevens to design the Wellington Memorial, and the unsuccessful Gilbert Scott to design the Foreign Office. Scott had his great secular building at last.

Had he been a man whose principles could resist his interest, he would not have had it now, because a change of government brought in Lord Palmerston, who insisted that the style of the new Office should be Scott's abhorred 'vernacular classic', pointing out that if Scott would not design it thus there were plenty of people who would. Scott was determined that none of them should, and was, therefore, in his own words, 'driven into the most annoying position of carrying out my largest work in a style contrary to the direction of my life's labours'. How thankful we may be that he was! The building that we have (Plate LXII) is inconveniently under-windowed (probably because Lord Palmerston had condemned Gothic buildings as 'dark' so that Scott was not indisposed to make an Italianate one even darker), but it is rich and stately, with much really beautiful sculpture, and suggests what has always been rumoured, that a good many accomplished hands besides his own were employed by Scott upon his uncongenial task.

The Scott-Palmerston battle was fought not in single combat, but by sides in Parliament, and has come to be known as the 'Battle of the Styles'. **Palmer-ston's** victory was merely local, since even before it was decided, the enemy Gothic had won ground at Manchester, which proved to be the first point held in a successful campaign of national conquest. The competition for the design of the Manchester Assize Courts (Plate XXVI) in 1859 was won by a young local architect, Alfred Waterhouse, with a project uncompromisingly Gothic, the choice and the subsequent execution of which were received with complete approval. Seen now in the light of all that it led to, this building shows a still incomplete emancipation of Victorian architecture from formalism: some of its Gothic details seem still to be in quotation marks, and not normal words in a natural language. But emancipation is what it stood for, emancipation from the tyranny of arbitrary formulas and obligations, of Corinthian columns ten diameters high of which one half-diameter must be given to the base and one diameter and a sixth to the capital, of Doric entablatures whose triglyphs were so spaced as to produce a terrifying crisis whenever they had to turn a corner, of rooms the proportion of whose length to breadth should not exceed the sesquialteral, and whose heights must be regulated by their several areas, of ideal construction and materials to be simulated and actual construction and materials to be dissimulated – in short, of everything which a rare Cockerell or Elmes could do by nature and which common men seldom attempt without some alarm.

Common men in France were well drilled in it, for there the discipline of the schools had percolated deep. Common men in England had picked up what they could in busy offices, and had not picked up very much. But common men in England had a great deal of common sense, and in the first principles of Pugin, as practised by Waterhouse and his school, common sense was the avowed and usually the active criterion. In modern eclectic Gothic evolved by them, English architects of the Victorian age were so greatly superior to those of other countries as in the international neo-Classical style they had been inferior.

Unfortunately this superiority in the handling of style did not at first bring even any equality with other nations in an architectural element far more fundamental. In the planning of buildings common sense is not enough, needing to be allied with deep wisdom and skill if it is not to sink into mere opportunism. The philosophy of planning is not what the common man can evolve for him-self, and although in some architects, particularly in Sir Charles Barry and Waterhouse, it seems to have been instinctive, most had to learn it, which in Victorian England they had few opportunities of doing. Few among the remark-able public buildings to which the Manchester Assize Courts led the way are planned with anything approaching the skill displayed in their forerunner. The beautiful town halls designed by Edward Godwin at Northampton and at Congleton (Plate XXIX) are small enough to have called for no special expertise in this respect, and in Crossland's larger building of the same kind at Rochdale the several parts are arranged with an insouciance allowable considering the nature of the site and disarming criticism.

Nearly all the best public buildings that date from the fifteen middle years of Queen Victoria's reign were designed in the contemporaneous style derived from Gothic, a style not only evolved by the age but fitting it like a glove. Its highest manifestation came at those years' close, in the splendid town hall at Manchester (Plate XXVII), opened in 1877, with which Alfred Waterhouse followed up his earlier triumph in the same city. This great work was described by a writer in a former edition of the *Encyclopaedia Britannica* as 'probably beyond dispute the most important municipal building in the kingdom, if not in Europe', and although many years have passed since those words were written, they can be truly repeated now. The building's importance may no longer inhere in its size – it has had itself to be enlarged, and for all I know may now be surpassed by many others – but its nobly architecturalised construction, the mingled grandeur and convenience of its planning, the magnificent massing of its composition, and the complete harmony of every decorative element in it with every other, have still to be surpassed.

Not only in Manchester but in London the defeat of Gothic by Palmerston had proved but a temporary set-back rapidly repaired. In 1866 eleven architects were chosen to compete for the designing of the new Law Courts, and all sent in projects that were unmitigatedly Gothic (Plates LXXV and LXXVI). One of them, indeed, nervously provided alternative elevations in a neo-Classical style, but nobody seems to have regarded these as anything but a joke. George Edmund Street, the author of the design executed, prevailed over Waterhouse, Burges, Deane, and Scott, four dangerous contestants, and six others whose emulation cannot have caused him serious anxiety, although a rumour went round that the fantastically showy proposals of one of them had their advocate among the jury. This jury consisted of the First Commissioner of Works, the Chancellor of the Exchequer, the Lord Chief Justice, the Attorney-General, and a member of the House of Commons, the two architects attached to it being consulted not about architecture but about compliance or non-compliance with the set conditions. It made a terrible mess of things at first, choosing the plan submitted by one competitor and the elevations submitted by another (who was Street), and requesting the two men get together and alter their work to fit. When this request had met with the reception that might have been expected, it was decided to dismiss Street's proposed collaborator, consoling him with a promise that if the National Gallery were rebuilt he should be the man to do it. The National Gallery never *was* rebuilt, which, considering that the architect thus appointed to do it was the designer of the Charing Cross station hotel, seems to me no subject for regret.

Street, once in the saddle, had a difficult ride. First he had to change his plan. Next, the Government changed the site from the Strand to the Embankment, and he had to redesign the whole building. Next after this, the site was changed back again to a site in the Strand much larger than formerly proposed, and he had to redesign the whole building again. During all these changes he had to retain, if he could, the characteristics of the elevations to which he owed their selection, and to convince or beguile a notoriously ignorant bully in the then First Commissioner of Works, Mr Ayrton.

What of the result? How much did Street, the sanguine, resilient Street, the idol of the young – with his poetical perception, his ready inventiveness, his knowledge and his skill – how much did Street make of his grandest opportunity? He has given us in the great hall of the Courts – the *salle des pas perdus* – the noblest room of the century, perhaps the noblest room in England (Plate LXXVII). He has given us in the three fronts of the building, to the Strand, to Bell Yard and to Carey Street respectively, compositions of street scenery as perfectly appropriate to their crowded surroundings as Barry's regiment of buttresses in line at Westminster is to the river-front it faces. He has given us a treasury of novel and beautiful details, none of them quite like what a thirteenth-century architect ever did produce, but all of them very much like what a thirteenth-century architect might have produced in nineteenth-century London. He has given us a model of beautiful and enduring construction. But he has given us something that common men could not make their own, as they could Waterhouse's gifts at Manchester. The fifteen years of general collaboration are over, what had been general language now becomes the metonym of Street's personality; eclectic Gothic has now become his, not everybody's. The Law Courts have been called the 'grave of the Revival'. If that is true, here is the reason.

But, whether buried in the Law Courts or not, the Gothic Revival had done its work before that great building was finished. It had provided the English architect with tools he could handle, tools useful in other tasks besides Gothic, and had made unnecessary his pretensions to a Classical education he seldom actually had enjoyed. It had given him a self-confidence that enabled him to cut not too poor a figure in the free-for-all scramble that followed the removal of its discipline. During its waning, Queen Anne had arrived, heralded by the architects Nesfield and Norman Shaw, and, although her popularity was greatest among artists at Hampstead, and in board schools, she was warmly welcomed by the councillors of Leicester, and condescended to shape their new town hall to her taste. This admirable building (Plate XXIII) might well, I think, claim the attention of the Society for Psychical Research. Its architect was a local man of the highest respectability, of whose other work I have not been able to get any information. In every particular down to the smallest it seems to bear the personal touch of William Eden Nesfield. Of three possible suppositions – that its architect had a phenomenal gift of mimicry, that Nesfield made a design to be submitted in his name, that the design was inspired by a spirit haunting the building in which the two men had their London offices – I do not know which to choose. None of these suppositions would have been considered to be necessarily discreditable at the time, and charity, therefore, would allow them equally. The particular significance of the design, whatever its authorship, lies in the still Gothic flexibility of its style: indeed it might be described, by a reversal of Pugin's phrase, as displaying 'Classic details on a Gothic body'. The rigours of neo-Classical conventions are still completely relaxed, actual construction is still frankly expressed, actual materials are still allowed their say in the forms they are made to assume.

The Leicester town hall ushers in the phase of Victorian public architecture that rocketed upwards for twenty years until it burst in starry glory over the Imperial Institute at the time of the Diamond Jubilee. Notable points in its upward career are marked by the town halls of Wakefield, Sheffield and Oxford (Plate XXIV), and the Victoria Law Courts at Birmingham. All these buildings, and innumerable imitations of them, were customarily described as exhibiting a 'free treatment of the Renaissance', and, even though the freedom may often be more apparent than the Renaissance, the description is not inappropriate. The style, which perhaps I may venture to entitle 'the bracket and overmantel style', affords harbourage to pretty ornaments from many countries, from France, Spain, Italy, Holland, with some few even from Japan. In adopting it architects escaped from a Gothic that in the last days of Street was in danger of becoming rarefied and esoteric, and got together again as closely as they had been brought together before by Waterhouse. The Wakefield town hall was designed by Collcutt, that at Sheffield by Mountford, that at Oxford by Hare, and the Birmingham Law Courts by Webb and Bell. Yet they are so much works of one school as almost to seem works of one man. The design of each was selected from among many of the same kind submitted in open competition. Each particular competition was eagerly watched by the local public, and fully commented upon in the local press. At the present day, when the public is supposed to open its mouth and shut its eyes and try not to make a face when it tastes what is given it by the Fine Arts Commission or the Arts Council, it is difficult to realize what the Victorian freedom was like. Architecture then was what we have not had for a long time, architecture by general consent.

And now I come to the last building I intend to mention. Thomas Collcutt, the architect of the Imperial Institute (Plate XXXI), 'the patriot architect' urged by Tennyson to 'work for eternity', and 'make it truly glorious' seems to me to have fulfilled these injunctions very well, although I know that some people do not agree with me. That nobody has ever been certain as to what the building is for is no fault of its architect. He was required to fulfil a monumental programme, and the monument has been put to various uses successively and is now full of a lot of people and things that would otherwise have to be somewhere else. The same is true of a great many of our monuments that started their existence with a use more definite. It is at any rate, a speaking memorial of its age and of the architecture of that age, and comes most fitly to close this my brief review.

CHARLES
ROBERT COCKERELL

E. M. DODD

'I HAVE made my choice, & know that I have now no time to waste.' This memorandum of 1804, written for his own eyes shortly before commencing his professional training, reveals the essential Cockerell in his power of lonely decision and his uncommon ardour. The particular choice was that of 'not resting content to be an *ordinary* architect, nor merely a successful one, but [of] ... aspiring with all the nerve bestowed upon me to be like old Sir Wm Chambers', and the attitude suggested by it already forecasts the position Cockerell was to occupy in the plebeian world of early nineteenth-century British architecture, where with his intense intellectual curiosity and his aristocratic disdain of the insensitive and the conventional he stands in solitary isolation. Almost from infancy he had known his ambition – that of 'restoring our Architecture to the heights from which it had sadly fallen' – and his whole career can be read as a sustained and deliberate effort to achieve that end. And 'old Chambers' epitomized how such a career might be constructed. Cockerell had barely known him, for Chambers had died when his admirer was seven, but his memory was to dominate the young architect's intellectual horizon, Cockerell was later to say, 'like a great golden eagle'; while Chambers's style of academic Classicism, exemplified in all its glory by Somerset House, was to signify for Cockerell the highest peak of English architectural achievement. Chambers was indeed his earliest idol, and there cannot be the slightest question that Cockerell sought, very consciously, to emulate him.

In this he was to be notably successful, for in many ways the two were wonderfully alike. Both were men of wide learning and of generous and constant humanity, who held and maintained ideals of sterling integrity throughout their long careers. Both were men of superlative technical ability and of fastidious taste and discrimination, for whom architecture served not only the needs of the material life but of the life of the intellect as well. Both were temperamentally conservative men, intent on consolidating the tradition rather than plunging headlong from it. And both, as Academicians, had as their political objectives the elevation of the architect's status in their respective societies. More than any other, Cockerell must be accounted the nineteenth-century equivalent of Chambers.

But there were wide differences between them, too, and as befitted an architect of a new age, Cockerell's stylistic orientation, though built on much the same eclectic foundation which Chambers had used, was destined to lead to an outcome which 'the last of the Romans' might never have foreseen. What was Cockerell's stylistic orientation? And what was its outcome? This little essay cannot possibly pretend to answer these questions in anything like detail, but will simply attempt to point out a few landmarks which may help to explain the continuity of his work, the story and the character of its development. The line which this development has traced strikes me as having a firmness, an absolute certainty of control, as impressive as it is rare. To draw attention to this is the limit of my aim in the following pages, in which I shall record a few relevant biographical facts and try to describe how Cockerell's very personal style of architecture evolved.

Charles Robert Cockerell was born in London in 1788, the second son of Samuel Pepys Cockerell, a descendent of the diarist and himself an able and affluent Late Georgian architect. A spirited and rather romantic youth, with a remarkable gift for drawing and a shrewdly analytical mind, young Cockerell put his abilities to use at a very early age, acquiring a wide knowledge of architecture and a passion for Greek studies which, undampened by the rigours of a Westminster education, emerged as one of the dominant influences on his whole life. Cockerell's mornings invariably began with a translation of ancient text. He could, we are told, read Lycophron with ease at first sight, which is no mean achievement, and he not only read Greek with ease and lively pleasure but followed with critical attention the debates of his day on questions of text and interpretation, in which he could hold his own with any professional scholar. Nor could this deep Hellenic bias fail to inflect his conception of architecture, his other consuming enthusiasm, the formal study of which he commenced in 1804, when he entered his father's office as an articled assistant. Cockerell never considered that he owed very much to his father's tuition, apart from a sound and intimate knowledge of building techniques, and, indeed, from the son's account one might easily gather that Cockerell *père* was a plodding practitioner of the dreariest description. There is, however, no reason to suppose that he was anything of the kind, and though not a man of strong originality, his surviving works show that he was much alive to the manifold artistic influences of his time and that he could use them in new and interesting ways. And they show, too, that many of these influences were precisely those on which the younger Cockerell was to draw for his – infinitely more imaginative – productions.

One influence in particular was to be of paramount importance for the son as it had been for the father – that of contemporary French Classicism. Among the elder Cockerell's works a distinct Gallic sympathy is betrayed at least as early as 1795 in the decorative elements of Daylesford, Gloucestershire, a house which he built for Warren Hastings; but for us interest focuses more emphatically on a later work, dating from the time that his son was his articled pupil, and a work in which the son, as his father's architectural amanuensis, had a share. This is the steeple which is all that survives of the Wren-designed church of St Anne, Soho, an altogether extraordinary performance quite evidently beholden, in its bare-bone simplicity, to the Père la Chaise monuments which the elder Cockerell must have seen on his visit to Paris during the short-lived Peace of Amiens. 'Papa has come home convinced that the future of Arch^{re} lies in France', young Cockerell wrote in 1803, about the time the designs for the steeple were begun; and it was not long after this that we find the pupil himself reading and carefully annotating his father's copy of the Abbé Laugier's revolutionary *Essai sur l'Architecture* and copying designs from the very recent treatises of Dubut and Ledoux. By then, Cockerell already accepted French supremacy in building as almost axiomatic. 'The best French works in Architecture are as superior to ours as Hyperion to a Satyr.' Here was a distinction, jotted into a notebook in 1806, which seemed no less valid to Cockerell years later when, as a visitor to post-Napoleonic Paris, he studied French works at first-hand and acquired a renewed appreciation of Parisian methods of planning and composition, which, in due course, he was to make completely his own.

Of comparable importance, though less positive in its ultimate influence, was Cockerell's early initiation into the theory and practice of 'the Picturesque'. In this, he enjoyed the direct intervention of his father's friends, the trio of 'Picturesque' aestheticians Payne Knight, Price, and Repton, some of whose precepts he was soon to apply in his first independent exercise, the landscaping of his family's Paddington estate, where Cockerell introduced a whole anthology of 'Picturesque' plantings and adjuncts, including a 'Gothick' conservatory and a prototypal Greek Doric temple, modelled on that described by Laugier. But this modest undertaking was vastly overshadowed by the building of Sezin-cote, his uncle Sir Charles Cockerell's fantastic 'Indian-styled' country house in Gloucestershire. Young Cockerell did not design it. That responsibility devolved upon his father, but there is a story that the young apprentice was a driving force behind the whole enterprise, he being the one who originally suggested that his uncle's house be based on 'ideas from the best Indian works', and a surviving notebook proves that, while engaged in the work as one of his father's draughtsmen, he was deeply as immersed in the study of 'the architecture of Hindustan' – and as thrilled by its 'Picturesque' potentialities – as were his father and the latter's consultants, Repton and the painter Thomas Daniell.

But though the new-found freedoms allowed by the 'Picturesque' etched an indelible impression on his developing sensibility, young Cockerell's infatuation with the Indian style was a passing mood, and well before his apprenticeship was over he renounced his association with his uncle's building adventure as a youthful indiscretion. Sezincote came to embody for him one of the shabbier aspects of the English mentality: 'our curious penchant for the make-believe', he called it as early as 1808. By then his taste for the work had been entirely superseded by an affection for Grecian architecture, the field to which he now subscribed his loyalty absolutely.

It was, at the time, a rather *avant-garde* interest, and one which, Cockerell tells us, he pursued independently of his father, Grecian architecture not being something which the elder Cockerell found especially sympathetic. For though he, like many of his contemporaries, could appreciate the *primitive* quality of Greek Doric, the younger Cockerell could denounce most of the men of his father's generation as 'blind as shrimps in a cave to the true Nature of Grecian Beauty'; and, in an amusing diatribe, he took particular pains to castigate his hero Chambers for his obstinate refusal to recognize any merit in Grecian architecture whatever. But Cockerell's own generation – the generation of Downing College and the British Museum – was also that of Byron, Keats, and Shelley (the first Cockerell's exact contemporary and friend); and they all shared the romantic predilection for Greece engendered by the climate of their time. Characteristically, Cockerell's interest in Greece was, first and foremost, a literary interest, and it was not until 1806, his eighteenth year, that he made the direct acquaintance of Grecian plastic art. For in the autumn of that year he was allowed a preview of the Elgin Marbles then arriving in London, and he was decisively and irrevocably spellbound by their impact. Approaching them with a mind nurtured on Winckelmann – but at the same time critically independent and extraordinarily quick and shrewd in his perceptions – he recognized that 'W[inckelmann]'s notion of Grecian Beauty is so shallow as to be positively absurd when one sees Ld Elgin's Marbles, which are so *True to Nature* & so *full of Life & Movement* that one might almost suppose they were cast from *living* models'. And with an eye on his own future works Cockerell already guessed that, by analogy, one might extend this interpretation to Grecian architecture.

In Greece, where he spent the years from 1810 to 1815, his guess was amply confirmed. First at the Parthenon, where by careful measurement he satisfied himself about the existence of entasis in the Greek column. The entasis of the Roman column had, of course, long been known, and had been copied by architects of the Renaissance, but archaeologists before Cockerell had failed to observe that the same feature, more subtly used and less easily detected is also to be found in Greek architecture. 'I have no doubt', wrote Cockerell, 'that it was a general rule with the Gk architects, though it has hitherto escaped the eyes of Stuart & our most accurate observers.' Other discoveries followed thick and fast, and in those relating to further Grecian 'refinements', such as the curvature of the stylobate, Cockerell found that his early intuition had proved correct. He wrote to his father:

> I have now concluded that the *vigourous, lifelike quality* of Ld Elgin's Marbles ... is the prime Beauty of Gk Arch^{re} as well, for contrary to all we have been told, the whole Temple, far from being a collection of inert masonry, is *alive with movement* ... for the deviations which I have found in its construction provide an effect *almost of breathing* to the solid marble slabs.

The implications of this interpretation were enormous. For by means of it Cockerell was allowed an altogether fresh vision of Antiquity, which he saw as something more intense, more alive, more Dionysiac – more really Antique perhaps – than anything that had ever been envisaged before; and from his notes it is evident that he already grasped that this dynamic dimension of Grecian architecture might provide a direct visual source of inspiration and a starting-point for new adventure.

The idea crystallized all the more in Italy, where he spent the two years following Waterloo. Here, Cockerell's scholarly interest was naturally directed to Roman archaeology, but his journals show that what really allured him most, and what he singled out as 'by far the most useful examples for our modern buildings', were Cinquecento and Seicento works, in which he pointed to what he called 'the elusive yet positive Grecian quality which must strike every sensitive observer'. It was a sharp and revealing observation, and something of its future importance for Cockerell can already be glimpsed in a series of surviving sketches in which he made his first imaginative attempts to reinterpret – and to exaggerate – this 'Grecian' component of Italian Renaissance and Baroque architecture. Herein are the earliest adumbrations of the mature and vigorously personal style which he was later to cultivate with such unswerving devotion.

Influential, too, were Cockerell's connections at the radiating-point of modernism, the French Academy at Rome, where (as later in Paris) he revived and extended his knowledge of contemporary French Classicism. How completely he absorbed its discipline is demonstrated in his one independent undertaking belonging to these years, his abortive project for a 'Wellington Palace'. In plan this is a familiar Palladian villa-scheme, inflated to grandiose proportions and recomposed with fresh references to Roman *thermae* (Cockerell had just completed a paper restoration of the Baths of Caracalla). But the way in which the whole complex is constructed, with its relentless (and unreal) emphasis on axiality and geometry, its extreme reticence of silhouette, its rooms deployed *en suite* round inner courtyards, its central 'Pantheon' dome – all this is as French as it can be, and were it not for the amateurish lack of decision permeating almost every part of it, the design might almost be mistaken for a Prix de Rome project of one of the architect's *pensionnaire* friends.

Back in London in 1817, Cockerell was soon surveying with new eyes the architectural scene on which he had turned his back seven years earlier. He found it, as his notes confirm, in the highest degree discouraging. Building after building, put to the test, failed to measure up to his incredibly stringent standards. There were some notable exceptions: St Paul's and the City churches (then little appreciated) passed with flying colours, while among more recent works he recognized two as bearing the stamp of some real architectural excellence. One was Soane's Bank of England; the other was Waterloo Bridge, the latest triumph of his future father-in-law, John Rennie. But the bulk of London building seemed to him beneath contempt. It lacked 'that logic & assurance & *finesse* which the French understood but is all but unknown here'; it was also 'altogether wanting that *vigour of effect* so evident in Grecian work but which our professors Smirke, Wilkins, *et al.* are content to ignore'. Supremely confident of his own powers, Cockerell's consciousness of being a potential innovator is conspicuous from the very beginning. He was determined – he confesses as much – to 'retrieve the lost art of Architecture in England'.

The first dozen years of his practice, from 1818 to 1830, were preparatory and experimental. A wide variety of commissions came to him – schools, churches, and country houses – and through all of them a galaxy of themes is to be detected. Not surprisingly, one of the most persistent influences is that of the modernism of post-Revolutionary France, and indeed there is hardly a building or a project belonging to this period for which, in plan or composition, a French source cannot be found. This is true of two very early works, Lady Boswell's School, at Sevenoaks, and the Literary and Philosophical Institute (now the Freemason's Hall), at Bristol, the one a neat little essay (since altered) in Laugierian fundamentalism, the other an adaptation (in plan) of a lecture-diagram Cockerell had seen at the École Polytechnique; while his later competition project for London University is a brilliant exercise in monumental Grand Prix planning which, compared to Wilkins's executed design, shows at once what a rich source of ideas French practice could offer to one who cared to study it with intelligence and sympathy (Plate XXXIII). So too did Cockerell's first ecclesiastical building, the long-demolished Hanover Chapel in Nash's new Regent Street, where for a frontispiece he adopted a Grecianized version of a recent Grand Prix expedient of twin towers flanking a central portico – Cockerell's answer to the traditional Gibbsian anomaly of a roof-riding steeple. France, however, never provided the whole answer, and there is a good deal in these early works which can be explained only with reference to other influences. Of these, none was more potent for Cockerell than Wren.

Wren was, in a way, his own discovery, and Cockerell was to be that architect's foremost champion throughout the early nineteenth century, For Cockerell, it was Wren's precise intellectuality which struck an answering chord, and in an age for which the seventeenth century's Baroque liberalities were still strongly suspect, Cockerell must have been one of the few who could perceive and appreciate Wren's genius as a rational and lucid planner. Not that Cockerell, for all his admiration, intended to initiate a Wren Revival. Nothing could have been further removed from his intention. But he did sense that from Wren he might derive an *approach* to a solution of his own, and on analysing his buildings one finds that this is exactly what he did, time and time again.

Hanover Chapel is an early and fascinating example of this. Here, behind its French-inspired façade, the architect was faced with an awkward problem. Not only was the site more a wedge than a parallelogram in shape, but also there was no alternative but to place the entrance in the east wall, the side which by ecclesiastical tradition (as well as by express condition of the Church Commissioners) had to contain the altar. Immediately, Cockerell saw that the problems which Wren had faced – and solved – in his City churches were closely analogous to those confronting him as he hammered out a scheme of his own: the requirements, both liturgical and practical, were virtually the same in the third quarter of the seventeenth century as they were in his own time; and if Wren had never had to wrestle with two tiers of galleries as Cockerell's programme dictated, he was certain that he understood Wren well enough to know how he might have handled them if he had. After several preliminary trials, Cockerell pitched on an extremely thoughtful variation of a favourite Wren-Hawksmoor plan-type which consisted, in essence, of a square within a square for the main theme, above which rose a glazed dome. For the rest, it was an extemporization, the subsidiary elements of the plan being wrapped round the central core to fill out the remaining space. The result was that rare thing, a 'Commissioners' Church' so compellingly logical that even its galleries, far from being treated as unwanted appendages, were inextricably fused with the body of the structure, which was in itself a model of simplicity and grace. And Cockerell's subsequent churches, notably Holy Trinity, Hotwells (Bristol), were, in their geometrical unity, no less distinguished contributions to the Wren-Hawksmoor tradition of centralized church design.

New methods and new materials must be allowed expression, too, and from the first Cockerell had a perfectly down-to-earth, practical-minded view of his art, recognizing the necessity of self-adaptation to an age of change. It was of supreme importance to him that the architect employ all the technical means at his disposal, an attitude pressed upon him by the example of his beloved Wren and fostered by his lifelong connections at the École Polytechnique. And so it is not surprising that he ardently advocated the use of cast iron, the most remarkable of the new materials invading English architecture. Nearly all of his designs ambitiously exploited it, and if in execution his works are technically less adventurous than on paper, the reason can invariably be traced to either the conservatism or the poverty of his early clients. Such had been the case at Lady Boswell's School, where Cockerell's projected cast-iron principles were pruned because they would have added nearly £200 to the cost – out of the question for a £500 building; while similar considerations curtailed his use of iron in his churches and his country houses. But in their conservatories, where the superiority of iron to timber easily outweighed its additional expense, his clients willingly enabled him to utilize 'ferro-vitreous' construction, and Cockerell's innovations in this field were widely acclaimed.

As a group, Cockerell's early works show what the works of a young architect ought to show, immense power of assimilation. Yet, by and large, they are still mainly traditional. Despite the freshness of many of the ideas embodied in them, their reticent serenity of outline and detail marks them as close approximations of the neo-Grecianism of Smirke and Wilkins, though to the scholarship of these architects Cockerell has added an imaginative factor which sets his buildings off as uncommonly distinguished examples of the contemporary idiom. About 1828, however, there are signs that his stylistic orientation was shifting, and we find him hankering after a more personal mode of expression, something which would allow a higher emotional ceiling than what was sanctioned by current Greek Revival practice. Symptomatic of his new outlook was changing loyalty to Wren. Earlier, it was primarily 'Early Wren' which had seized his imagination, but about 1827 'Late Wren' began to exert an attraction, and from this Cockerell was inevitably lead to the exhilarating discovery of the more theatrical originalties of Hawksmoor and Vanbrugh, whose works he now referred to in terms of a most intimate appreciation. And besides these studies of his native Baroque he was also addressing himself with renewed intensity to Mediterranean Baroque as well. With these immensely suggestive sources at his elbow, Cockerell's mature conception of the architecture crystallized rapidly, and it was not long before he was ready to make the decisive plunge beyond 'Smirkism', of which his earlier works had only hinted.

An interesting portent of his new style was his (unexecuted) design of 1828 for a projected University Library at Cambridge. Here, the main lines were still thoroughly conventional. The plan was a French conception of no particular excellence, while the exterior, broadly considered, can be connected with two late-eighteenth-century Dublin buildings which Cockerell had seen the previous year: the Royal Exchange and the Four Courts, themes from which he revised and reconstructed with reference to his Grecian studies. But in the handling one senses at once that he strained every nerve to be different. Instead of a 'stuck-on' portico *à la* Smirke, Cockerell integrated his with the main block by recessing the wall behind it; instead of unrelieved wall surfaces, Cockerell invigorated his by girding the building with two interpenetrating Orders, both fully articulated, and by projecting single columns from the double pair at each end of the façade. The resulting conception, it must be admitted, is not altogether successful. A curious, but explicable, *malaise* runs through all of it. But as a harbinger of Cockerell's developed Classicism, it is a document of first-class importance, being far and away the most compelling evidence we have of his defiance of the frigid pedantry of his rivals. Nor in this was he alone. The young Barry's Travellers' Club and the aged Soane's (demolished) State Paper Office show that other architects were as concerned as he with imbuing English architecture with a new luxuriance of texture and shadow.

Their approaches, however, were worlds apart. Barry's and Soane's pioneering gestures were based on Italian palazzo prototypes. As a whole and in detail both works followed this precedent fairly closely – too closely, Cockerell thought, and indeed he early registered his disapproval of the new 'Italian Revival', which seemed to him 'fraudulent & surreptitious use of the past ... which is conceived as a collection of "styles", to be put on or taken off as Fashion dictates'. Not that he discounted the relevance of Italian Renaissance precedent in itself. Far from it. But he considered that it should be but one component among so many, and though his own theory was firmly based on a belief in the didactic importance of the architecture of the past for that of the present, he dismissed at once the question of revivalism with a personal conviction that:

Scholarship in architecture means a broadening, not a constricting, of the field of thought. Therefore, if our new buildings are to be something more than servile & lifeless copies (which too many of them are), we must dispassionately study *all the acknowledged masterpieces of the past*, absorb the ideas embodied in them, & then with *our own needs & methods* in mind, develop those which are capable of being developed, & abandon those which are not.

Thus, at a moment when his leading rivals were laying down an ever-stricter code of historicism, Cockerell spoke rather of a 'modern architecture ultimately released from the shackles of the past', and set for himself the task of evolving a personal style of his own, a style which, however, would be fluid enough to assimilate characteristics from many other styles.

An important stage in this evolution was his (demolished) Westminster Fire Office in the Strand, a commission of 1831 (Plate XXXIV). Here, once again, we find him working with themes with which he had worked before. The plan, for instance, can be partially traced to a French paradigm, while the space-conception of the main first-floor room had interesting affinities with several of Wren's City churches. The elevations, on the other hand, embodied something new, for with their colossal piers and two sentinel Doric half-columns, their high plinth, their sculptural detail, and the bold pedimented attic storey, there is a powerful Baroque emphasis which is hardly evident in Cockerell's earlier works. Now, as never before, he went all out for bigness of scale, boldness of articulation, and richness of decoration, and the resulting synthesis, intensely original and unique at its date, can be considered the first fully mature manifestation of a personal style which Cockerell was to continue to expand and develop throughout the rest of his career.

As the composition was new, so were the details. In Cockerell's earlier works these were generally quite literal copies of Grecian prototypes, distinguished from those of his contemporaries by reason of the fact that they were based on examples which he had himself discovered. The Ionic and Corinthian Orders from the Temple of Apollo at Bassae were especially valued trophies of his Grecian travels. And so they were to continue to be. But from this time onwards, Cockerell insisted that all his borrowings be converted in accordance with his developed ideas as to how Grecian examples should be modified for their use under a northern sky, and we now find him altering them in the most intrepid manner. Similarly, by analogy with his theories regarding Grecian 'refinements' the seemingly straight lines of his buildings were now rendered as curved ones and the verticals were made to lean inwards – understandably an expensive procedure which, combined with his meticulous standards of craftsmanship, he was for ever lamenting only his most ambitious works would permit. But the results were extraordinary, and can still be appreciated in some of the few Cockerell buildings which have come down to us. For they are 'alive', as Cockerell had discovered Greek buildings are 'alive'.

The competent handling of the Westminster Fire Office, completed in 1832, made its architect's reputation, assuring his appointment the following year as architect to the Bank of England in succession to Soane. As this had been a plum for Soane, so in a rather different way it was to be for Cockerell. For though there was little in the way of new construction required at the Bank itself, the position offered a prestige foothold in the fast-expanding City at a time when the rising financial world was first seeking monumental architectural expression; and it was to the task of fulfilling these ambitions that Cockerell was to concentrate his energies during the ensuing two decades, consolidating his talents in a field where he was to emerge as a designer of very special distinction.

His first important City building was the head office (demolished) of the London and Westminster Bank, in Lothbury, which he undertook in 1837 in collaboration with William Tite. Cockerell's contribution to the work was an exemplary demonstration of how a street-front, flanked by abutting buildings, could be imbued with enormous dignity and richness of effect with the utmost directness and economy of means (Plate XXXV). Taking his cue from ideas with which he had been occupied before at the Westminster Fire Office, he provided a series of horizontally rusticated piers, rising from a high podium to a cornice, which was carried forward over slightly projecting piers at the extremities, where they performed the double function of isolating the bank from its modest neighbours and of providing pedestals for seated statues of 'London' and 'Westminster'. Above there rose an attic and a balustrade masking the roof. The careful articulation of the volumes, each subtly evaluated and having its due weight in the whole, the effective recession of one plane behind another, and the sustained level of craftsmanship were all worthy of note, but what showed the architect to best advantage was his forthright acceptance of plate glass as a viable new material demanding expression; and Cockerell's treatment of the ground-floor windows, filling nearly the full width of the bays, represented a daring innovation which he was to repeat over and over again. An interesting existing example, contemporary with the bank, is the block now occupied by the Squire Law and Seeley Historical Libraries at Cambridge, the sole executed fragment of a projected complex for the University Library, where the ground-floor windows are similar exercises in maximal fenestration.

Another rare survival of Cockerell's work of this time – and indeed his only surviving London building – is the Sun Fire Office in Threadneedle Street, next to the Bank of England. It remains not entirely as he left it. The interior has been rearranged and the exterior has had an extra storey thrust into its middle, but despite these indignities it remains an impressive witness of his genius, and interesting as Cockerell's closest approach to the palazzo style, which, in his hands, was completely reconsidered and reinterpreted. Moreover, the building is a monument of some historic importance as establishing a pattern for commercial work which was to be imitated far and wide. One detail in particular was to prove wildly infectious. This was the ground-floor arcade of haunched-segmental arches resting on square moulded imposts, evidently the first appearance of a window-type which, descending to the lowly London villa-builder, was to be applied and misapplied deep into the High Victorian future.

But what Cockerell himself considered his best work of these years was destined to remain unbuilt. His courageous and magnificent design for London's Royal Exchange, a casualty of what was certainly the most notorious of all nineteenth-century architectural competitions, would easily have taken its place near the apex of his achievement. Its plan, announcing his sympathetic understanding of current French practice, provided a skilful utilization of a difficult trapezoidal site and consisted of a large central court with shops and offices radiating round it and lining an adjoining arcade, which bisected the main axis at the rear of the building; while the spatial disposition of several of the principal rooms harked back to his early studies of the City churches. But the chief glory of the project was its main front, which Cockerell dramatically and picturesquely enhanced by disposing a series of six giant Corinthian columns in the manner of a triumphal arch, each supporting salient entablatures carrying detached standing figures: a grandly Roman theme which, as some of his boyhood sketches show, had haunted him for nearly a lifetime (Plate XXXVI). So too had numerous other features of the design, not least of which was his brilliant application of an inter-threading and subsidiary Greek Doric Order which, sweeping round the structure at string-course level, penetrated through the main entrance and culminated in a carefully-calculated climax of spatial drama. In every way it would have been Cockerell's most personal building, at once a summary of previous developments and a herald of new departures; and a measure of its meaning to him is suggested by his decision to display his superb wash-drawing for the project directly above his drawing-board whence, as a permanent office fixture, it was to find an echo in nearly all his subsequent works.

In none is this more clearly seen than in what is now Cockerell's best-remembered work, the Ashmolean Museum and Taylor Institute at Oxford, for which he won the commission, after a competition, in 1839 (Plate XXXVII). Here again the plan-form is firmly rooted in French practice and resulted from a careful consideration of the exigencies of the site and the needs of the two foundations which the building was to house. Two wings are linked by a lower portico-fronted connecting block to form three sides of an open quadrangle, the whole shelved on a high, boldly rusticated platform and grilled by a giant Ionic Order of pilasters, half-columns, and full-columns, the last arrayed, on the street-front, like those of the Exchange in the form of a statue-bearing screen. Cockerell himself described the work as 'something of a tribute to the memory of Nicholas Hawksmoor' (his famous drawing, 'A Tribute to Wren', had just achieved a considerable success at the Royal Academy), and, indeed, Hawksmoorean features are not hard to find, as, for example, in the triumphal-arch motifs at the ends of the wings which, with their round hood arches breaking through the entablature, reflect very distinctly those of the tower of Christ Church, Spitalfields, Cockerell's favourite Hawksmoor church. But with what imagination he fuses this with his Grecian and Italian Baroque sources! And how skilfully he uses his borrowings. Notice, for instance, how he deploys the elements at the junctions of the main block and the wings, where with almost breath-taking adroitness he discharges the 'tension' of the corners. There is a fine ease in this which is the earned ease of genius.

So one feels, too, about Cockerell's last important independent works, his provincial Branch Banks of England at Bristol, Manchester, and Liverpool, which he had in hand by 1845, when the Ashmolean was finishing. All of them share features in common and with the architect's earlier works. Thus the main banking rooms once again affirm his devotion to the City churches, while the principal elevations all have an attached Order bracketing the lower storeys, an attic storey above in which at least one of the windows is round-headed, and a crowning pediment. But compared to most of his earlier works Cockerell is now infinitely more suave and more confident in his own idiom, and the variations in composition and detail among the Banks are as striking as the similarities. Perhaps the finest (and Cockerell's own favourite) is the wonderfully allusive Branch at Liverpool, of which an admirer has not untruthfully suggested that a thorough analysis would, in itself, constitute a liberal education (Plates XXXVIII and XXXIX).

It is the kind of education which most Englishmen of Cockerell's time were happy to ignore, and, apart from stolen details commonly misapplied, one looks in vain for any very intelligent emulation of his achievement. But in France it was different. There as the architect himself had frequent occasion to observe, his work was both better known and better appreciated than it ever was at home, and his personal style clearly forcasted later Parisian developments. Those most directly indebted to him were younger architects like Hittorff and Labrouste, men who, having followed up Cockerell's Grecian researches, remained in close contact with him at nearly every stage in their formulation of what was to be known as *le style néo-grec*.

But in England Cockerell's course was running out, and the provincial Branch Banks, completed by 1848, mark the close of the most fruitful period of his life, though his Liverpool Bank Chambers, an undertaking of 1849, show that, late in life, his powers were by no means diminished, and that in a work calling not for architectural 'display' but for the straightforward accommodations of an office-force, he could turn his back on the opulent and sensuous Classicism of his more characteristic works, and design a block of almost uncompromising plainness, in which the bare stone is treated with the fullest feeling for its crystalline quality. Cockerell himself was to affirm that this work represented his ideal solution to the problem of commercial architecture, and a series of hypothetical designs, dating from the early 1850s, show how, in future applications, the ideas embodied here might even more brilliantly have been carried into practice.

But for the most part the last fifteen years of Cockerell's life present the sad picture of a great man who had outlived the period to which he belonged, and of an architect who, loaded with decorations, was rarely called upon to build. The enthusiasm for Greece which had thrilled his generation was all but extinct, and to progressive young architects fresh from their sketching-tours of medieval France the Royal Academy's Professor of Architecture must decidedly have seemed an anachronism. Nor could he for his part muster interest in their work. He had been left entirely unmoved by the Pugin revolution, and was utterly antipathetic to the orthodoxy of *The Ecclesiologist*, while those of his colleagues who sought with him (now and again) to perpetuate the Classical tradition – men like Pennethorne and Gibson – he discounted as positively incompetent in comparison with the French. And it was the French and the French alone who (as he exclaims in a letter of 1842) 'understand as our architects never will that the Requirements, the Construction, & the Materials of a building are the essential things, not the superficial application of a "Style" '. What in England, Cockerell asked himself during a visit to Paris in 1849, could be even remotely compared with his friend Labrouste's new Bibliothèque Ste Geneviève? He could think of nothing, though in the next year – 1850 – he saw rising in Hyde Park a work which did momentarily restore his faith in the future course of British architecture. The Crystal Palace seemed to him 'confirming evidence of an impending revolution which may leave us with an architecture as brilliant in its way as any we have known before'.

Indeed, so enamoured was he by Paxton's Palace that during the last years of his life he harboured as his great ambition the challenge of building a ferro-vitreous railway station, for which he tossed off a number of projects, designed to exploit 'unprecedented spans & unprecedented lightness of construction & effect'. But no such commission came to him, and Cockerell had instead to content himself with the few final commercial works which continued to devolve upon him, and with the task of completing two works left unfinished by younger colleagues. Basevi's Fitzwilliam Museum and Elmes's St George's Hall assured that Cockerell's career would close with much the same Classic dignity with which it had opened.

Apart from the superb library, the fittings of which are entirely his, Cockerell's plans for the Fitzwilliam were so curtailed and later mutilated that this work can easily be ignored. St George's Hall, on the other hand, has survived more nearly as Cockerell left it, and remains as we know it, a magnificent monument to the two architects whose names are associated with it.

Here, Cockerell's first important contribution was the decoration of the Great Hall. With this, as with the building at large, he had assisted the young Elmes as early as 1839, when the work was in its formative stages, and no doubt it was Cockerell who was the controlling mind behind the Wren prototype which provided one of its starting-points. Now it was Cockerell's task to design those fittings and enrichments for which Elmes had left no drawings. It was a labour of love, and there can be no denying that he discharged the commission with quite exceptional skill. However, for all the beauty of the individual components – the coffered ceiling, the Minton-tiled floor, the bronze doors, and the great organ case – the ensemble fails to make a perfectly unified impression, and the cause, no doubt, can be attributed to that outside interference which the architect continually complained of. This, fortunately, was very much less the case with Cockerell's other main contribution to the building, the adornment of the Small Concert Room; and the result was an unqualified triumph (Plate XL).

From the beginning it was apparent that Cockerell conceived the room as something of a *jeu d'esprit*. 'Our architecture has become too deadly earnest', he wrote in 1853, while his designs for the work were in progress, and it was as an antidote to what he called 'the joylessness of most modern works' that he intended the work. Never before had he had such an opportunity, for the interior decorations of almost all his earlier works had been baldly severe, severity being the order of his commissions. But it had been a difficult restriction for Cockerell, whose vision called for greater ebullience than he had been allowed, and from time to time throughout his career he sought release in hypothetical decorative exercises of the kind his imagination demanded. And it is in these that one finds the sources for his decorations of the Small Concert Hall, the first – and the last – commission of his life in which they could be used.

Indeed, many of the decorative elements can be traced back to sketches belonging to the very beginning of Cockerell's career, and it is this fact which explains the dominant character of the Hall, which in its elegant sumptuousness seems rather to belong to the eighteenth, rather than the nineteenth, century. One early sketch in particular, based on Gabriel's Opéra at Versailles, provided a number of themes; while for other ideas Cockerell drew on studies dating from the later years of his practice. The gentle undulating sweep of the caryatid-supported balcony, for instance, was a theme with which he had been occupied during odd moments in 1835; the arabesques adorning the columns and pilasters first made their appearance in his sketches of 1842. In fusing these disparate themes together, however, Cockerell was not in the slightest hampered by his sources, and the developed design was a synthesis of rare and consummate fluency.

The work at St George's Hall dragged on till 1856. A year later Cockerell resigned his surveyorships and his professorship, gradually handing over his practice to his son Frederick, who had collaborated with him in his last commercial building, the Liverpool and Globe Insurance Office. The six years that were left to him were years of quiet study – in 1860 he published the final fruits of his Grecian researches – and of quiet contemplation of an architectural scene which must have seemed to him as noisy and as crowded as Frith's painting of 'Derby Day'. The few glimpses we have of him during these twilight years reveal him as the Grand Old Man of English Architecture, a towering eminence in every way, but tired and disillusioned and no longer a fighter for the cause he believed in: the man who, in 1858, told his friend Viollet-le-Duc that, were he to begin again, he would give up the impossibility of being an architect and be an engineer instead; the man to whom, in 1859, Palmerston sent Gilbert Scott with his design for the Foreign Office – that 'regular mongrel affair' which, says Scott, Cockerell 'had the greatest difficulty in swallowing'; the man on whom, in 1860, the Royal Institute of British Architects settled its presidency while the opposing camps within its membership rallied for the next skirmish in the 'Battle of the Styles'.

❖

Cockerell died three years later, and was buried next to Wren in St Paul's. He was not soon forgotten, for he had been too commanding a figure to be easily erased from men's minds; but his works, so studied and so eclectic, exercised no very penetrating influence on the future of Victorian architecture, and his son's Freemasons' Hall in London, commenced a year after the father's death, was to be one of the last reminders of the Cockerell tradition.

Three decades passed and then, about the time the Victorian age was drawing to its close, a renewed esteem for Cockerell and his work crept into English life. His younger students gradually recalled that their late professor had said that Wren was an architect worth looking at, and before long Cockerell's works were looked at, too. Norman Shaw publicly praised him; students of the professor's own students, bred in a less exacting school, were sent to measure his buildings; he was written about; and it was only a matter of time before an

Edwardian generation made him its patron saint. It cannot be said that the buildings inspired by this reverence mark a very distinguished phase of English architecture. Perhaps a later generation, more assured of its own standards than ours is, will be better able to overlook its deficiencies than we **are**. But certain it is that none of its exponents will ever be esteemed anywhere **near** the master whom they all tried to flatter.

SIR CHARLES
BARRY

PETER FLEETWOOD-HESKETH

INTRODUCTION

No nineteenth-century architect reflects in his works more clearly the changing ideas of his time, the change from Grecian elegance to Victorian ostentation, than Charles Barry, whose span of life reached from the age of Robert Adam and Sir William Chambers to the zenith of the Gothic Revival. He was born in Bridge Street, Westminster, on May 23rd, 1795, the son of a prosperous stationer, was educated privately, and from the age of fifteen was articled for six years to a firm of surveyors. He then travelled, from 1817 till 1820, in France, Italy, Turkey, Egypt, Palestine and Syria, and acquired a reputation for the beauty of his sketches, many of which were exhibited at the Royal Academy.

Barry began practising as an architect on his return to England, at a time when Greco-Roman Classical was still the prevalent and indeed the traditional style. Its only competitor was the Gothic Revival, still in its infancy. Barry, not surprisingly, could, like many of his contemporaries, handle the first of these with ability, as we may see in his Royal Institution (now the City Art Galley) at Manchester, 1824–5; and the second with considerable success, as in his churches at Stand, in Lancashire (All Saints, 1822), or at Brighton (St Peter, 1823).

His earliest major Gothic building, more mature though perhaps less attractive than these churches, was King Edward VI's Grammar School at Birmingham, 1833–6. This was really a modest prelude to the great work of his life, the Houses of Parliament. It was the first occasion on which he had the assistance of Augustus Welby Pugin, as a designer of details and of John Thomas, the stone-carver, both of whom were to work with him later.

Meanwhile a desire for change and adventure, for something more florid, more extravagant, and obviously richer, had already begun to pervade the atmosphere, a desire felt by no one more strongly than Charles Barry himself. He found an escape from the Greco-Roman tradition in the Italian palazzo style of Florence and Rome, massive and without applied Orders, but with a bold, crowning cornice and visible roof – proof that the building was solid and not a mere shell. His first, and best, essay in this style is the Travellers' Club in Pall Mall (1830), the result of a competition for which Edward Blore, J. P. Deering, Henry Harrison, Thomas Hopper, William Wilkins and Benjamin

125

Watt also submitted designs. Barry's design was an 'improved' version of the Florentine Palazzo Pandolfini, and marks a turning-point in English architecture.

If a graph were to be made showing the changes in the quality of Barry's work, it would rise from a high level in the 1820s to a peak in 1830, represented by the Travellers', which possesses the originality of his advance into the palazzo style, but has not yet lost all the refinement of his earlier Classic manner. This level was maintained until the building of the Reform Club, next door, in 1837. But from then onwards the graph would show a steady decline, a gradual coarsening which one can only attribute to an inherent insensitiveness, notwithstanding his thoughtfulness and undoubted artistic integrity. Maybe he worked to much from theory and too little on impulse. Perhaps, with an ever-growing amount of work, he became too busy to pay much attention to refinement of detail. More probably he actually came to prefer the somewhat florid coarseness we see in his later work, which seems also to have accorded with the tastes of his employers. Indeed it can truly be said that, as a professional man, he gave them exactly what they wanted.

From this general downward trend we must, however, exclude the great work of his life, the Houses of Parliament, won in competition in 1836, begun in 1840 and opened in 1852. It would hardly be surprising if the exhaustive and unremitting demands made upon him in the planning and supervision of this gigantic undertaking had a damaging effect upon his other work. But even here a deterioration of taste is apparent in his proposal, in 1853, to enclose New Palace Yard with two additional ranges of building, joined by a diagonally-placed gateway at the corner, surmounted by a conical roof of almost grotesque design. Fortunately this extension was never built.

Meanwhile, 1837 saw the erection of the Reform Club, next to the Travellers'; bigger, grander, more magnificent and of very high quality. By comparison it is perhaps, a trifle pompous, but certainly not ostentatious or vulgar like Barry's later work and still in the first and favourite phase of his Italian manner – that which, indeed, he would probably have used for Westminster had the choice of style been his. Realizing the adaptability of Italian architecture, but the purity of Greek, he for long tried to invest the former with Grecian refinement. The Reform Club, though not creating such a sensation as had the Travellers' eight years earlier, consolidated Barry's reputation as the first master of this newly-revived Italian manner. At the time of its erection, his son wrote, the building stood almost alone as a model to foreigners of what a great English club could be.

The second Italian phase is represented by Bridgewater House, London, built for the Earl of Ellesmere in 1847, a fine symmetrical building with a splendid interior with arabesques by Crace. (For Lord Ellesmere's cousin, whose fortune was also founded upon the Duke of Bridgewater's Lancashire coal, Barry had designed the great staircase of Stafford, now Lancaster, House near by. Splendid though it is, Barry's coarse ostentation is here brought into unflattering contrast with the superb Régence interiors of Benjamin Wyatt.)

In Bridgewater House (Plate XLVI), Barry repeated the idea he used at the Reform Club (borrowed from Cockerell), of roofing in the courtyard to make a central saloon. But the outside is heavy with corner chimney-stacks and coarse balustrade. It is an example of what his biographer-son described as 'greater freedom of treatment and a desire for greater richness of effect'. He seems to have been always ready to provide his clients with whatever 'effects' they wanted. Profuse Gothic ornamentation, which had now become habitual through the building of the Houses of Parliament, led him to apply the same profusion of surface ornament to his Classic designs.

In spite of Barry's great experience and knowledge of architecture, he seems to have been curiously lacking in positive taste. The treatment of the top storey of Bridgewater House is a typical Barry compromise, resulting in a very distorted 'frieze', in which the windows are unduly cramped and crushed down by the heavy bracket cornice. A less 'adaptable' architect would have made this top storey into an attic, or even let its inhabitants live in darkness, rather than be guilty of such ill-proportioned fenestration – Barry himself was not happy about these façades.

Finally, in the third phase of his Italian manner, we find Halifax Town Hall, designed by him in 1859, the last year of his life, and executed by his son, who added a high roof to the design. This, the corner pepper-pots, and the almost Oriental tower, are more ostentatious than beautiful, but the rest is good, rather rich Classic, with superimposed orders and plenty of depth.

Meanwhile, like most Victorian architects, Barry was quite willing to work in other styles, as circumstances seemed to him to demand. Highclere, for example, and Gawthorpe, were both made Jacobean; the first (in 1837 for the Earl of Carnarvon) from Greek Ionic, the second (c. 1850 for Sir James Shuttleworth) from Elizabethan Tudor. More successfully and with less ostentation he added in Tudor, for Sir John Guest in 1848, to Canford Manor in Dorset (Plate IX), already Tudorized by Blore between 1826 and 1836.

Charles Barry thus emerges a man of great versatility, but questionable taste. He was certainly very able. He could rise to grandeur. But it would be difficult to speak with unqualified enthusiasm about everything he did.

His greatness lay principally in the lucidity of his planning. In this respect he might be compared with Sir Christopher Wren and, like Wren, was fortunate in being given opportunities not granted to some of his greater contemporaries. Yet his plans are extraordinarily extravagant and wasteful and lack the compact economy of their Palladian predecessors. Endless corridors, lobbies, anterooms and *dégagements* were introduced for scenic or perhaps snob effect. Similarly his formal gardens spread out to tire the eyes and obscure the landscape with their miles of balustrading, their innumerable urns, flights of steps and terraces, their formal beds and parterres. While his façades became in time ever more wrought and overwrought with panelling and rustication and any enrichment that would fill up. As Nature is said to abhor a vacuum, so Barry seems to have developed a horror of blank spaces. Wolfe, his lifelong friend, writing of Barry at the time of his early travels, tells us:

I know not whether the taste for ornament, for which he subsequently became remarkable, was natural or acquired. But he was full of admiration for the Egyptian practice of completely covering their buildings with sculptured hieroglyphics or painting; and he exulted in the (then recent) discovery, that the Parthenon, the model of Greek purity, was itself overlaid with ornament. His opinion was that ornament should be so limited in size as to increase the apparent scale of the building, and that it should be so kept down by lowness of relief, or by marginal framing, as not to interfere with the main outlines. These rules observed, he seemed to think that enrichment could never be overdone – an opinion which he continued to hold to the end of his career.

This may sound very well in theory, especially when fortified by Greek and Egyptian precedent, but in fact Barry seems in some degree to have lost his sense of balance between ornament and blank spaces, and the values of one in relation to the other, which he had so well understood in his earlier work. He seems to have forgotten one of the important functions of ornament, in emphasizing the shape of the object to which it is applied, and that, in the case of a building, the ornament should either be still intelligible when seen from far enough away for the building to be appreciated as a whole, or, at that distance, to have become invisible. Such things were better understood by Barry's near contemporary, Charles Robert Cockerell. One has but to think of Cockerell's firmness of line and strength of form to become aware of Barry's weaknesses. Cockerell's Ashmolean and Taylor Institute look richer than anything of Barry's by the very accuracy of the placing of detail. Barry's ornaments cancel each other out; Cockerell's, by judgment and delicacy, tell by their discrimination.

SIR CHARLES BARRY

THE HOUSES OF PARLIAMENT

Let us turn to his greatest work, that which inevitably earns his place among the great architects of history. For twenty years the building of the new Palace of Westminster absorbed his attention. The anxieties, disputes and disappointments arising during its execution at last exhausted the health and strength of even his iron constitution.

Nothing worse can happen to a creative artist than to have his work interfered with by others. This happened to Barry recurrently at Westminster, with invariably detrimental effect on the work.

On the night of October 16th, 1834, as Barry watched the old Houses of Parliament burning, thoughts were already in his mind of the opportunity their destruction presented. Sir Robert Smirke was at first called upon to provide designs for the new building, but this idea was soon abandoned in favour of a competition, in 1835, for a design in the Gothic or the Elizabethan styles, of which Barry, then aged forty, was declared the winner on February 29th, 1836.

The period for its completion was optimistically fixed at six years, and upon this basis were determined the architect's fees. This led to controversy later.

The choice of Barry's design was, on the whole, popular, but there was some criticism, partly from unsuccessful competitors, and partly from others with a genuine dislike of Gothic architecture. There was, indeed, a determined effort on the part of his professional rivals to upset the award, culminating in a petition to Parliament on June 22nd, 1836. The matter was hotly debated, Joseph Hume representing the attackers, Hanbury Tracy the defence. The question was quickly settled, however, by Sir Robert Peel, who pointed out that if Hume's suggestions were adopted, the whole principle of competition would be destroyed and the public faith endangered. Barry naturally kept out of the controversy, but was somewhat distressed by it and was particularly hurt by an insinuation that Sir Edward Cust (a strong supporter at all times) was the real author of the winning design and he merely the draughtsman!

These troubles over, he embarked upon the great work with enthusiasm, and for quite a long time all went well. Presently, however, fresh difficulties arose. Inevitable delays; the appointment of independent authorities to superintend certain parts of the work without reference to the architect; the Government's attitude with regard to his fees. Building began in 1837, with the river wall, completed two years later, and on April 27th, 1840, Mrs Barry laid the foundation-stone of the main building.

The design (Plates XLI, XLII, XLIII) is too well known to require description here – essentially Classic or Renaissance in conception, Gothic in dress; a symmetrical front to the river, a great tower at one end and a grandfather clock at the other, with smaller features in between. (It has been suggested that the basic plan, with the Central Lobby at the crossing of the principal and subsidiary axes, may have been inspired by the plan of Beckford's Fonthill Abbey, by James Wyatt. Though the scale is far larger, the arrangement is the same.)

Work proceeded piecemeal, as first one part of the site, then another, was cleared of the old buildings. Delays were caused by controversies with Dr D. B. Reid, appointed in 1840 to superintend the heating and ventilation, and by a masons' strike in 1841. Then the Peers, who had surrendered their old house for the use of the Commons, became impatient for their new one and appointed a Committee of Enquiry in 1844, which accused Barry of making alterations to the design 'without due authority'. He was, however, defended and encouraged by Lord Lincoln (afterwards Duke of Newcastle), First Commissioner of the Board of Works, and the Committee was thus mollified. Meanwhile, the House of Commons appointed a similar Committee, which also ended by giving its blessing to Barry's alterations.

The trouble began when it seemed as though Barry was not carrying out the design originally selected. But after the decision of the two Committees, opposition died down. It had the effect, however, of acting as a useful corrective to the architect's natural tendency towards alteration and development of plan.

Meanwhile, Barry's difficulties were not at an end. The appointment of Dr Reid to take charge of all heating and ventilation of the building, without any consultation with the architect, led to an impossible situation. Reid introduced a system of his own invention which did not fit Barry's plan and was quite different from the system for which Barry had made provision. Alterations had to be made, at great expense and considerable delay, only to be undone again when Dr Reid (whose scheme was found to be dangerous) was removed from the scene and Barry was allowed to resume control.

Similar difficulties arose over the great clock. They began in 1844 and continued for the rest of Barry's life. Most of these troubles were caused by the appointment of specialists to work independently and without reference to the architect. For instance, the lowering of the ceiling in the House of Commons, by the insertion of a false ceiling with sloping sides, was insisted upon, contrary to Barry's wishes, in an attempt to improve the acoustics. Barry was very unhappy about the consequently ruined proportions and this defect has been perpetuated in the recent rebuilding after 1945.

A further example of divided responsibility was the appointment in 1841 of a Fine Arts Commission under the presidency of the Prince Consort, to decide upon the painting and sculpture to be introduced into the building. It is a somewhat outrageous fact that Barry was not given a place on the board, and there were naturally, and partly as a consequence, many points of disagreement.

Barry's aim was to make the Palace of Westminster a treasure-house of the visual arts and a sculptured memorial to our national history, and to establish in the course of its erection a School of Gothic Decorative Art.

Barry and Pugin worked in perfect harmony from the time they first co-operated over the Birmingham Grammar School in 1835, till Pugin's death some twenty years later. Upon his appointment as architect for the Palace of Westminster, Barry at once invited Pugin to join him, because he admired his genius for Gothic detail, his draughtsmanship and his enthusiasm. Pugin accepted, and worked willingly under Barry. In an historic letter dated September 3rd, 1845, and published in *The Builder* three days later, Pugin makes it perfectly clear that his engagement 'is simply to assist in carrying out practically Mr Barry's own designs and views in all respects'.

If we were to write of 'Contrasts in Character' as Pugin did of architecture, we could have no finer illustration than these two collaborators. Barry as architect-in-chief and originator of the whole concept; Pugin, the skilled Gothic decorator. Barry the practical, catholic and adaptable planner and man of business; Pugin the sensitive, dedicated, bigoted medievalist. The correct apportionment of credit for the whole work may remain unsolved. But it can truly be said that nowhere else among Barry's works can we find Gothic ornament of this quality; nor among those of Pugin such grand, straightforward planning, though, to be fair, he never had another such opportunity. It was only after both Barry and Pugin were dead that Pugin's son tried to claim that Barry stole credit that should have been Pugin's.

Second only in importance to Pugin, among those working with and for Barry at Westminster, was John Thomas, the stone-carver, discovered by Barry while working on the Birmingham School. Barry placed the whole of the stone-carving at Westminster under his direction.

The Houses of Parliament, begun in 1840, were opened in 1852. Soon after the completion of the main parts of the building, in 1852, Barry was knighted. His son tells us that this recognition by the Sovereign was doubly appreciated at a time when he had begun to feel deeply the attacks made upon him and the harassing controversies in which he had become involved. The Houses of Parliament now stand as Barry's great memorial, as St Paul's Cathedral does for

Wren. With their wonderfully varied skyline, as seen from the river, or from Lower Regent Street, framed by Carlton House Terrace, or from any other angle; with their glittering towers and spires, caught in the evening sun – they rank high among the world's greatest architectural groups.

Within, there can be few finer interiors than St Stephen's Hall, the lofty Central Lobby, the House of Lords, or the Royal Gallery, rich with carving, gilding, painting and mosaic.

For this great work, which for some twenty years absorbed almost the whole of his time and destroyed most of his private practice, Barry was, of course, grossly underpaid by a Government which in this matter proved to be no less mean and dishonourable than most.

PRINCIPAL OTHER WORKS

The buildings which Charles Barry designed in their entirety are far outnumbered by those he altered, but in the former we find his best work. In this category we have already referred to the Manchester City Art Gallery and his early churches; to the Travellers' and Reform Clubs, Bridgewater House and the Houses of Parliament. He also, in 1842, built the British Embassy at Constantinople (modified 1847–8), for which brown London bricks were specially shipped out. His later alterations and adaptations, though sometimes amounting to complete recasting, were too often detrimental to the original. For his fidgety pencil was always titivating and fiddling about with perfectly good buildings that had far better been left alone.

A remarkably successful alteration was that made in 1833 to the College of Surgeons, in Lincoln's Inn Fields. Against his principles he was, fortunately, obliged to retain the existing Ionic portico, the main face of the building behind it being kept plain and crowned with a massive cornice and low blind attic. The detail is excellent and the whole front is extremely distinguished. If he had exercised the same reticence and taste fourteen years later at Bridgewater House, a building of somewhat similar proportions, how much better the result might have been. Another successful alteration was at Walton House, Walton-on-Thames, called Mount Felix, a reconstruction for Lord Tankerville in 1837. Here Barry added a tower belvedere, and an entrance corridor similar to that at the Travellers' Club. The whole composition might be described as an early stucco variant of Osborne House.

Rather different was his treatment of Highclere House in the same year, for Lord Carnavon. Without making any but surface additions, he transformed the simple, pedimented Greek Ionic house that he found into a turreted and pinnacled essay in 'Jacobean', with a central tower. It is significant of Barry's personal taste that Highclere was one of his favourite works.

The following year saw the beginning of his work at Trentham Hall, in Staffordshire, for the Duke of Sutherland, for whom he had already worked upon the grand staircase at Stafford House (now Lancaster House) in 1835. Trentham was perhaps his largest engagement outside London. Immense additions were made to the house (now demolished), and formal gardens created upon a colossal scale. These remain among the most important of their kind in the country, with belvederes and balustrades, terraces and fountains, vases, statues and flights of steps. His work at Trentham was perhaps among his best in his picturesque Classic manner; for example, the tower now re-erected at Sandon.

In 1843 Barry enlarged Duncombe Park, in Yorkshire, for Lord Faversham, and in 1844 was called upon to alter the Board of Trade building in Whitehall. In rebuilding and heightening the Whitehall front, he made it more elaborate. He was obliged, against his own taste, to re-use the existing Corinthian columns, raising each one on to a rusticated podium, at the same time breaking the entablature and balustrade, along which he placed a row of urns. In connection with these alterations Barry prepared vast unexecuted schemes for extending the building along and on the other side of Downing Street to incorporate various Government offices, with a huge dome, and the Horse Guards made higher and more elaborate. The designs for these may make us feel thankful that they were not carried out.

Meanwhile work in the North continued. Between 1843 and 1850, at the behest of the then Earl of Harewood, Barry turned his attention to Harewood House, in the West Riding of Yorkshire (Plate XLIV), a remarkably beautiful house begun by Carr of York in 1759 and completed by Robert Adam. The following extract from the Rev. A. Barry's memoir describes his father's alterations to Harewood, which are characteristic of his treatment of a Georgian house, and of his attitude towards such buildings:

It needed finish, life and variety. The treatment of the work by Mr Barry (additional accommodation being required) was simply to raise the wings, altering their design so as to bring them into greater harmony with the centre, and to improve the centre itself, by adding a handsome balustrade, and by raising the chimney-stacks to the dignity of architectural features, so as to vary the flat and monotonous lines of the former roof. Little else was done except that some beautiful carving (by Mr Thomas), in the pediment and elsewhere, gave the greater richness and life which the original

133

design wanted. But the effect was considerable, and the house now commands attention, not only by its scale and proportion, but by the evidence of taste and design visible throughout.

Those who have seen drawings of Harewood as it was before Barry laid his hands upon it can judge for themselves whether or not he improved it. But we do find here the key to one characteristic shared by Barry and his clients – the desire to *command attention*. Whatever their motives may have been, Barry as a man of business would be alive to the advantage of his works being noticed.

His alterations for Sir William Middleton at Shrubland Park and its garden, near Ipswich, were similar in principle to those at Harewood and Trentham, on a smaller scale but far more successful, helped by the natural contours of the site. He 'Italianized' the house and, from a terrace commanding a distant view, threw down an escalade of five flights leading to a formal garden and arcaded 'gloriette' below. The effect is one of singular beauty.

Cliveden (Plate XLV), reconstructed by him about 1851, with its great terrace, is perhaps, because of its basic simplicity, the most successful of these adaptations of older houses. It is remarkable for its date. Avoiding the vulgarity of most of Barry's late work, it possesses considerable grandeur and actual beauty. And of course, a wonderful position.

Between 1845 and 1848, alterations were carried out for the Duke of Sutherland at Dunrobin Castle by W. Leslie, of Aberdeen. The style adopted was Scottish baronial, with high roofs, based upon the designs of Barry, who from time to time supervised the work. As with so many of Barry's undertakings, the scheme was altered and augmented as the work proceeded. At Gawthorpe, in Lancashire, an Elizabethan house of 1600, Barry's perforated parapet and large chimneys, done in 1849 when he heightened the tower, can hardly be said to have improved the proportions or the general appearance of the house.

In 1853 he was put on a Committee for carrying out the decoration of St Paul's Cathedral, which, as a great admirer of Wren, he entered upon enthusiastically.

Unexecuted work

In addition to his plans for Whitehall, already mentioned, there was, among Barry's unexecuted designs, a magnificent scheme for prolonging Pall Mall westwards through Cleveland Row, with the Marble Arch (removed from in front of Buckingham Palace to make room for Blore's new range facing down the Mall, later refaced by Aston Webb), forming an entrance to the Green Park, flanked by Stafford (now Lancaster) House and Bridgewater House.

Less attractive was his unexecuted design made in 1857, for the Duke of Newcastle for recasting Clumber, a dull Georgian house now demolished. This was an ambitious scheme to make it into an elaborate Renaissance pile with corner towers and a monstrous spiked dome. There was more to be said for the idea of putting domes and minarets on the Crystal Palace, but this, too, only reached the design stage. He had a peculiar gift that enabled him even to deprive a dome of its essential balloon-like quality and make it spiky.

Nevertheless, whatever our final assessment of the work of Charles Barry, it possesses one quality that should not be overlooked – its essentially human character. It retains something of the urbanity and gaiety of an earlier age and has much more sophisticated charm than the ponderous Greek of his early contemporaries or the earnest Gothic of his immediate successors, however much better, purely as architecture, theirs often was. To appreciate this we have but to compare his gay and glittering, and yet practical, Houses of Parliament with George Edmund Street's noble but somewhat forbidding Law Courts, the austere and ascetic work of William Butterfield or the beautiful but almost unreal conceptions of William Burges.

One suspects that Barry was at heart more Roman than either Greek or Gothic – easygoing and liberal. In his Pall Mall Clubs we find cornices far more Roman in feeling (as we would expect from their Italian models) than Greek. Mouldings and details that are even Palladian and look more like 1730 than 1830. The fire-places in the Travellers' library are almost early Georgian in style and the whole room has the proportion and atmosphere that we associate with that era. This seems quite deliberate and is wholly successful. It represents Barry at his best.

Sir Charles Barry died during the night of May 12th, 1860, eleven days before his sixty-fifth birthday. A man of determination and energy, he was unquestionably a great planner with an inventive mind and, to begin with, a genuine love of architecture, but with curiously unreliable taste. He leaves us wondering whether he really had any positive taste at all. When designing for British grandees the sumptuous palaces they certainly wanted, had he perhaps, behind his bland and easy manner, become a little cynical towards their desire for pomp, so easily, and so profitably exploited?

135

A. W. N. PUGIN

ALEXANDRA GORDON CLARK

PUGIN is always thought of as an Early Victorian, the major architectural figure of the first decade of the reign. Though this is, historically, accurate, it does obscure the fact that in terms of years he was a contemporary of R. C. Carpenter and S. S. Teulon, both born in 1812 (as was Pugin), Benjamin Ferrey born in 1810, Gilbert Scott born in 1811, Butterfield and Ewan Christian born in 1814. All these men were profoundly influenced by Pugin; their careers must have been different but for his precocious achievement. They appear rather as Pugin's successors and his contemporaries would seem to be Cockerell, Barry and Salvin, but Cockerell was his senior by twenty-four years, Barry by seventeen years and Salvin by thirteen years. Although Cockerell had done distinguished work while Pugin was only a child, his major commissions came when Pugin's productive years were all but over, and the same is true of much of Barry's work and nearly all of Salvin's. The tremendous outburst of creative energy during which all Pugin's important work was done is contained in the span of years 1836 to 1844; it is hardly conceivable that anybody else could have assimilated so much, and given so much, with prodigious talent and generosity in so few years. A detailed catalogue of that period – of the constant designing, the travelling, the writing, the reading of ancient and modern works on theological history and the liturgy, the essays on contemporary Roman Catholic politics – would make any explanation of the final breakdown needless. Towards the end of his life he wrote: 'My medical man tells me that I have lived an hundred years in forty.'[1]

That there was about Pugin a personal greatness no one has ever thought of disputing. His life was a remarkable and fascinating one. He wrote better than any other English architect – and better than most English writers – he designed buildings of distinction, the best stained glass of its time, and exquisitely in wood and metal. Yet generally his buildings have seemed disappointing, with none of the thrill or grandeur that the obvious genius of the man would have led one to expect, and do not by themselves explain the profound revolu-

[1] The major biographical accounts are M. Trappes-Lomax's *Pugin* (1932), and B. Ferrey's *Recollections* (1861). The two key critical studies are those which appeared in H. R. Hitchcock's *Early Victorian Architecture* (1954), and 'Some comments on the life and work of Augustus Welby Pugin', by P. B. Stanton, *Journal of the R.I.B.A.* 3rd ser., IX (1952). Dr Stanton's thesis (University of London, 1950) is the definitive work on Pugin, but it has not been published in full.

tion in architectural theory and practice that was brought about by him single-handed. Indeed, his total importance is not expressed by his architecture alone, but in conjunction with his activities as a discriminating antiquarian, a decorator and a zealous propagandist for the Gothic way of life which involved far-reaching political and religious reforms as well as stylistic ones.

It was as Pugin the antiquarian scholar that he began his career. Simultaneously with the playful treatment of 'Gothick' forms in Georgian country houses and villas, an aspect of dilettante sophistication and aristocratic whimsicality, went a new seriousness of research into the artistic achievements of the Middle Ages through the direct study of the buildings themselves. The most outstanding of these new historians of the early nineteenth century was John Carter, 'antiquity's most resolute friend', a man in many respects like Pugin, who gave his life to the study of medieval buildings. This passion and research passed to Pugin together with the knowledge accumulated by his father, who, in order to assist Nash in the great demand for gentlemen's residences in the castellated style, had gained vast experience of Gothic buildings and details, which he gave to the world in his *Books of Specimens* and *Examples of Gothic Architecture*, profusely illustrated with measured drawings. At his father's death the series was continued by Pugin, then aged twenty, who travelled extensively in this country and abroad making drawings of ancient monuments to use in its completion. This inherited knowledge was something new – Carter and the elder Pugin had been pioneers – and allowed for a greater inwardness.

The early revived 'Gothick' was almost entirely scenic; it could be laid on, but it could not be bent round corners or adapted to difficult sites. In essence it was decorative and not constructional. Pugin's understanding of the style was basically different. From an early age he could design in Gothic shapes and forms as naturally as contemporaries could with Classical features. Before him architects could, from learning and imitation, add Gothic details; after Pugin they could design as if the medieval building tradition had never been broken. This is his historical importance. It could be compared with the revival and bringing into unselfconscious and regular usage of an almost dead language. The only near analogy, and not an exact one, in English architecture is to be found in the career and influence of Inigo Jones, a comparison which Pugin would not have much enjoyed.

Complementary to his antiquarian studies was his precocious early work as a decorative artist, where his passionate love for Gothic was united to his great ability to draw and his instinctive feeling for linear patterns which he knew how to vary endlessly. His designs included scenery at Covent Garden, Gothic furniture for Windsor Castle, and volumes on *Gothic Furniture in the style of the*

A. W. N. PUGIN

15th Century, Designs for Iron and Brass Work in the style of the XV and XVI Centuries, and *Designs for Gold and Silversmiths.* With his delicate and fluent pen he easily provided the required Gothic detailing for both Barry and Gillespie Graham in their entries for the competition for the new Palace of Westminster held in 1835. It was, however, his writings that ensured his immediate recognition and influence and decided his career as an architect. Apart from the highly personal design of his own house, St Marie's Grange, near Salisbury, he had had hardly any practical experience as a builder when, in 1836, he published his first architectural pamphlet, *Contrasts; or a Parallel between the Noble Edifices of the Fourteenth and Fifteenth Centuries and Similar Buildings of the Present Day; shewing the Present Decay of Taste: Accompanied by an Appropriate Text.*

On comparing the Architectural Works of the last three centuries with those of the Middle Ages the wonderful superiority of the latter must strike every attentive observer: and the mind is naturally led to reflect on the causes which have wrought this mighty change and to endeavour to trace the fall of Architectural taste, from the period of its first decline to the present day; and this will form the subject of the following pages.

In this formidable little work Pugin fiercely proclaimed his deepest beliefs, beliefs which were to determine his every action for the rest of his life. This is Pugin the Catholic, writing in the first flush of his conversion from Presbyterianism, which he had announced the previous year in the following words: 'I can assure you that, after a most close and impartial investigation, I feel perfectly convinced the Roman Catholic church is the only true one, and the only one in which the grand and sublime style of church architecture can ever be restored.' The main ideas propounded in the book were direct expressions of the amalgamation of his faith and his admiration of Gothic architecture, 'everything grand, edifying and noble in art is the result of feelings produced by the Catholic religion on the human mind', the destruction of art and irreverence towards religion are the result of Protestanism, and finally 'that the degraded state of the arts in this country is purely owing to the absence of Catholic feeling'. The Middle Ages had produced great architecture at a time when all professed the Catholic creed. Therefore, the only conceivable style for Christians to use was that of the pointed arch. Gothic and Christianity were synonymous and therefore comprised all that was good and true; Classical forms were irrevocably associated with Paganism. Pugin had thus established an ethical standard for architectural criticism, embodying the idea that a style is some-

141

thing organically connected with society, and from this he deduces that the better the society the better the architecture. Good men build good buildings.

This theory was brilliantly and wittily illustrated in the principal part of the book, the 'contrasts' themselves, where each page consists of two etchings, the one of some medieval building or architectural feature, the other of its early-nineteenth-century counterpart. These set out to give the opportunity for an unbiased comparison of architectural styles, but they necessarily also pass judgment on the societies of the two epochs. Everywhere the happiness and simple goodness of life in the Middle Ages were juxtaposed with the brutality and meanness of contemporary life, the kindly discipline of the ancient Poor House and the harshness at the modern Panopticon, the Catholic town with its churches and abbeys and the new town with its jail and factories, the splendid decorated parish church and the cheap Commissioners' one, and so on. Nowhere was the satire more biting than in 'Contrasted Episcopal Monuments', where the incised brass figure of an austere medieval prelate surrounded by the saints and emblems of his faith is compared with a podgy Georgian divine, the Right Reverend Father in God, John Clutterbuck, D.D., whose bust together with those of his two wives, one of which is supported by an ugly putto, are set against a marble pyramid (Plate XLVII). The drawings are wonderful examples of Pugin's skill; the Gothic appears rich and solid, the nineteenth-century styles skimped and unpleasant. They clearly revealed the attitude of a generation that was bored with the regularity of late Georgian architecture and was longing for variety and elaboration.

The impact of *Contrasts* was profound. The enlarged edition of 1841 sold in vast numbers. No more could the Gothic style be used altogether lightheartedly or carelessly; its intense religious purpose was clear to all. Pugin's views have often been derided for their exclusiveness and logical inadequacies, but he probably needed this utter conviction and intellectual certainty to fulfil the work that he felt called to do. The confusion of beauty and morality in his doctrine was one that had a great appeal in the nineteenth century; it appeared a few years later in the manifesto of the young Pre-Raphaelites, who must have learnt much from Pugin, and received its definitive exposition in *The Seven Lamps of Architecture*, by Ruskin.

The buildings of all the major architects of the day had been pitilessly pilloried. They were not only ugly, they were wrong: but an alternative was there. The newly-emancipated English Catholics had found a champion and rushed to employ him on ecclesiastical commissions. By the time he came to write his next treatise five years later, he had built or was building more than twenty-five chapels, churches and cathedrals. Having established the moral necessity for building in Gothic, now in *The True Principles of Pointed Christian Architecture* he dealt with the practical aspects of the style, and it was primarily as a practising architect – Pugin the functionalist – that he spoke. His approach was rational throughout; the violently Catholic bias was tempered and Gothic was represented as the only sensible and natural style for building in this country. He never abandoned his sense of religious mission but in analysing the Gothic architecture that he loved he proclaimed his two great principles for design that are indeed fundamental for good work in any period. 'First, that there should be no features about a building which are not necessary for convenience, construction, or propriety; second, that all ornament should consist of enrichment of the essential construction of the building.' His beautiful illustrations showed how deep was his understanding of Gothic construction and ornament. He lucidly explained the purpose of drip-moulds, buttresses, crockets and pinnacles, showed how their use conformed to his second great principle, and gave examples of good and bad practice. Vividly he ridiculed the nightmarish effects obtained by the unrestrained use of ornament in contemporary furniture, for example modern grates 'which are not infrequently made to represent diminutive fronts of castellated or ecclesiastical buildings with turrets, loopholes, windows and doorways, all in a space of forty inches. The fender is a sort of embattled parapet, with a lodge-gate at each end. The end of the poker is a sharp-pointed finial; and at the summit of the tongs is a saint.' Pugin was undoubtedly a good teacher. His writing was powerful and persuasive. Moreover, his advice was sound in his efforts to give clear directions for the use of ornament and to cure it from the worst excesses of ignorant yet ostentatious industrial design.

His approach to construction was even more fundamental. He asked 'that the external and internal appearance of an edifice should be illustrative of, and in accordance with, the purpose for which it is destined'. This was an attack on the rules and formulas of architectural theory, generally accepted for centuries, which had dictated the conventional shapes and proportions for houses and churches. Pugin wanted buildings to express their character naturally. To his rational mind rigid symmetry and picturesque effects were equally false. 'Yet notwithstanding the palpable impracticability of adapting the Greek temples to our climate, habits, and religion, we see the attempt and failure continually made and repeated; post office, theatre, church, bath, reading-room, hotel, methodist chapel, and turnpike-gate, all present the eternal sameness of a Grecian temple outraged in all its proportions and character.' He loathed showy façades which had no relation to the building behind, and he castigated the 'modern castellated style' with its mock turrets and donjons. Similarly deplorable was the fictitious dome of St Paul's. '*So in fact one half of the edifice is built to conceal the other:* miserable expedient! worthy only of the debased style in which it has been resorted to.' The Gothic style alone, Pugin proclaimed, allowed buildings, both ecclesiastical and domestic to be functional, natural and appropriate, not squashed into a predetermined shape for the sake of an aesthetic ideal. 'An old English parish church, as originally used for the ancient worship, was one of the most beautiful and appropriate buildings that the mind of man could conceive; every portion of it answered both a useful and mystical purpose.' This book powerfully reinforced his earlier arguments and gave them further substance. Gothic is not only true; it is common sense.

With his belief in rational construction as the basis of good architecture and his overthrow of neo-Classical standards Pugin was in fact anticipating the functionalism of the twentieth century. His two great principles, with their emphasis on a way of building and not style, gave the exciting promise of an architecture not based on period precedent. Pugin indeed realized the necessity for it but could not accomplish such a profound change without more preparation, and in his own work he tied himself to Gothic details. The final statement of his theory appeared in *An Apology for the Revival of Christian Architecture in England,* published in 1843. He continued the battle against the disordered eclecticism of imported and revived styles in contemporary architecture with his usual shrewdness and Dickensian sparkle. Describing a cemetery entrance he wrote:

This is generally Egyptian, probably from some associations between the word catacombs, which occurs in the prospectus of the company, and the discoveries of Belzoni on the banks of the Nile; and nearly opposite the Green Man and Dog public house, in the centre of a dead wall (which serves as a cheap medium of advertisement for blacking and shaving-strop manufacturers), a cement caricature of the entrance to an Egyptian temple, two and a half inches to the foot is erected, with convenient lodges for the policeman and his wife, and a neat pair of cast-iron hieroglyphical gates, which would puzzle the most learned to decipher; while, to prevent any mistake, some such words as 'New Economical Compressed Grave Cemetery Company' are inscribed in *Grecian* capitals along the frieze, interspersed with hawk-headed divinities, and surmounted by a huge representation of the winged Osiris bearing a gas-lamp.

But the general tone of the book was cheerful; Pugin realized that the Gothic Revival was well established in England, the number of Roman Catholics was growing rapidly and there were purposeful reform movements at work within the Church of England. The Promised Land was within sight. He could look to the future with confidence. 'We do not wish to produce mere servile imitators of former excellence of any kind, but men imbued with the consistent spirit of the ancient architects, who would work on their principles, and carry them out as the old men would have done, had they been placed in similar circumstances and with similar wants to ourselves.' His essential aims for nineteenth-century architecture have been sympathetically described by the late H. S. Goodhart-Rendel: 'Always before his eyes and before those of the more enlightened of his followers was a vision of a time near at hand when natural building should have been relearnt by Christian workers – all workers of that time having become Christian – in a service that was perfect freedom.'[1]

That the influence of Pugin was more the result of his writings and that the buildings are disappointing has been said so often, not least by Pugin himself, that there is a danger of the latter being undervalued. That they are disappointing was due in part to the circumstances of his life. The remarkable frontispiece of the *Apology* shows gathered together in a single perspective twenty-five buildings (Plate XLVIII), and this is by no means Pugin's total production. His energy was phenomenal, but not an unqualified advantage. 'Clerk, my dear sir, clerk, I never employ one. I should kill him in a week.' The speed at which he worked and the number of projects on which he was engaged never allowed for revision, for second thoughts, for perfection, for the complete statement. Moreover Pugin constantly had to work with insufficient means, in spite of his two wealthy patrons, the Earl of Shrewsbury and March-Phillips.[2] St Mary's church, Southport, cost £1,500, including the full complement of furniture, St Mary's, Dudley, a spacious church, cost £3,165, and St George's, Southwark, cost £20,000; whereas St Pancras church, of 1819–22, by the Inwoods, cost over £70,000, and Butterfield's All Saints, Margaret Street, cost approximately £70,000, and they were, in comparison with St George's, small buildings. These difficulties were often aggravated by the pressing demands of the Roman Catholic authorities to get the churches finished and open as soon as possible. Pugin was always prepared to sacrifice architectural considerations in order to further the advance of the Church.

[1] 'Victorian Conservanda', H. S. Goodhart-Rendel, *The Journal of the London Society*, February 1959.
[2] Denis Gwynn, *Lord Shrewsbury, Pugin and the Catholic Revival* (Hollis and Carter, 1946).

The major and most influential part of his architecture consisted of ecclesiastical work. Without producing any one church to stand comparison with those of Butterfield, Street, and Pearson, he provided the Victorian Age with a completely new type of church. Naturally his style originated in the fanciful and play-acting Late Georgian 'Gothick'. As Professor Hitchcock has proved, St Marie's, Bridgegate, Derby, of 1838–9, shows the influence of Barry, the only experienced architect with whom Pugin had been closely associated. Similarly his early scheme for a great church at Southwark betrays a Romantic concern for overwhelming vastness. His first church on a large scale was St Chad's, in Birmingham, begun in 1839 and opened less than two years later (Plate XLIX). It is an unusual design and one without either immediate precursors or successors in this country. The two west towers with their thin spires, the red brick and the continuous slope of the roof to nave and aisles all give the church a Germanic character, and it would seem to derive from some medieval examples that Pugin had seen on his continental travels. The view of the exterior shows his appreciation of the adaptability of the Gothic style and his skill in obtaining an effective composition on the steeply sloping site. There was perhaps no other contemporary architect who could produce such an ingenious plan. The interior is essentially a huge room; the tall, slender columns to a rather mean roof hardly punctuate the space at all. Here there was enough money for a big church, but not an elaborate one. His other large church, St George's Cathedral, Southwark, of 1840–2 was again a necessarily economical building and from Ruskin onwards, has been much reviled. Justice was finally done by H. S. Goodhart-Rendel in an obituary to it after its partial destruction by bombing during the Second World War.

This perspective view is one of great beauty, preserving as it does, the best characteristic of the unruined church – its rich simplicity. Pillars and arches are subtly carved and moulded, window tracery is diverse and complicated, yet the broad design is uninterrupted by any of those needless variations to which Victorian architects were mostly so much addicted ... Internally the architecture of St George's was good for any period, externally it was merely good for 1840.[1]

Very swiftly, Gothic with Pugin had ceased to be decoration and, fortified and strengthened by the reasoning of his own True Principles, became architecture. He is at his most typical and successful in his parish churches which became the standard models for such buildings. Good examples are St Wilfrid's,

[1] 'Four Gothic Revival Casualties', by H. S. Goodhart-Rendel, *Architectural Review*, February 1942.

Cardiff Castle, Glamorgan. 1865–81.
ning room chimney-piece. *William Burges*

II Overstone Hall, Northamptonshire. c. 1860. *William Milford Teulon*

III St. George, Camden Hill, London. 1864.→
E. Bassett Keeling

IV 26 South Audley Street, London. c. 1860.
Thomas Harris

V Thoresby, Nottinghamshire. 1864–75. *Anthony Salvin*

VI Harlaxton, Lincolnshire. 1834–c. 55. *Anthony Salvin*

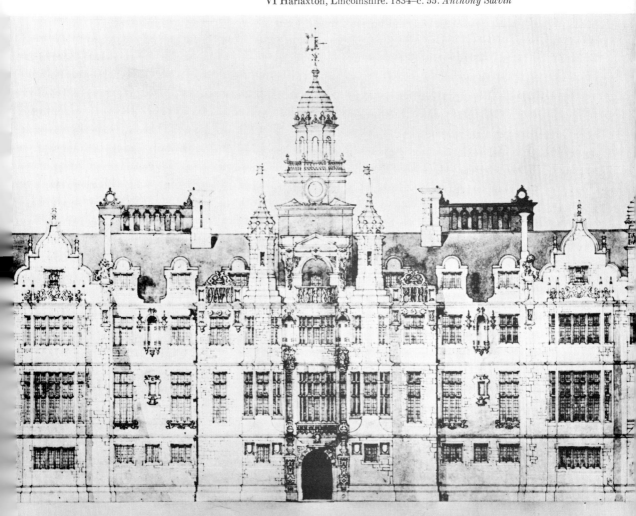

← VII Scotney Castle, Kent. 1837–40.
Anthony Salvin

← VIII Peckforton Castle, Cheshire. 1846–50.
Anthony Salvin

← IX Canford Manor, Dorset. 1826–36.
*Edward Blore. Enlarged and altered by
Sir Charles Barry,* 1854–55

← X St. John's Hospital, Alton,
Staffordshire. South side of quadrangle.
1840–42. *A. W. N. Pugin*
(Copyright Country Life)

← XI Kelham Hall, Nottinghamshire.
1858–62. *Sir Gilbert Scott*

← XII Aldermaston House, Berkshire.
1848–51. *P. C. Hardwick*

← XIII Betteshanger House, Kent. 1856–.
George Devey

← XIV Cardiff House for Mr. McConnochie.
Before 1874. *William Burges*

← XV Cloverley Hall, Shropshire. 1862–70.
(Demolished.) *W. E. Nesfield*

← XVI Eaton Hall, Cheshire. 1867–80.
(Largely demolished.)
Recasting of earlier house by *Alfred Waterhouse*

← XVII Shiplake Court, Oxfordshire.
Sir Ernest George

← XVIII Goldings, Hertfordshire. c. 1870.
George Devey

XIX Bryanston, Dorset. 1890. *R. Norman Shaw*

XX Knightshayes, Devon. 1869–c. 73. *William Burges*

← XXI Scarisbrick Hall, Lancashire. Red drawing-room 1837. *A. W. N. Pugin* (Copyright Country Life)

← XXII Kinmel Park, Denbighshire. c. 1866–68. *W. E. Nesfield*

← XXIII Leicester Town Hall. 1874–76. *F. J. Hames*

← XXIV Oxford Town Hall. 1892. *H. T. Hare*

XXVI Manchester Assize Courts. 1859–64. (Demolished.) *Alfred Waterhouse*

XXIX Congleton Town Hall, Cheshire.
1864–66. *E. W. Godwin*

XVII Manchester Town Hall. 1868–77.
fred Waterhouse

XXVIII Leeds Town Hall. 1853–58.
Cuthbert Brodrick

XXX Portsmouth Town Hall, Hampshire. 1886. *William Hill*

XXXI Imperial Institute, London. 1887–93. (Demolished except tower.) *Thomas Collcut*

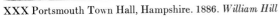

XXXII St. George's Hall, Liverpool. 1842–56. *Harvey Lonsdale Elmes.* (*Completed R. Rawlinson and C. R. Cockerell*)

XXXIII London University. Unexecuted design. 1825–26. *C. R. Cockerell* (Victoria & Albert Museum. Crown Copyright)

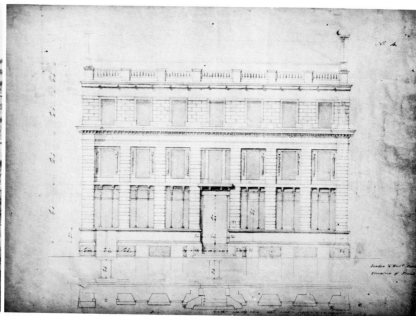

XXXIV Westminster Life and British Fire Office, Strand, London. 1831–32. (Demolished.) *C. R. Cockerell*

XXXV London and Westminster Bank, Lothbury, London. 1837–38. (Demolished.) *C. R. Cockerell* (Victoria & Albert Museum. Crown Copyright)

XXXVI Royal Exchange, London. Unexecuted design. 1839. *C. R. Cockerell*

XXXVII Ashmolean Museum and Taylor Institute, Oxford. 1839–45. *C. R. Cockerell*

XXXVIII Branch Bank of England, Liverpool. Castle Street elevation. 1845–48. *C. R. Cockerell*

XXXIX Branch Bank of England, Liverpool. Cork Street elevation. 1845–48. *C. R. Cockerell*

XL St. George's Hall, Liverpool. Small concert hall. 1851–56. *C. R. Cockerell*

XLI Palace of Westminster. 1840–60. House of Lords
Sir Charles Barry and A. W. N. Pugin

XLII Palace of Westminster. 1840–60. Peers Lobby
Sir Charles Barry and A. W. N. Pugin

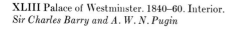

XLIII Palace of Westminster. 1840–60. Interior.
Sir Charles Barry and A. W. N. Pugin

XLIV Harewood House, Yorkshire. Alterations, 1843–50.
Sir Charles Barry

XLV Cliveden House, Buckinghamshire. 1851.
Sir Charles Barry
XLVI Bridgewater House, London. 1847–49.
Sir Charles Barry →

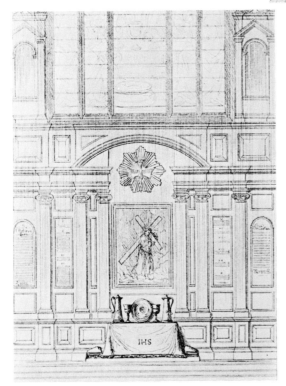

XLVII Contrasted altar screens from *Contrasts,* by
A. W. N. Pugin (2nd edition 1841)

← XLVIII Frontispiece from *An Apology for the Revival*
Christian Architecture in England, by A. W. N. Pugin. 1843.

XLIX St. Chad's Cathedral, Birmingham. 1839–41.
A. W. N. Pugin

L St. Giles Church, Cheadle. Staffordshire. 1841–46.
A. W. N. Pugin

LI St. Giles Church, Cheadle, Staffordshire. 1841–46.
A. W. N. Pugin

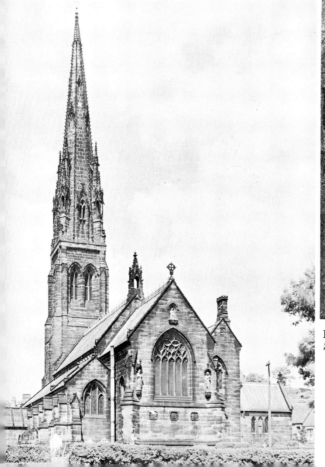

LII Crystal Palace. Original design on blotting paper. 1851.
Sir Joseph Paxton

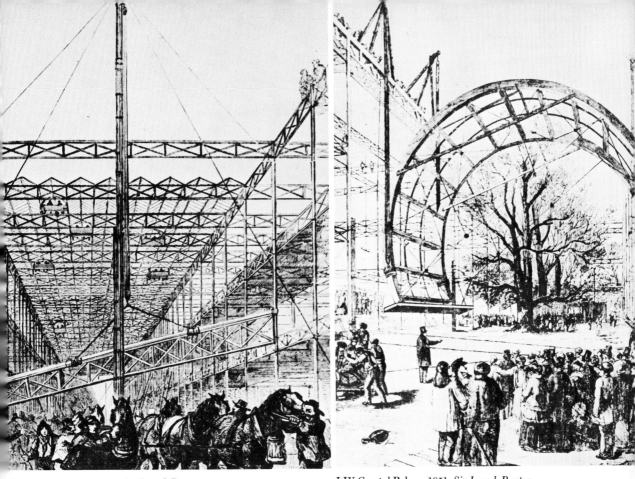

III Crystal Palace. 1851. *Sir Joseph Paxton*

LIV Crystal Palace. 1851. *Sir Joseph Paxton*

LV Crystal Palace. 1851. *Sir Joseph Paxton*

LVI

LVII

VIII

X

LIX

LXI

LXII Government Buildings, Whitehall. 1862–75.
Sir Gilbert Scott →

LXIII Albert Memorial, London. 1864–72. *Sir Gilbert Scott*

LXIV Exeter College Chapel, Oxford. 1856–59. *Sir Gilbert Scott*

LXV St. Pancras Station, London. 1867–74. *Sir Gilbert Scott* →

LXVI Trinity College, Hartford, Connecticut. 1875–82. *William Burges*

← LXVII Cardiff Castle, Glamorganshire. 1865–81. Clock Tower. *William Burges*

LXVIII Gayhurst, Buckinghamshire. Additions of kitchen, privy and stables. 1859–. *William Burges*
↓ (Copyright Country Life)

X Cork Cathedral. 1865–76. *William Burges*

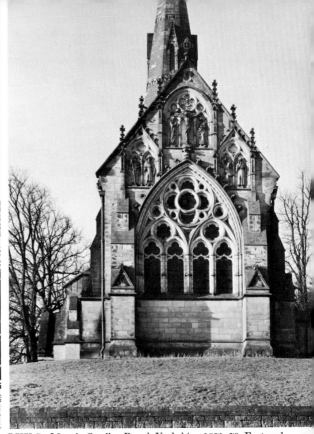

LXX St. Mary's, Studley Royal, Yorkshire. 1871–78. East end.
William Burges

← LXXI Cardiff Castle.
1865–81. Dining room
ceiling. *William Burges*

LXXIII Castell Coch, →
Glamorganshire.
1875–81. Dining room
dome and gallery.
William Burges

← LXXII Cardiff Castle.
1865–81. Arabic room
ceiling. *William Burges*

LXXIV St. Mary's, →
Studley Royal,
Yorkshire. 1871–78.
Chancel dome.
William Burges

LXXV Royal Courts of Justice, Strand, London. Competition design. 1866. *G. E. Street*

LXXVI Royal Courts of Justice, Strand, London. Competition design. 1866. *William Burges*

LXXVII Royal Courts of Justice, Strand, London. 1871–82. Great Hall. *G. E. Street*

LXXVIII Royal Courts of Justice, Strand, London. 1871–82. Main Entrance. *G. E. Street*

LXXIX New Zealand Chambers, Leadenhall Street, London. 1872–74. (Demolished.) *R. Norman Shaw*

LXXX 185 Queen's Gate, Kensington, London. 1890. *R. Norman Shaw*

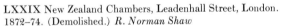

LXXXI 180 Queen's Gate, Kensington, London, 1885.
R. Norman Shaw

LXXXII 6 Ellerdale Road, Hampstead, London. 1875.
R. Norman Shaw

XXXIII Bedford Park, Acton, Middlesex. 1875–. The Hostelry and The Stores. R. Norman Shaw

LXXXIV 170 Queen's Gate, Kensington, London. 1888. *R. Norman Shaw*

LXXXV Bell Brothers offices, Zetland Road, Middlesbrough. 1890. *Philip Webb*

LXXXVII Clouds House, Wiltshire. 1881–87. Hall. *Philip Webb*

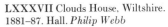

LXXXVI Leys Wood, Sussex. 1868. (Demolished.) *R. Norman Shaw*

LXXXVIII Clouds House, Wiltshire. 1881–87. *Philip Webb*

← LXXXIX Smeaton Manor, Yorkshire. 1877. *Philip Webb*

← XC Rounton Grange, Yorkshire. 1872. (Demolished.) *Philip Webb*

Red House, Bexley Heath. 1859. *Philip Webb*

Beaumont College. Domestic wing. *J. F. Bentley*   XCIII Westminster Cathedral. 1895–1903. *J. F. Bentley*

XCIV Westminster Cathedral. 1895–1903. J. F. Bentley

XCV Sanderson's Wallpaper Factory, Chiswick, Middlesex. 1902. →
C. F. A. Voysey

XCVI Broadleys, Windermere, 1898. *C. F. A. Voysey*

XCVII Worcester College Chapel, Oxford. James Wyatt. Recast 1863–64 by *William Burges* (Copyright Country Life)

Hulme, Manchester, of 1839–41 and St Oswald's, Old Swan, Liverpool, of 1840–2. Pugin is putting his theory into practice. It is his interpretation of architectural propriety in church buildings, that is to say their purpose and the requirements of the liturgy, that determine their architecture and composition. His description in *True Principles* illustrates his conception of the ideal medieval church.

> These towers served a double purpose, for in them hung the solemn sounding bells to summon the people to the offices of the church, and by their lofty elevation they served as beacons to direct their footsteps to the sacred spot. Then the southern porch, destined for the performance of many rites – the spacious nave and aisles for the faithful – the oaken canopy carved with images of the heavenly host ... the fretted screen and rood loft – the mystical separation between the sacrifice and the people, with the emblem of redemption carried on high and surrounded with glory – and the great altar, rich in hangings, placed far from irreverent gaze, and with the brilliant eastern window terminating this long perspective; while the chantry and guild chapels, pious foundations of families and confraternities, contributed greatly to increase the solemnity of the glorious pile.

This is the image that Pugin tried to reproduce on a modest scale.

His many little churches, often in the industrial areas of the Midlands and the North, have asymmetrical towers and spires, south porches, a characteristic feature of the English medieval parish church, low aisles, and deeply projecting chancels with a little belfry on the east gable of the nave to hold the Sanctus bell. The result is an effective, complex and irregular composition, the plan and each part of which depends on some requirement of the ritual. The symbolism is expressed in three dimensions. The Picturesque has become Functional. Pugin knew well how to make variations on this basic plan and his designs are always sensitively related to their site, for he appreciated that different elevations are needed in built-up or open situations. Moreover Pugin always respected local materials and traditions. The vitality and enthusiasm of the man himself, however, so evident in his writing, are alas lacking in these sensible but bald and meagre buildings which can hardly stand comparison with their medieval prototypes. His designs reached a large public when two articles illustrated with his architecture were published as a book, *The Present State of Ecclesiastical Architecture in England*, in 1843, which undoubtedly contributed to their swift acceptance as standard patterns.

His intentions were most successfully realized in St Giles's, Cheadle (Plates L and LI). 'It is the only place – excepting the hospital at Alton – where I have had an opportunity of showing a *real* revival.' As originally designed for Lord Shrewsbury and begun in 1841 it was to have been relatively inexpensive, but greater funds were made available and the finished church that was consecrated in 1846 is of a lavish completeness unparalleled in his work. The general plan is very close to that of St Oswald's and the style is his favourite, Decorated, but the detail is unusual in its quantity and quality and the spire is of true grandeur. The exterior gives a good example of his typical asymmetrical church compositions, with each feature standing out clearly, and here accented and outlined by the sturdy ornament. The pleasant dull-red sandstone of which it is built hardly prepares one for the great splendour and richness of the interior where every square inch is painted with patterns and boldly coloured. Pugin has throughout followed his own advice and the ornament is kept in its proper place. It was the most satisfying Gothic Revival church that had yet been built and its high accomplishment was undimmed by the works of his successors.

Another important church of these years was St Barnabas's, Nottingham, later a cathedral, the plan of which is more complex than before in his work. The exterior with the complicated shapes of the east end piling uphill to the great central tower makes an excellent composition. Inside, the planning of the ambulatory and chapels around the sanctuary shows Pugin to be an architect who can mould space effectively. Here one feels the awe and mystery of the central place of God's House. Unfortunately the intended rich decorations were never executed. The summit of his architectural achievement was reached within the years 1840–4, and very few churches date from the last years of his life. Of these the most attractive was St Augustine's which he began to build for himself beside his house at Ramsgate in 1846 and was almost finished at his death.[1] It is notable for the obvious pleasure that was taken in the use of local materials, and that medieval attribute of genuineness in all the work.

The same development from fanciful to natural Gothic appears in Pugin's domestic architecture as in his ecclesiastical, but necessarily its characteristics are different. Of course, he had greater freedom of design when he was not concerned with emphasizing symbolical functions. In his first building, a house for himself, St Marie's Grange, Salisbury, of 1835, there are obvious signs of the earlier Gothic; it has similarities with Mr Wemmick's, of *Great Expectations*, though there were no cannons and it was substantially built.[2] Lord Shrewsbury employed him in his Midlands palace of Alton Towers, where Pugin began in 1836 his grandiose alterations and decorations which were to take several years

---

[1] 'Pugin at Ramsgate', by John Summerson, *Architectural Review*, April 1948.
[2] 'St Marie's Grange', by John Piper, *Architectural Review*, October 1945.

to complete and of which sadly little remain today.[1] His first considerable domestic work was the recasting of Scarisbrick Hall between 1837 and 1840 for Charles Scarisbrick. Externally the building is impressively solid and confident, but more particularly it is essentially Gothic in its correspondence with the interior. The Gothic detail is more obvious than in his later work, but even here the process of shedding the earlier extravagances and starting again from a thorough appreciation of the purpose, plan and materials, as well as detail, of medieval buildings had gone far, very far from the mock castles of his predecessors, which he was to scorn so amusingly in *True Principles*. Inside Pugin provided a most authentic medieval Great Hall, with a screens passage and an open timber-roof. The decoration throughout is of a sort of Prince Regent lavishness. The Red Drawing-Room (Plate XXI) is intensely and overpoweringly patterned, as if its designer intended to get in as many of his ideas as he possibly could. The Oak Room is similarly mannered and both are impressive examples of his remarkable powers of invention, It was surely the case of the young man coming into a lot of money; he was determined to spend it gloriously.[2]

Pugin received several commissions for buildings for monastic and collegiate foundations, and here his rational approach produced appropriate and effective designs. Good planning and simple construction are to be found at the Convent of the Sisters of Mercy, Handsworth, begun in 1840, the Bishop of Birmingham's Palace, which, before its demolition in 1960, made an impressive counterpoint to the Cathedral opposite, and St Marie's Presbytery, Derby. It was again Lord Shrewsbury who provided Pugin with his greatest opportunity for this type of building. Designing the Hospital of St John, at Alton[3] (Plate X) which stands with its chapel, schools and alms-houses on a magnificent site above the precipitous valley of the Churnet, excited him enormously, and he called it the 'perfect revival of the true thing'. This was indeed a practical attempt to re-create the medieval collegiate life which Pugin admired so much and advocated so strongly. In 1840 the building of the Hospital began. It is grouped round three sides of a quadrangle, consisting of the Guildhall with adjacent schoolmasters' houses on one side and on the other two a cloister behind which are the original quarters of the almsmen, the priest's house, the tower and the chapel. These are so unaffected, so firm and solidly built, so

---

[1] 'Alton Towers, Staffordshire', by Christopher Hussey, *Country Life*, June 2nd and June 9th, 1960.

[2] 'Scarisbrick Hall, Lancashire', by Mark Girouard, *Country Life*, March 13th and March 20th, 1958.

[3] 'Alton Castle and Hospital, Staffordshire', by Mark Girouard, *Country Life*, November 24th, 1960.

honest that they seem good medieval building; of course, the signs of their real time are there, particularly the rather precious bell tower, but the whole group has great repose and naturalness. The Castle, possibly intended as a dower house and begun in 1847, is even chaster and more restrained, massively walled, simply and regularly fenestrated and thoroughly competent. Perhaps the key building of his career and one of the key buildings of the Gothic Revival, it is a complete vindication for the use of the style; it is real solid building, it works, is handsome, finely grouped, interesting in silhouette and suitably rises to dignity in the Castle and elegance in the chapel. All the flash and theatrical Gothic of previous generations had been unlearned; this was Gothic from the ground up. It must have appealed to Butterfield, Street and Webb.

Mention has already been briefly made of Pugin's work as a decorator in churches and houses, which, in fact, comprises a large part of his total *œuvre*. This activity is so often underestimated in accounts of his achievement, but it is perhaps the one which reveals most directly his genius. The purely linear patterns of his stained glass, tiles, wall-paper and textiles are often of the greatest beauty. Many fine examples are to be found in his fantastically learned *Glossary of Ecclesiastical Ornament and Costume*, of 1844, and his *Floriated Ornament*, of 1849. It is surely remarkable that a man who had such an instinctive feeling for two-dimensional design should also be able to plan space so effectively in his buildings. To an age that was much preoccupied with ornament, which it frequently used excessively and eccentrically, he gave sound advice in his *True Principles*. In the influential *Grammar of Ornament*, of 1856, by Owen Jones, Pugin's second great rule of design is only paraphrased: 'Construction should be decorated. Decoration should never be purposely constructed.' The furnishings of his churches were as important to him as the architecture and he always provided many.[1] Ruskin charged him with 'starving his roof tree to gild his altar'. Possibly he did. Pugin clearly loved processions and ceremonial and wanted the settings to be worthy. In his almost pathological attachment to the rood-screen, while low rails were preferred by progressive churchmen, one is inevitably reminded of the proscenium arch.

Unrivalled scope on a grand scale for his ceaseless inventiveness was offered by exterior and interior decoration of the Palace of Westminster (Plates XLI, XLII, XLIII) which formed his major professional commitment from 1844 until his death. The enthusiasm and vitality of his personality is here translated into the endless variations of eminently suitable, lavish, palatial décor which are never oppressive or repetitive. There was no other architect who could provide

[1] Several good examples are given by Peter F. Anson, in *Fashions in Church Furnishings, 1840–1940* (Faith Press, 1960).

such details, fine and intricate, rich in colour and noble in scale, the Perpendicular tracery, the pinnacled *flèches* of the ventilation ducts, panelled ceilings, broadly-patterned flock wall-papers, encaustic tiles, even coat-stands and light-fittings. The throne in the House of Lords is the climax and epitome of the inexhaustable wealth of invention of the whole. Throughout the building balance is kept between the structure and the ornament; Pugin had remained true to his own principles. All this activity did something to improve the debased standards of craftsmanship, and Pugin even built up a workshop of his own, where, with occasionally as many as ten workers, stained glass, metal objects, textiles and wall-paper were made. His standards were high and there were frequent difficulties in the interpretations of his designs, particularly those for stained glass. Warrington and Wailes were succeeded by John Hardman Powell (the nephew of the Roman Catholic Birmingham manufacturer who was a generous patron), who remained a faithful and successful collaborator until Pugin's death. Many metal objects were produced in Birmingham factories to his designs. All in all, Pugin was the greatest maker of the nineteenth century before William Morris.

'My writings, much more than I have been able to do, have revolutionized the taste of England. My cause as an architect is run out.' Só Pugin wrote to John Hardman, despairingly, in 1851. One must agree with his judgment; he had revolutionized the taste of England, completely and quickly. Nevertheless, St Giles', Cheadle, the cathedrals of Birmingham, Southwark, and Nottingham, Scarisbrick Hall, Alton Castle and Hospital and the detail of the Palace of Westminster are positive achievements. The many implications of his work were fulfilled by the High Gothic architects, his contemporaries in years, in the next generation.

SIR JOSEPH PAXTON

ROBERT FURNEAUX JORDAN

JOSEPH PAXTON was not a great Victorian; he was a typical one. Quite astonishingly so in almost every way. First, he was a self-made man, if ever there was one. The son of a humble Bedfordshire farmer, he ended up with honours and successes thick upon him. He owed much to his master, the Duke of Devonshire – far more to his own efforts. Standing at the meeting-point of two ages, he served as a gardener, loyal but never sycophantic, in a great Whig household. This savoured more of the eighteenth century than of the nineteenth. And yet, as a believer and exponent in full-scale Victorian *laissez faire* capitalism, it was through the stock-market, the railway boom and mechanical ingenuity that Paxton made his fortune. If a Duke provided Paxton with the lower rungs of the ladder, it was the Railway Age that provided the upper ones.

Again Paxton personified many opposite Victorian qualities – commonsense and romanticism, also piety and scepticism, optimism and caution. Self-educated, he knew his poets – even versified a little – his novelists and painters, but in real life he always kept both feet firmly on the ground. He adored exotic plants, strange lands, curiosities and medieval architecture, but all these things he was apt to turn to some most practical purpose in the furtherance of his career. He had a most typically Victorian strain of simple piety – the 15th Psalm was his guide – but a great contempt for any form of religious excess, including, of course, all Continental clericalism. He 'did' the Grand Tour, as the Duke's amanuensis, with extraordinary thoroughness; his John Bullish contempt for foreigners was no less thorough. If domestic bliss was one sign manual of the Victorian Age, then again Paxton was a child of his time. He might engage in many great enterprises – horticultural, mechanical, architectural, *Punch*, the *Daily News*, Parliament – but everyone of these he shared with his dear Sarah, conducting them all from his home on the Chatsworth Estate. His life was simple, his ingenuity unfailing, his energy unbounded, his health robust, his taste dubious. Such was the man who, in 1826, was appointed head gardener to the sixth Duke of Devonshire. He reached Chatsworth at five o'clock in the morning, climbed the garden wall and set his men to work. Thereafter he never looked back.

If Paxton served his master faithfully for forty years there was never any cringing nonsense in the attitude of the gardener to the aristocrat. In the nineteenth century a duke was a duke and commanded respect; equally, however, in

155

the nineteenth century, a gardener was sturdy and independent. More important was the fact that the sixth Duke was in his own right a man of very considerable parts. If Paxton's affection and loyalty were based upon genuine regard, as well as upon gratitude, the Duke on his side, though always a little apt to distribute largess, was never patronizing. As the gardener gradually became in effect, bailiff, stockbroker, courier, mentor, critic and, finally inseparable companion, the Duke depended upon him more and more for advice and guidance at every turn of his not uncomplicated life. So, indeed, did the whole of the great Whig circle, of which Chatsworth was only the centre, the perimeter being studded with such jewels as Haddon Hall, Bolton Abbey, Lismore, Devonshire House, Castle Howard, and a dozen other great mansions. It was a circle within which Paxton had his beginning and moved easily.

That Paxton should rise to great heights, directing railway companies, undertaking great public works and advising the whole world upon matters architectural and horticultural, was something that might well have come between master and man. In fact it never deflected Paxton from loyal service; it only served to increase the Duke's pride in his most admirable Crichton.

From his earliest days at Chatsworth, Paxton displayed, as fully as any man of his time, that thoroughly Victorian blend of romanticism and realism. If the Chatsworth cascades and fountains were conceived as a faerie fantasy, the pumps and pipes and jets, designed in the Estate Office, were efficient and durable. It was the marriage of these two opposed ways of thought which lifted Paxton's talents to the level of genius.

The circumstance that brought this about was a tragic one. The Duke had been in the very heaven of delight when his cousin and ultimate heir, William Cavendish, had married his beloved niece, the Lady Blanche Howard – a love-match well within the charmed circle. Ten years later, in 1840, she was dead. The Duke was as crushed, as was the widower. A marble vase at Chatsworth still bears mute testimony to his grief. Only Paxton, and his works, could be a diversion from that grief.

Paxton had already achieved some horticultural fame. As early as October, 1832, the Princess Victoria – of course, with her mother and Lehzen – had visited Chatsworth, to be duly impressed with the mansion, with the gold plate, the cricket match, the mill at Belper, with the monkeys, ponies and the curious plants in the conservatory. Her abiding memory, however, was of all the autumn leaves being swept away while the household slept, and – above all – of the illuminations. These were not merely fireworks and set-pieces which were a strange forecast of the Crystal Palace a century later; the Chatsworth cascades and fountains and basins were all ablaze with thousands of Russian lights all throwing their sheen upon the water. It was the head gardener who had arranged every-thing. His name remained in the royal memory.

It was Paxton's horticultural activities, however, which went so far beyond the ordinary duties of a head gardener – even those of a head gardener of a great estate. For us to be taken back to the early nineteenth century would be to discover an amazing dearth of now familiar plants. If Humphry Repton and others, just before Paxton's day, had added richness to the foliage patterns of our parks; the herbaceous border and the rock garden, as we know them, simply did not exist. Only with the building of large conservatories did exotic plants and shrubs come into their own ... only with Paxton. Then they became all the rage.

For Chatsworth, Paxton obtained valuable and quite unique specimens of tropical and rare plants, many of them unknown in Europe. The dwarf banana tree, which he first spotted on a Chinese wall-paper in a Chatsworth bed-room, was one of the more famous. At that time, however, botanical expeditions were being sent all over the world. Paxton was not behindhand in this. He organized more than one expedition. The first was to Calcutta. He sent an intelli-gent young man from the Chatsworth Estate. He loaded him with plants and seeds – all most scientifically packed. These were exchanged in Calcutta for very rare and valuable specimens. It was thus that eighty new varieties of orchid came to this island, and thus also did the Monkey Puzzle enter our lives.

Paxton's next expedition, westwards to the Pacific Slope, was more ambitious. Its object was the collection of hardy trees, firs and pines. Paxton himself raised the finance, mainly from nurserymen, but once again it was Chatsworth gar-deners who were sent. The route, however – unlike that to Calcutta – was uncharted. The whole enterprise was perilous. The two gardeners were sent across Canada, over the Rockies and down the Columbia River. Paxton warned them against bears and women. He never thought of rapids. Their canoe was overturned. All was lost. The news filtered back to England where the disaster, having been duly attributed to an all-ruling Providence, passed into the annals of Victorian heroism and adventure, and thus into the pages of the *Boys' Own Paper*.

Meanwhile, Paxton himself, having wisely declined a post at Windsor, was busy transforming the gardens at Chatsworth – creating his 'Eighth Wonder of the World'. The transformation was radical, efficient and imaginative. It would have been difficult to find a more suitable field for Paxton's diverse talents, or a better way of assuaging the Duke's melancholy. Shrubberies, cascades, vineries, wall-conservatories, a Grand Canal with an Emperor Fountain – de-signed in honour of the Tsar who never came – the Grand Rock Garden, the Arboretum, the circular Lily House, and, above all, the Great Conservatory.

Humbler folk, although naturally kept in their proper station, were not ignored. Nash's village, at Blaize, a generation earlier, had realized for the first time the Romantic qualities of the English cottage, of the vernacular, of thatch and leaded lights. That was part of the cult of the Picturesque. It had little or nothing to do with better housing, with comfort or hygiene. *That* was part of the cult of the Philanthropic. At Edensor, near Chatsworth, the Duke and Paxton, typically enough, combined these two cults. If Edensor, to our eyes, displays a bewildering variety of architectural styles, it is nevertheless the first of the model villages. Paxton described the cottages as 'commodious and comfortable'. They were supplied with water; there was sanitation of a sort; there was a drying-ground and a playground. Edensor was, in fact, the forerunner of much in housing that we now take for granted.

The Great Conservatory was begun in 1837. It was finished and fully planted by 1840. It was planned with a central and side aisles, also a gallery, the staircase to which was concealed by a rockery. The Conservatory was 277 feet long, 123 feet broad and 67 feet high. It was the largest glass building in the world, and the vast curvilinear roof – so strong in fact, so delicate in appearance – taxed Paxton's powers to the full. A carriage and pair could be driven through the Conservatory – a privilege reserved for the Duke. It housed a collection of plants, creepers, shrubs and trees that all the world came to see. 'After St Peter's,' wrote Lady Carlisle, 'there is nothing like it.' It was, even in those days, an expensive luxury, and in 1923, owing to the cost of upkeep, it was demolished. Looking back to 1840, however, we see it as the forerunner of something even greater.

However dubious the design of the objects displayed, however vulgar the taste, however crazy the gadgets, the Great Exhibition of 1851 had a social and technical significance that can hardly be exaggerated. Housed in Paxton's Crystal Palace it resolved, in a most curious manner, the great Victorian schizophrenia – that dichotomy that split so disastrously what might have been one of the great cultures of history, the dichotomy between romanticism and materialism.

The fascination and the failure of the Victorian era is that its quintessence was in itself a conflict. Tennyson's *Idylls of the King* was written for stockbrokers' daughters; Darbishire's feudal and romantic pinnacles were for the Bethnal Green Market; Rossetti's paintings sold in Liverpool and Belfast. The Conway Bridge had on it everything from the Barons' Wars except a portcullis. This combination of social disintegration and vast resources was historically unique. When once the island's harbours and coal measures were linked together by water and by iron, the stage was set to rebuild London and change the world. The international character of the Great Exhibition was not due to any enlightened interest in foreigners; on the contrary it was a patronizing and Philistine gesture from a Herrenvolk, fearless of competition.

Victorian achievements, in both halves of that divided society, were stupendous; but just because it did have two halves and was not, like Periclean Athens or Angevin Christendom, at one with itself, its achievements were always just below the top line. The Pre-Raphaelites, for instance, really do matter, but they are not the Italian Primitives; the Midland Railway really is a monument to the energy of Man but it is not the Pont du Gard. But then the Italian Primitives and the Pont du Gard could never have existed together; the first was contemporary with only primitive engineering, and the second with only crude painting. The Pre-Raphaelites and the Midland Railway, however, were robust if monstrous Siamese twins: the patrons of the former being the magnates of the latter.

Between these two worlds, between materialism and romanticism, it was a cold war. There was very little appeasement. It can never have seemed very likely that those seething, turbulent years of wealth and poverty, cruelty and philanthropy, piety and scepticism, fanaticism and hypocrisy, elegance and squalor, could leave behind them any symbol of their monstrous two-headed nature. In the event they did, and that symbol was the Great Exhibition of 1851.

Thus, we can see the Crystal Palace as a most elegant shelter for exhibiting steam-engines, *or* as a useful iron structure for housing very bad sculpture. In both cases the fundamental Victorian incongruity is there. We can never make up our minds whether – like the age to which it belonged – the Crystal Palace was supremely great or rather comic. Remembering the sincerity, the optimism and the prayers, it was also supremely pathetic.

Above all it was a miracle. The industrialists were far too busy and too prosperous to need an exhibition. The aristocracy were too comfortable and too obtuse, while the rebels – the Carlyles and the Ruskins – saw no reason for thus celebrating the triumph of filth and cruelty. It is indeed difficult to conceive of any neutral guiding force which would bring together those three warring elements – offically described as 'Machinery, Science and Taste'. This neutral force must not be insular and yet, since the whole mood had to be one of fervent self-assurance, it must be intensely patriotic. It had to be earnest about economics, romantic about science and scientific about art. Obviously, therefore, it had to be German. Every dog has its day and May 1st, 1851, was most emphatically Prince Albert's.

In spite of Thackeray's reference to:

> God's boundless heaven is bending blue,
> God's peaceful sunlight's beaming through,

the morning of May 1st was in fact showery, the sunlight intermittent. But it had cleared by midday when the Queen left the Palace. The guardsmen's horses, the Sovereign's escort to the nine State carriages, were still those delicate high-stepping beasts with curved necks and big nostrils that come to us from Regency prints. The flags in serried lines along Paxton's eaves all flew bravely while the raindrops sparkled on the glass and on Owen Jones's brilliant paintwork. The procession of the season-ticket holders: 1,050 noblemen's carriages, 800 brough-hams, 600 posting carriages with postilions, 1,500 cabs, 300 clarences and 380 other vehicles, formed a twinkling, glittering line – glossy coachwork, glossy horses, glossy toppers – all the way back to the Strand where it met the chimes from the City churches. The gentry and nobility were not alone that morning. From dawn the labouring classes, with the help of excursion tickets from the north, had been picnicking on the sward. As the balloons went up into the spring sunshine and the music stopped, the cheering became a great roar of huzzas from Notting Hill to Trafalgar Square.

That buoyant morning was all meant to be the celebration of iron and steam and yet – with the flurry of ostrich plumes, the red velvet, the little girls in pantalets, the parasols, the high-sprung carriages and the breakfasts at Brooks's and White's, it might equally well have been part of the peace celebrations of 1812, and still the perfect back-cloth was the Crystal Palace. The Palace was crystalline, it was elegant and it was slender. Somehow it contained within itself just the ghost of a ghost of Carlton House or a Sussex Terrace drawing-room writ very large. Halve the scale, put some fronds round the top of Paxton's columns and you are back in the simpler rooms of the Pavilion at Brighton.

And yet – the whole form and structure of the Crystal Palace was dictated by expediency. It is an illustration, if ever there was one, of the thesis that only through inspired obedience to all the circumstances of a moment does an artist succeed. The Crystal Palace was poised magnificently and accurately in mid-century. In its transparent Regency elegance it was the perfect setting for the Winterhalter scene of May 1st, and yet in its scale and structure it is not and never could have been a product of the age of Nash or Soane. The biggest unbroken floor space of *that* generation had been Porden's Riding School, at Brighton – a mere 178 feet by 58 feet – a *tour de force* in laminated timber. Some-how the Carlton House elegance of the Crystal Palace was begotten by Paxton out of the Palm House at Kew and the Chatsworth conservatories, but essen-tially it was a triumph for big Midland contractors. The conservatories were only collateral, the real ancestors were iron train halls and Paris markets. A building reveals its designer as mercilessly as it does its era, and the more one studies the Crystal Palace the more plain does it become that Paxton was a romantic, but not an an educated genius, who had dabbled very competently in railway shares *and* water-lilies. The Crystal Palace was by Euston Station out of Lilia Victoria Regina.

In spite of Prince Albert's earnest care for the 'Fine Arts' it seems to have been taken for granted that this would be a building with which professional architects were to be hardly concerned at all. They were far to busy fighting the 'Battle of the Styles' at the end of a cul-de-sac; it was the engineers who were now the master spirits of the age. It was the great Brunel, in fact, who had proposed a competition – one in which he was to play the dual role of assessor and winner. The competition, as it turned out, committed nobody to anything and the 233 schemes submitted were all rejected in favour of Brunel's own design for a dome – a monstrous bulb of sheet iron 200 feet across. If Paxton, through the science of construction, managed to bring south the grace of a Chatsworth garden-party, Brunel would have brought us little with this bulb except the robust stink of Smethwick and Wolverhampton.

Prince Albert was in despair. It was on Friday, June 7th, 1850, two weeks before Brunel's tenders were due, that Paxton told Mr Ellis, M.P., manager of the Midland Railway, that he had 'had an idea'. On Tuesday, at a Midland Railway Board meeting at Derby, Paxton had made the famous blotting-paper doodle (Plate LII). In nine days the Chatsworth Estate office turned the doodle into plans and a vast set of calculations. On the tenth day Paxton, waiting for a connection at Derby, 'fell in' with Stephenson who had been visiting his great job at Menai. Twenty-four hours later Paxton was inside Buckingham Palace. It was not quite 'jobbery', but it was what we would call 'swift'. Even on the 1850 railway map Derby was not on the line from Menai to Euston. The electric-telegraph clerks must have been busy. In any case, if you have an age of *laissez faire* you mustn't grumble when the devil takes the hindmost.

Brunel, whose successes were now behind him, could afford to be chivalrous about the death of his 'bantling'. Paxton, with the spur of royal approval, acted quickly. His arrangements with Fox and Henderson, the engineers, and with Chances, the glass-makers, were so advanced that by July 16th (five weeks after the blotting-paper doodle) the Building Committee unanimously adopted the plans. The Committee were embarrassed by their own conduct, but they realized that they were being got out of a very nasty hole – in at least five ways. One: ever since Paxton's appeal to public opinion – through the *Illustrated London News* – Brunel's dome had been wildly unpopular. Two: Brunel's very permanent-looking brick sheds had fanned the flames of controversy over the desecration of the Park. Three: it couldn't be built in the time. Four: it would cost more to remove than to build. Five: the exhibits would have been inadequately lit. Albert's black despair would alone have forced the Committee's hand, but Paxton – if this gardener was really to be trusted – had solved the whole problem. With our brilliantly illuminated exhibitions and displays, it is not always realized how essential it was that the Crystal Palace should be crystal – that its roof and walls should be ninety-five per cent glass. In 1851, with the incandescent mantle still forty years over the horizon, the artifical lighting of a building as long as Portland Place and twice as wide, could never even be attempted. The Great Exhibition always closed at dusk.

For all that, the Building Committee were taking enormous risks. It was all paper and promises, and the prefabrication of building components was something entirely novel and untried. Victorian optimism had never been so blatant. As Charles Dickens wrote in *Household Words*: 'Two parties in London, relying upon the accuracy and goodwill of a single ironmaster, the owners of a single glass-works in Birmingham and of one master-carpenter in London, bound themselves for a certain sum of money, and in a few months, to cover eighteen acres with a building upwards of a third of a mile long.' That was July 16th, 1850; on January 31st, 1851, the building was handed over to the Royal Commissioners for the reception of exhibits. Between those two dates lies the first miracle of prefabrication – a miracle *almost* without a sequel.

A miracle ... because the essence of prefabrication is adequate preparation. There were hundreds of sheets of exquisite and entirely original full-sizes; even the beautifully designed column heads and joints which Brunel had used at Newcastle Central or at Paddington were no sort of precedent. There were, also, all the details for the ingenious devices – the famous glaziers' trucks running in the gutters, the mechanically-controlled louvres to frustrate prophecies that everyone would be roasted alive in such a giant greenhouse, or such beautiful examples of the new aesthetic of iron as the spiral stairs to the galleries. And all these on a module, so that even the fence round the site could eventually go down as the floor-boards. Paxton prepared everything and thought of everything, but when we examine his time schedule there just isn't room for that preparation ... we can only deduce, quite literally, gallons of midnight oil.

I have tried to see the Crystal Palace (Plates LII, LIII, LIV, LV) as one should see any great building – giving it, first, a social or historical setting, glancing at its antecedents (conservatories and railway stations) and then going on to judge not only whether it met its technical and functional circumstances, but whether those circumstances were or were not the mainspring of its inspiration or its poetry. On the whole the Crystal Palace stands the test well, failing only where any work of art in the nineteenth century was bound to fail. The design by Brunel or one by, say, Pugin, would have been a mistake, for either would have been an over-emphasis of one half only of that dual world. The Crystal Palace was a mirror – more or less – of Victorian England. As such it was, in one sense, a colossal success; as such it was also, like the age it mirrored, necessarily a failure.

When we have done our best for the Crystal Palace, we still know in our hearts that it was not the Parthenon or Chartres Cathedral, nor even – since we must be fair to it as a temporary building – the marquees of the Field of the Cloth of Gold. It fascinates us because of its social and technical significance. It fascinated the Victorians. In a wave of self-congratulation and gusto they even wanted it to remain permanently in central London, on that stretch of turf that still lies empty behind the Knightsbridge Barracks. In 1852 a very special plea was made in a pamphlet by a 'medical man' – but probably inspired by Paxton – that it should become a Hyde Park *Kurhaus*, combining 'all that is desirable in the spas of Germany with all that is decent in the Roman Thermae'. The plea failed and so, in the end, the Crystal Palace went to Sydenham where, much enlarged but not improved, it was described by Ruskin as 'a cucumber frame between two chimneys'. On the whole we would not have it otherwise. The Crystal Palace, unlike churches and castles, could never have passed into history as a venerable monument. It was destroyed in 1937 by fire; perhaps being no longer visible it will be all the more revered. Like so many modern buildings – of which indeed it is the forerunner – its qualities lay in its mechanical ingenuity, its glitter and its novelty, not in its greatness as a work of art. If it had survived as a monument it would have been almost wholly as a monument to the determination and courage of a man whom Queen Victoria described as 'a common gardener's boy'.

WILLIAM
BUTTERFIELD

PAUL THOMPSON

[The sources for this essay, which condenses material from researches which I hope to publish separately, are too numerous to list here; but because of the scarcity of written material for Butterfield's life before 1860, the main evidence remains in his buildings. My interpretation may be altered by further discoveries, such as those which have eliminated most of his traditional early works – including the tile tracings at the Victoria and Albert Museum, and Llangorwen Church, Cardiganshire. The more familiar view of Butterfield, based on his later work, is cogently expressed by Sir John Summerson in his essay 'The Glory of Ugliness'.]

THE MOST familiar buildings of William Butterfield are the hard works of his middle years, complex compositions in tightly-patterned coloured brick, town churches in London and elsewhere, and those forbidding homes of Christian instruction, Keble College and Rugby School (Plate LVII). Butterfield himself is remembered as a narrow relentless bachelor, insular in his ideas, savage to his staff, crochety with his clients, allowing himself but one personal pleasure, a daily walk from his office to the Athenaeum; a volcano of constricted passion who spoke only in the pent-up power of his architecture. There is no doubt that in this architecture can be found the spirit comparable to that of Gerard Manley Hopkins in poetry – and Hopkins when young was much impressed by Butterfield's churches – taking medieval English Gothic details and constructional colour and juxtaposing them with disconcerting discord and power. In his defiance of traditional harmony Butterfield is a modern, an Expressionist, and as such he has appealed profoundly to modern critics. It is certainly hard to forget his church at Babbacombe, seen perhaps in the gloom of a winter afternoon, the nave held tightly horizontal by a long, low raftered roof, the severe nave arcades on brown marble cylinder-columns, the wall-space above patterned with bold diagonal ribs on grey-black and red brick walls, the nave floor of harsh wasp-yellow, red and black tiles; and beyond this the soft colours of the chancel, a wide floor marbled in broad patterns, pinks, grey-blues, a little black, sea-green, veined yellow, much buff; open in effect, but two great double side-arches thrusting sharply upwards beside the vertical columns of the sanctuary, reaching up into the arched vaulted roof – the whole spatial effect intensely contrary and victorious; or the church of St Augustine, Penarth, crouched grey-white on a hill above Cardiff harbour, concealing an interior of yellowish ashlar and pink sandstone and raw, red brick with harsh white and black diapering which is only held together by the tough simplicity of its architecture; or, caught in the sunlight after a storm, confronting the mean streets of Rugby, a chimney and corner of the school, a restless abstract pattern of materials and modelling.

This is not, however, the whole Butterfield. He is not simply an eccentric extreme of Victorian architecture; he is as complex and paradoxical as the whole Victorian scene. Despite his Gothic dogmatism he produced neo-Norman and neo-Georgian decorations and furnishings when appropriate, restored a dozen

167

Classical London churches without leaving a Gothic mark, patronized the Grecian Athenaeum, and lived and worked all his years as an architect in an office in the Adelphi with an Adam chimney-piece and grate, a rich plastered ceiling with a painted central medallion, an ancient Turkey carpet and a few pieces of Georgian furniture, Gothic apparently confined to the mind. Butterfield is often regarded as the most complete contrast to William Morris; yet he was one of the first patrons of Morris and Company, and, in a spirit strongly reminiscent of Morris, worked in a blacksmith's forge to master the art of wrought ironwork. His furniture of the 1850s is remarkably similar to the early productions of the Morris firm, and his buildings were sketched in admiration by Philip Webb. It might in fact be argued that the later Butterfield resulted from a complete distortion of his real genius.

Butterfield's architectural work and theories after 1860 are well recorded in the accounts and papers which he left at his death in 1900, but the evidence for his earlier life is sadly thin and confusing. The son of a London chemist, he was articled to a London builder and subsequently to more than one London architect. He found his feet as a pupil in Worcester, where he measured and sketched the cathedral and the churches of the country-side in the company of the head clerk of the office. By 1844, at the age of thirty, he seems to have been well established. He was settled in the Adelphi, paying a handsome rent, and at his own suggestion was supervising the publication of designs for church furniture, books and plate for the Cambridge Camden Society. He had trained his first pupil, Henry Woodyer, whose early buildings in 1845 and 1846 are clearly under his influence. It is hard to believe that Butterfield had not had a respectable practice for some years. Yet such was his talent for avoiding publicity that all that undoubtedly survives from his hand before 1844 is a Nonconformist chapel built at Bristol in 1842–3. Was it the last of a series of buildings which preceded a conversion in 1842 to the High Church ecclesiological party?

From his first contact in 1842 with the Cambridge ecclesiologists, Butterfield led rather than followed their taste, at first from eclecticism to a belief in 'correct' Gothic based on precedent, and after 1849 back to an acceptance of High Victorian originality. In the first phase he was a disciple of Pugin. He was sufficiently so recognized at the time to complete at least three of Pugin's architectural projects, and in later years Pugin designed a number of windows and a nunnery seal for Butterfield, which were executed by Hardman's, of Birmingham. Butterfield was associated with a testimonial raised for Pugin's family at his death. In Pugin's *True Principles of Pointed or Christian Architecture*, published in 1841, may be found the sanction for the characteristic features of Butterfield's work in the 1840s – his use of good natural materials, honesty and clarity in construction, porches with wooden barge-boards, coloured floor tiling, steepish roofs, battered chimney-breasts with coped flues, proudly displayed door-locks and hinges – even the Turkey carpet on his office floor. The school and house at Wilmcote, which may be Butterfield's earliest domestic building, are strikingly similar in detail to designs published by Pugin in 1843 in his *Apology*. Butterfield in the 1840s and early 1850s can be fairly described as the most successful of the Puginists, building without the cheapness and fussiness which made most of his master's work an aesthetic failure, but both in his functionalism of plan and structure and in his concern for English Gothic precedent, building strictly within the canons of the true principles.

His first major work was in assisting the leader of the Cambridge ecclesiologists, Beresford-Hope, in the reconstruction of the ruined abbey of St Augustine's, Canterbury, then a provincial brewer's Vauxhall Gardens, into a training college for Tractarian missionaries. They based their design on archaeological evidence from excavations, but in the detailing (wherever it has not been mauled by recent alterations) in the stone and tile fire-places, the great stilted tie-beam roof of the library, the chapel stalls and kitchen cupboard, Butterfield's strong clarity of design is evident. This first venture into neo-monastic architecture was followed by the building of two entirely new convents, at Cumbrae and Plymouth, which are the finest examples of Butterfield's Early Gothic style.

The College of the Holy Spirit, at Cumbrae (Plate LXI), was founded by a Scottish nobleman for 'the frequent celebration of Divine Service by a Collegiate Body under circumstances favourable to religious learning'. The first stone was laid in May, 1849, the Canon's house completed by November, 1850, and the rest during 1851. Its intended conventional character was emphasized by its inaccessible situation, and it is extremely surprising and fortunate that it has managed to survive, since 1876, as the Cathedral of the Isles. Cumbrae is a low, green island in the Clyde, like a long farm, with Millport in a bay at the south end, a rocky beach, an old stone pier and houses, and round the bay stone-built terraces and villas for a few retired officials, captains and colonial governors. Its genteel remoteness must have appeared ideal for a house of religious canons. The college hides itself behind the town, presenting to College Road a long buttressed wall, a stone arch and big wooden gates with Butterfieldian ironwork. Behind the wicket door and through a wood a path leads steeply up to the terraced hill-top site.

The buildings are immediately attractive, absolutely devoid of the alienating hardness which was to become typical of Butterfield. A long line of green-grey slate roofs running north-south on the brow of the hill, the roofline broken by dormer windows, big battered chimneys and the collegiate church spire, enclosed by trees, the distant craggy mountains of Arran providing a romantic background, sparing and sensitive in detail, well constructed in local island stone, the whole group is the perfect realization of the early Tractarian ideal. The church projects to the west, very plain, windowless to the north, with finely massed roof shapes; beyond it is a small, terraced graveyard, a fat, hunched, stone arch forming a lich-gate. Projecting to the east is a small chapter house, a charming timber-roofed refectory with a miniature dais, long tables and a big east window, and two sides of a cloister with generous middle-pointed tracery in a whiter stone and a spidery, timber roof on corbels. To the south of the church lived the canons; a long upper corridor with rows of cells, one for the sick with a tiny window opening into the chancel of the church, a room for conversation, and a library below, and outside trefoiled windows, a little turret with a spirelet recalling the French influences on Scottish Gothic, a tiny hip gable, and a big oriel window. The whole composition is extremely original and attractive. Even more so is the house for the choristers to the north, which depends for its effect on a section of mansard roof at each end, and simple Gothic windows contrasted with a battered chimney corbelled out above a buttress in the centre of the west wall. Despite the eccentricity of the design, which allows a window to pierce the chimney as it springs from the buttress, the detail is kept perfectly simple, and the quality of the craftsmanship is always evident; the masonry of the chimney itself, for example, from its springing to its tapered coping, could not have been better constructed. Cumbrae may have been a vain dream; there may never have been sufficient funds or enthusiasm to maintain the chanting of the choristers in the high, cool, black-and-green-tiled church, or the scholarly canons in their library; but no building more perfectly illustrates how convincing and winning the architectural dream of the Puginists could be.

Butterfield's second convent is in a less attractive but more challenging position, among the slums of Plymouth overlooking Stonehouse Creek. The buildings were begun in 1850 for a sisterhood known as the Devonport Society, most of whom came from Pusey's community of sisters at Regent's Park village to help in the cholera epidemic of 1849 under the leadership of Lydia Sellon, the daughter of a naval commander. St Dunstan's Abbey, as it was known, did not prosper financially. Butterfield took no fee for his services, and his designs were adapted during building to a smaller scheme carried out under local supervision. The Abbey is now a school, and has been much added to over the years. Nevertheless, the main building remains, with Butterfield's characteristic chimneys, fine random masonry, hipped gables, steep roofs, an oriel window corbelled out above a long thin buttress, and a circular staircase tower which gives it the air of a feudal Highland castle. It is an attractive fragment.

Abbey-building was probably the highest ambition of a medievalist like Butterfield, and his first churches show much less inspiration. Nevertheless, in the 1850s it was in his churches for country parishes that he maintained his early style. The best are probably Langley in Kent, Wykeham in Yorkshire, which has a detached spire, and Milton in Oxfordshire, of dark golden ironstone, high tile roofs crouched against a central tower whose buttresses paw impatiently to the ground piercing the lean-to vestry roof. Milton, built in 1856, impeccably furnished, bare of constructional polychrome, is the last church in this manner. Langley is perhaps the best, a Tractarian paragon designed for Pusey's brother, a well-lit interior strongly and simply detailed throughout, with glass by Hardman under Butterfield's direction, a plain arcade, attractive floor tiles, and a very pretty painted sanctuary roof. Outside, its firm window tracery is set off by soft ragstone walls, and the splendid simplified ashlar broach spire stands as singly as monumental sculpture.

Although these churches and convents would alone call for some reassessment of his reputation as a fanatic in pursuit of pure ugliness, they are not the most rewarding part of Butterfield's architecture. By the date of Milton his domestic style had developed far beyond Puginist Gothic, and he had produced a small group of buildings which may have had more influence than any others which he built. There were no satisfactory medieval precedents for village schools and parsonages, and the architects of the Gothic Revival were obliged to work out their own solutions to the problems of style and plan which they presented. Pugin himself failed in this challenge, but Butterfield was able to pursue Pugin's functional principles to their logical conclusion and evolve a wholly new secular architectural style.

This style was never his only style for schools or parsonages, and in larger stone parsonages in particular he stuck to his fine Tractarian Gothic. But two of the four schools which he designed before 1849 had cottages attached in a local vernacular style shorn of Gothic trimmings. They have segment-headed doors, casement square-headed windows, and a lively variation in their roofs. The same manner appears in a brick school by Woodyer, built in 1846. There may well be many more similar buildings by both of them. After 1849 in six years Butterfield designed seven more schools and six parsonages. Three of these schools are in brick, but one is altered beyond recognition. The earliest is at Alfington, near Exeter, standing beside an extremely mean little church also by Butterfield. It is a very complex composition in brick, tile-hanging and in part half-timbering, with big brick chimneys and hipped tile roofs, intended to build up to a central bell-cote. A water-colour in the church vestry shows the original design, in pinkish brick, with strainer arches inset over the windows. It is still a little stiff, a little too complicated, but Philip Webb and the Red House spring at once to mind. The foundation stone is dated 1850. In the same year, or shortly afterwards, West Lavington School was built, again with big hipped tile roofs and battered chimneys, but more striking for its extraordinarily generous areas of window. The contrast with the somewhat dull church and the delightful Gothic parsonage is pronounced.

During 1853 and 1854 Butterfield had an extensive series of commissions in Yorkshire. In the Ouse river plain, near Snaith, he built three groups each of a church, parsonage and school, and further north, at Baldersby, a whole village complete with church, rectory, alms-house, school and cottages. The three Snaith groups are wholly, and Baldersby mostly, in brick. The best of these buildings, the schools at Cowick and Pollington, the parsonages at Pollington (Plate LIX) and Hensall (Plate LVI), and three groups of cottages at Baldersby (Plates LVIII, LX), rely entirely for their effect on the grouping of battered chimneys, hip gables and varied roof slopes. The plain brick is unornamented. The windows are mostly sash and casement windows of a traditional kind, except in the schools, where much bigger windows are used, wood-mullioned grids which look forward to the best modern school architecture. Only very occasionally is a Gothic touch allowed to creep in. The parsonage at Hensall could easily be mistaken for a house by Philip Webb, and challenges the Red House as the first example of a conscious Victorian return to an honest unpretentious style of house-building. And if at Hensall, as at the Red House, a vaguely Gothic air is not absent, the parsonage at Pollington is further advanced, absolutely devoid of imitative flavour. The Baldersby cottages are the prototype of the tradition of brick-cottage housing of garden suburbs and municipal estates, which for many decades stood alone in England for architectural decency and honesty against the flood of speculative building.

Butterfield himself did not follow this path. These buildings were never publicized, and like the Red House were not illustrated in contemporary periodicals. His influence found its way quietly through the domestic works of Philip Webb and G. F. Bodley in the 1860s. Some of his own later domestic work was remarkable, occasionally strikingly modern in feeling, but in general his progress was towards individual Expressionism. Why did this happen? Why did he turn his back on his own achievement?

Firstly because the Gothic Revival origins of these functional buildings concealed from him their true importance. Although for a moment in 1854 this new domestic style dominated his work, he can have never regarded it consciously

172

as more than the humblest aspect of his architecture. This was not because he lacked social concern: the opposite was probably true. The challenge of Pugin to the England of his day had been social as much as architectural; hence the poignancy of some of his 'Contrasts', for example, the venerable alms-house of St Cross and a Benthamite workhouse. Butterfield himself was peculiarly inspired by St Cross, and as its architect for forty years took a marked interest in its general affairs. His interest in 'the old Guilds' suggests that like Pugin he felt that 'the Church is the true Mechanics Institute, the oldest and the best', and wanted a return to a society of Christian craftsmen. And the general social concern of the Gothic Revival architects can be found expressed even by Gilbert Scott, who argued that the landlord held his land 'subject to the moral condition that his peasantry are allowed a fair share in the produce', and warned that slum housing was 'a smouldering volcano'. It was not merely fortuitous that one of the first two churchwardens of All Saints, Margaret Street, was a leader of the Christian Socialist Co-operative Movement. But social responsibility and not socialism was the Gothic precedent. Butterfield might build good cottages, but they must keep their place in the feudal social hierarchy, and this stratified society must be reflected in his choice of style. At Baldersby the merit of the cottage is not shared by the rest of the village, which grows progressively more elaborate, reaching a climax in the outstandingly ugly rectory. An architecture in which styles represent status cannot remain functional.

The second cause was the development of Butterfield's personal character. The glimpses we have of him in his early years are of a happy enthusiast, optimistically scheming with Beresford-Hope, travelling the country and Continent with his sketch-book. His first pupil and friend, Woodyer, a man of flamboyant Bohemian manner habitually dressed in an Inverness cloak and a crimson tie, and smoking a rare cigar, was the kind of person who would not have been able to cross the office doorstep in later years. The change in Butterfield's mood set in during the 1850s. His friendships with Hardman and with Beresford-Hope both deteriorated into quarrelling and bitterness. The youthful hopes of the recovery of a Christian society became obvious illusions with the fashionable but shallow victory of the Gothic style; and the pioneering spirit which as late as 1849 led him to experiments in iron construction had turned by 1860 to a pessimistic dislike of Victorian progress, of iron ships and international exhibitions, of the tendencies of scientists to lose their faith and clergy to lose their commonsense. He felt increasingly alone against the world.

His change in architectural attitude manifested itself in the development of his interest in constructional polychrome. At first a mere aspect of his feeling for natural building materials, it grew into an overwhelming concern. In spite of the

178

English precedents for the use of naturally coloured building materials, it was fundamentally a reaction against the bonds of historicism, to some extent even a consequence of Victorian scientific progress, of the fascination in geology and the evolution of rocks. But to architecture it proved a deviation from scientific progress, and for Butterfield an abstract evasion of the real architectural problems of his time.

SIR GILBERT SCOTT

DAVID COLE

GEORGE GILBERT SCOTT was born, one of the curate's family of thirteen, at Gawcott parsonage, near Buckingham, on July 13th, 1811. He died, after some years of uncertain health, of coronary thrombosis on March 27th, 1878, as Sir Gilbert Scott, R.A., F.S.A., Past President of the Royal Institute of British Architects, Royal Gold Medallist, late Professor of Architecture at the Royal Academy, Hon. LL.D., and widely regarded as the most successful and prolific architect of the century. Into the intervening years is packed a success story almost of Smiles proportions, giving rise to a reputation which, already attacked in the closing years of his life, lent itself so handily to the iconoclasm of the 1920s that no proper consideration of his life and works has ever been made. The iconoclasts have been much assisted by his preferring autobiography to allowing a prosy official biographer to incant *nil nisi mortuis bonum*.

Yet Scott's importance for us is threefold. Firstly, we may learn a good deal about the study and practice of architecture in the nineteenth century from his life and works – the output of his office was very large; almost a thousand buildings, many of considerable importance were designed or altered. Secondly, a few of these new buildings are architecture of a high order, though there are others quite the reverse. Thirdly, in order to understand the history of many of the country's most important medieval buildings, it is essential first to understand what he did to them, and his reasons for so doing. We cannot afford to take refuge in the shifts of a lazy mind, the stock phrases of 'a modern building of no interest', or 'heavily restored in modern times'.

How came Scott, almost by accident, to occupy such a position in Victorian England? He grew up in a country parsonage, receiving little formal education, nurturing no particular ambition, but developing a taste for drawing like some young lady of good family. On this slender foundation, and with some instruction from a clerical uncle, he was at sixteen articled to an architect, a shadowy figure, in the City of London. After this, and two and a half years as assistant to Henry Roberts, mostly spent working on Fishmongers' Hall at London Bridge, and some other desultory work, his father died in February 1835. The family dispersed, and he had to earn his own living. He was nearly 24.

He had lately been working on Poor Law institutions, made necessary by the legislation, the brain-child of Edwin Chadwick, which reversed the official attitude to poor relief by removing all the paupers to the workhouse. So he set up in practice and bent every energy towards getting commissions for such buildings.

He had, although he probably did not realize it, three great advantages. One was that the Scotts, descended from his grandfather Thomas, an Evangelical Christian of great force of character who wrote a lengthy Commentary on the Bible, were both prolific and clerical, and usually both at the same time. So when he wrote round to his relations and their friends, many of them were able to find him jobs to do on their churches or church schools or parsonages. Another was that he had been born at the right time to plunge boldly into a great expansion of building activity, especially the church-building activity which started in the 1840s and carried on past the end of his life. The third was in being able to team up with W. B. Moffatt, who had been a fellow pupil, and whose character and attainments complemented his own. The two rushed up and down the country on stage coaches – these conveyances were at their short-lived prime – entering competitions not always conducted fairly by present standards, and calling upon Poor Law guardians, and with considerable success. In the four years 1836–9, 323 Poor Law institutions were erected at an average cost of under £5,000 apiece, so, especially considering the competitive fee-cutting rife at the time, it was not particularly lucrative work for the architect. Scott and Moffatt did some 53 up to 1845: all were designed on a wholesale basis and the locations of the majority are now untraceable. The earlier ones, such as Tiverton, in Devon, were plain, had a minimum of Classic detail, and could pass for barracks or factories: Scott was much ashamed of them in later years. A handful like Amersham, were richly Tudor and quite pleasing. They were followed by a few orphanages and lunatic asylums: meanwhile, the Scott connections had been bringing in odd rectories and churches, and other churches had been gained in competition, starting in 1838 with one in Lincoln.

The study of the Victorian church is a fascinating subject. At about the same time Scott started in practice, there came into being a curious, almost accidental, amateur body, the Ecclesiological Society, which succeeded early in its existence in laying down the law that all churches had to be in the style of the late four-teenth century, without box pews or galleries, with a long chancel, using 'real' materials, not plaster, and to conform in other details too numerous to mention but mostly tending to make the building quite unsuitable for Anglican worship: anyone departing from the party line was earnestly vilified. The Society's tone was High Church – too high for most people's comfort – but despite his family's evangelical background Scott joined early in 1842 and at once found that his first thirteen churches had been conceived on entirely the wrong principles. He dramatized this revelation until in retrospect it appeared rather like the light that shone on Saul on the road to Damascus; at any rate, it ushered in a period when the many small and few large new churches he designed conformed to the Society's principles. He dared neglect no avenue of advancement, for in 1838, though he could not afford it, he had married his cousin and taking up quarters in the very expensive Spring Gardens, off Trafalgar Square, very soon gave hostages to fortune in the persons of two sons.

His office by now contained pupils, and one of the earliest was G. F. Bodley, who developed into a most accomplished and sensitive church designer. He was also building up a nucleus of reliable practical men like J. Drayton Wyatt, who drew and detailed fluently and quickly, and found fulfilment in doing this well for years; John Burlison, who made the estimates and surveys and looked after many large jobs at the constructional stage; and, somewhat later, John Bignall, a mine of information on building construction. This meant that Scott could travel, much against his inclination, for he was conscious of a certain diffidence in such company, to dine with bishops, and, more to his taste, to survey and measure country churches which were to be, or might be, restored.

1844 was Scott's *annus mirabilis*. His third son was born; he moved to a gentleman's residence in Avenue Road, St John's Wood, the office remaining at Spring Gardens; he took his first, albeit brief, trip abroad; but above all, he competed for the replacement of the burned Nikolai-kirche at Hamburg. In this competition he was placed third, but the clients, dissatisfied with Gottfried Semper's winning Greek temple, referred the matter to Zwirner, the architect of Cologne Cathedral, who advised that Scott's scheme be built. This very great undertaking was in construction for nearly twenty years, at a cost of £175,000, before it was consecrated, and the tower and baptistery were added later. And when help had been wanted to finish the competition drawings, along came twenty-year-old George Edmund Street, who stayed for nearly five years and gave distinction to some of the output of the office, before setting up on his own and becoming a much better designer than his master. Scott always had a respect for Street.

Meanwhile, Moffatt had cultivated the utilitarian buildings with fair success, and did some church restoring also, like St Mary's, Nottingham, where no one has quite been able to decipher what was done. But Scott and Moffatt had grown rather apart. The latter was not a shrewd business man, and Scott could now stand on his own feet. So Mrs Scott drove up to the office to tell Moffatt that the partnership was to be dissolved, and dissolved it was at the end of 1845. After this, Scott, working hard because he was living up to his income and had saved nothing, settled down to a steady output of churches, half a dozen new and half a dozen restored each year, varied by major works such as the restoration of Ely Cathedral, his first cathedral work, which he took over in 1847, or his appointment to look after Westminster Abbey in 1849 – another milestone – by trips to Germany, and by attempts, attended with a certain amount of ill success, to obtain commissions to design country mansions and public buildings of various types in Gothic. This no doubt started as much from a wish to cultivate more lucrative forms of practice (so that, paradoxically, he could devote more time to the antiquarian detective work which he was beginning to love) as from a deep conviction that Gothic was the only proper way of designing.

In the event, these attempts led Scott into, no doubt unforeseen, deep waters. In 1856, at the same time moving into a fine late-eighteenth-century house at the top of Hampstead, he completed a manuscript (he had taken to writing on the long and tedious train journeys which his country practice entailed) published the following year and entitled, *Remarks on Secular and Domestic Architecture, present and future.* The argument advanced was that domestic architecture was unworthy of the times, and should be reformed by ending the unnatural division between ecclesiastical and secular architecture and recognizing the fourteenth-century Gothic as being able infinitely to embrace changed habits and changed methods of construction. This is, of course, much the same argument as that advanced by the Georgian Revivalists of the 1920s, and contrasts with the attitude of A. W. N. Pugin, Scott's mentor, that the nineteenth century should adopt idealized fourteenth-century habits as well as fitting into idealized fourteenth-century buildings. The perfected result of Scott's theory may well be studied in three designs: Kelham Hall, in Nottinghamshire, built during 1858–62; the unexecuted Gothic design for the Government Offices facing St James's Park; and St Pancras Station, in London.

Kelham (Plate XI), of hard brick, stone and slate, carefully planned to be asymmetrical, with carefully studied picturesque rooflines, and detail from England, France and Italy, is now, rather appropriately, a theological college. The long and complicated history of the Government Offices is well known in its essentials, and repays study in its fascinating if verbose details. Scott much coveted the commission, and, though not the successful competitor – his erstwhile assistant, Coe, had won first prize for one part of the competition – he complained at irregularities in the judging, and he and his friends eventually managed to get the First Commissioner of Works, who was in any case so disposed, to appoint him. But then events in Italy brought about the Derby Government's fall, and Scott finally found himself outmanœuvred by the wily Palmerston – who detested Gothic architecture – and forced to build a classical design, the heavy façades of which we see today. Scott prepared elaborate drawings of more than one Gothic scheme, and took most meticulous care over the design and especially the ornament; he was able to point in the end to a building that pleased no one, in supposed vindication of his beliefs.

St Pancras Station (Plate LXV) is a different matter. The well-managed and expanding Midland Railway had at last attained its own London terminus, and in 1865 asked several architects to compete for the design of a station and hotel. Scott produced drawings for a building of greater bulk and much greater cost than had been envisaged, having two more storeys of bedrooms than any of the others. But its greater prominence appealed, it seems, to the Midland directors, so that his plans were accepted; the construction went ahead with no delay, and most was completed by 1874.

Scott's practice had by now grown to a size at which contemporaries marvelled, and his familiarity with much of what his office was producing was of the sketchiest nature. Indeed, there were all sorts of apocryphal stories told: a specimen being to the effect that, visiting a northern church under construction, Scott sent for the clerk of works and began finding fault. The clerk of works heard him out, then explained, 'You know, Mr Scott, this is not your church, this is Mr Street's; your church is further down the road.' Nevertheless, Scott designed St Pancras with his own hand and with loving care; he disposed the towers and *flèches*, he drew out the elevations and thoughtfully related the openings in the walls, and then he applied the riches of fifty sketch-books to ornament the construction, inside and out, with eclectic fourteenth-century Gothic detail according to his stated philosophy. The result is a building which, had it been his only major work, would have placed him at once among the first half-dozen of Victorian architects.

Scott himself wished to be judged as an architect on the success or failure of what he regarded as his finest original work, the national memorial to Albert, Prince Consort, which was erected with great trouble in Hyde Park during 1864–72 (Plate LXIII). His declared purpose was to realize to full size one of those ancient shrines of jewellers' work which he conceived as being models of imaginary buildings, in the style of Gothic of the time of the Eleanor Crosses. Here there was no difficulty about fitting in register grates and sash windows, and funds allowed of sculpture and decorative work of the greatest perfection the mid-century could produce. The work was brought to a successful conclusion by his proceeding to Osborne to be knighted in 1872.

But in middle life he was giving more and more thought to the theory and practice of the restoration of medieval buildings. He had, as early as 1850, published *A Plea for the Faithful Restoration of our Ancient Churches*, and in 1862 he spoke before the Royal Institute of British Architects 'On the Conservation of Ancient Architectural Monuments and Remains'. This, considered in theory alone, would give him, rather than William Morris, the credit for being the pioneer in demanding a serious, a conservative, approach to the matter: but practice controverted theory in the shape of a number of unfortunate restorations done by his office, about which he probably knew little, but for which he bore the responsibility. Unlike Morris, he had his living to earn, and always feared a recurrence of the insecure days of his late twenties.

Scott gave a list of principles on which he tried to base his work. Structure must be stabilized: stonework repaired only where absolutely necessary. Plaster should not be stripped from the walls, while whitewash should only be removed with a blunt instrument, a careful watch being made for old painting, which should be retained. The existing roof, even if not of the original date, should be kept and repaired: the windows show the church's building history and so should not all be altered back to match the original. Reseating would no doubt be necessary for the proper functioning of the church, but old parts, such as screens, remaining should be re-used. The floors must be levelled and freed from damp, but monumental slabs and old tiles should be replaced. For all this properly to be carried out, it should be done as daywork and not by contract.

In practice, however, it was difficult to match up to these high standards. Scott could be weak, assistants and clerks of works were careless, workmen were ignorant, and clients liked to see where the money had been spent and were naturally chary of embarking upon a restoration without a contract with the builder, in case it might turn out rather like writing a blank cheque. So terrible things happened, such as at Exeter College Chapel, in Oxford (Plate LXIV), which in 1856 was condemned as unsafe, allegedly blown down with gunpowder, and rebuilt on the lines of the Sainte Chapelle, at Paris. Against such cases must be set others such as the Baroque porch of the neighbouring church of St Mary the Virgin, which Scott defended against all comers as being good of its kind, and it remains to this day.

The most notable body of Scott's restoration work was in the English and Welsh cathedrals. He worked at the majority of these: indeed, it is difficult to resist the conclusion that he was actively collecting cathedrals, rather as lesser men collect and repair veteran cars. Of the twenty-six cathedrals of the Old and Monastic foundations, in only three was Scott totally unconcerned – St Paul's, in London; Carlisle; and Llandaff. His share in the others ranged from the slightest – Bristol, where his advice was asked and disregarded and he took umbrage; Norwich, on which he wrote a report; and Wells, where he lent his name to assist his friend Ferrey; through Lincoln and York, where he designed furniture, and Durham and Canterbury, where he refitted the choirs, to such places as St Asaph, Chester, Hereford, and (perhaps his best work of this kind) St David's, where considerable reconstruction, the bulk spread over six to eight years, of necessity took place. The list of those where significant work was started reads like a roll of battle honours: Ely, 1847; Hereford, 1855; Peterborough, 1855; Lichfield, 1856; Durham, 1859; Salisbury, 1859; Chichester, 1861; Worcester, 1863; Gloucester, 1864; St David's, 1864; Bangor, 1866; Chester, 1868; St Asaph, 1869; Exeter, 1870; Oxford, 1870; Rochester, 1871; Winchester, 1875; Canterbury, 1877. Besides this, he operated as extensively on abbeys, notably St Albans (where he crossed that unpleasant character Lord Grimthorpe), Tewkesbury, and Westminister (a very early charge); he designed colonial cathedrals, and – something given to very few men at whatever period of history – he designed a complete new cathedral, that at Edinburgh, which was mostly built in the five years 1874–9.

Much has been made of his destructiveness. But in such cases, *ars summa est celare artem*, and his careful conservative work at Salisbury, and his success at Chichester in rebuilding the collapsed central tower to the old design largely from the old stones, go unnoticed, while he may be blamed unwittingly for earlier and less scholarly work, such as Hopkins', at Worcester, or the Cottinghams', at Hereford. Granted that much of his work might have been better done, it is certain that much might have been a good deal worse.

In the winter of 1870–71 Scott, while visiting Chester, fell very ill. He had, since middle life, much distrusted exercise, and at forty inclined very much to plumpness. He recovered, but, approaching sixty, he was probably never in robust health again. Next year, his wife died, and he took this badly, shortly afterwards giving up his country house near Godstone and moving back to a previous home, a big Georgian house at Ham, near Richmond, living there with his two youngest sons and his second son and assistant, John Oldrid, now aged 34, who had married the daughter of a clerical client of his father's and had a growing family of boys.

His eldest son, also named George Gilbert, had by now gone his own way. He had been articled to his father, had been to university, had had a Fellowship, shared in the family's prosperity and had just married a young wife. He had a practice of his own based on quality rather than quantity, and had developed into a most distinguished designer.

In 1873 Scott was elected to the Presidency of the Royal Institute of British Architects – the summit of the profession. But then he fell seriously ill again, and spent the next six months of the year abroad recuperating. The office was now clearly much in the hands of John Oldrid Scott, a somewhat unimaginative and uninspiring figure, and the work still continued to grow. In the hope of lessening the fatigue of journeys, Scott, a year before his death, moved, most improbably, to a newly-built house in Courtfield Gardens, South Kensington, typical of its place and time.

His last year of life was saddened by William Morris's famous and intemperate attack on him regarding the proposed restoration of Tewkesbury Abbey, which others, notably the irascible J. J. Stevenson, who had been in his office, joined, and which resulted in the formation of the Society for the Protection of Ancient Buildings. (It is ironic to think that this Society now shares premises with the Victorian Society, active against the demolition of good buildings of Scott's time.) Perhaps there was material for a libel case of the Whistler *v.* Ruskin class, but Scott contented himself with pointing out that for years he had, with whatever lack of success, been active and vociferous in the manner of his critics. What, he asked had they done for so long? They had not supported him. They remained ignobly silent.

He was also sad at the way the so-called Queen Anne style was gaining ground in domestic architecture, under the influence of such men as Norman Shaw. It meant that his vision of a universal fourteenth-century style for secular buildings had failed to establish itself, in spite of all his pains. But still he remained outstandingly successful in the volume of work which his reputation brought. At his death in 1878 there were over sixty buildings being built or altered from his designs. Abbeys, cathedrals, minsters, churches, chapels and monuments, even a castle, a hall, a court, a university – all were there, and they helped to swell the fortune of £130,000 which he left. And John Oldrid carried the practice on. He must have been used to the responsibility by then.

WILLIAM BURGES

CHARLES HANDLEY-READ

[Material] which throws new light on several of Burges's major buildings has been discovered since this article was written, notably a volume of letters revealing the sequence of building and decorating at Cork Cathedral. Other information which will illuminate his relations with certain patrons and artists, and amplify the record of his furniture and metal work, will be published in a fuller study of William Burges, now in preparation.]

THE IMPRINT of Burges is nearly always unmistakable, not only on his designs but also on his possessions. His touch as a designer is equally memorable whether we find it on a painted cupboard, a bronze door, or the slabs of stone surrounding a window. Similarly the provenance of the archaic vellum sketch-book proclaims itself at a glance, and the same may be said of the working portcullis, the dropped H, and assuredly of the elephant ink-stand. Long familiar to Burges enthusiasts, this curious little miscellany could be associated with no other Victorian architect – moreover each item may be taken to symbolize the more obvious features of his work: his reliance on the Middle Ages, his architectural play-acting and his visual jokes, not to mention his love of a monster scale. The vellum sketch-book – more accurately an album of careful pen-and-ink drawings – was perhaps compiled as an act of homage to Villard de Honnecourt, draughtsman and master builder of the period admired by Burges above all others. His debts to the thirteenth century stand out in many of his buildings, but the most spectacular translations from High Gothic into High Victorian, the basis of his popular renown, are to be found in his work for Lord Bute.

The castles in Wales, very different in size and appearance, are rivalled in the sphere of pictorial romanticism by few Victorian buildings. Smoothly shaped and compact in the case of Castell Coch, which is equipped as a model fortress, high-towered and rugged, and with a superb sky-line in the case of Cardiff, they are each endowed with a hint both of mystery and of menace. Seen from outside they evoke a picture of torchlight and dungeons rather than of the magnificent rooms they actually contain, but they deserve to be taken seriously since apart from their intrinsic architectural merits they embody a great deal of careful research. Burges was after all a considerable scholar, one who relied for many of his ideas on the past, yet in spite of his learning his imagination could erupt in unique fantasy, above all in his decorations. It is true that as a designer he is apt to be aggressive rather than charming, indeed there are times when he threatens to overwhelm us with his onslaughts; yet it is probably the sheer bulk and weight say of a tower or a chimney-piece – coupled with the equally forceful decorations – that his admirers are now learning to enjoy. At the same time they acknowledge in his work the grounds for a good many criticisms, including the charge of 'sham'.

187

Yet extreme romanticism is not the key-note of all his work, nor did he embrace Gothic merely for the glamour of its associations. Burges was endowed with a fair measure of common sense, he rarely approached a problem with a formula up his sleeve, and on the drawing-board he could exercise remarkably sound architectural judgment. His ability to meet the demands of his day in straightforward terms is proved by the small churches, all of them simple, well designed and cheaply built. Trinity College in Hartford, America (Plate LXVI) is indebted for its plan to tradition, but this does not make the building anachronistic, nor by High Victorian standards could the Cardiff house for Mr McConnochie (Plate XIV) be called pretentious: both are excellent buildings, neither is a sham. His work of this kind, it may be agreed, is inaccurately symbolized by the vellum sketch-book or the working portcullis, since they represent only one side of the picture. So another symbol is needed, and perhaps it is to be found in the exposed iron beam across the warehouse in Upper Thames Street: practical and unexpected, it would serve to remind us of a material he used prominently in several buildings; it would emphasize also his willingness to experiment and his love of daring juxtapositions. Above all it would remind us that as a romantic he could swoop to earth.

No autobiography has so far come to light, and while we may read of a 'mass of unpublished letters' a substantial collection has yet to be found. The few I have seen reveal little of Burges's personality and of his private life nothing at all. The approach to his work must for the time being be made through his own publications, the obituary notices, and the routine articles in the building press – a body of material which is backed up by the invaluable books and folios published by his brother-in-law, R. P. Pullan. Equally instructive and more enjoyable there remain the enormous collections of his drawings and sketches, also the dozens of notebooks and albums which offer a very close view of the way he set about his work.[1]

Born in 1827, Burges died in 1881. He was outlived by his father who was a prosperous civil engineer, a partner in the firm responsible for some of the principal harbours and lighthouses which served the shipping of those days. Burges was never at a loss when it came to the execution even of his most elaborate designs – for instance, several of his internal roofs and ceilings; indeed a

[1] *See* Bibliographical Note; also E. W. Godwin, *British Architect*, April 29th, 1881. (It is Godwin who mentions the letters.) *The Builder*, 1881, pp. 531, 534, 581, 648, 811. *The Building News*, 1881, pp. 473, 480, 575. Hundreds of drawings, and over twenty large albums, are distributed chiefly between the R.I.B.A. and the V. and A. At the R.I.B.A. I count over 60 notebooks besides the vellum album. Another album (Coch Report) is in the M.O.W. Library, while Burges's Estimate Book (entries from 1875 onwards) is in the Library at the V. and A. Groups of drawings are also preserved at Cork, Knightshayes and Cardiff; at Worcester College, Oxford, and at Trinity College in America. Only the most important items are mentioned here.

sound grasp of construction is to be seen in nearly everything he built, and for this asset he may to some extent have been indebted to his engineering background. In 1839 he went to King's College School where he spent five years; in 1844 he was articled to Edward Blore; and in 1849 he went to assist M. D. Wyatt. While he was with Blore he made three sketching tours in England, and perhaps it was at this time that he first became seriously interested in Gothic; but we must remember that from 1846 to 1848 Blore was chiefly occupied with the new, non-Gothic front for Buckingham Palace, and in any case it seems unlikely that Blore's example would have been particularly inspiring. I can imagine that Burges might have got on well with Wyatt – whose three publications up to 1849 were all on the subject of medieval mosaic.[1] To Burges, this interest in the applied arts would have been highly congenial, and we should remember that he made a feature of mosaic floors in many of his own buildings. Yet Wyatt at this time was only just beginning to make his way as an architect, so his influence on Burges was probably no more decisive than that of Blore.

Just how much time Burges spent with Wyatt and in what capacity remains for the present uncertain. Pullan tells us that in 1849 and 1850 he spent about eighteen months travelling in France, Germany and Belgium, also that in 1854 he again visited France, and Italy perhaps for the first time. In 1850 he had reached the age of twenty-three, and in that year he published what I believe to be his first article – on Damascenery – but his second article – on Incised Slabs and Pavements – did not appear until 1855. This period of five years was no doubt important to his development, but few facts are available apart from what we know of the visits to France and Italy in 1854. He could have learned much from the Great Exhibition, particularly the Medieval Court, and there is evidence that he watched the progress – to use his own words – of that 'not very satisfactory building' the Palace of Westminster. Several letters to Sir Frederic Madden of the British Museum inform us that in 1852 he was studying manuscripts in the Museum collection.[2] Then in 1855 – the year of his second article – came the competition for Lille, the first important event of his professional life, to which we shall return.

It is worth remarking at this point that although the competition drawings submitted by Clutton and Burges included a few touches that were slightly archaic,[3] they were at the same time simple and informative, quite without prettifying deceptions. For their final appearance it is difficult to say which of

[1] N. Pevsner, *M. D. Wyatt* (C.U.P. 1950), pp. 2, 30.
[2] B. M. Dept. of Manuscripts, Eg. 2845 ff.
[3] G. G. Evans and R. P. Pullan, *Photographs of Designs for Lille Cathedral* (Wimborne Minster, n.d.).

the two men was responsible, although Burges's hand may perhaps be detected in some of the more intricate details. Certainly one of his chief assets was his ability to draw, when he chose, with unequivocal precision, even if as a draughtsman he absorbed a wide variety of influences. While his admiration for Villard de Honnecourt comes out very often in a style which, though fluent, is apt to be blunt and at times even graceless, a few drawings survive to show that he could learn from more elegant draughtsmen of a later date – even indeed from his contemporaries. Thus many of the sketches for his decorative designs show unmistakable influence from certain of the Pre-Raphaelites; nor is this surprising since several of them, including Rossetti, were among his friends. Again, in one of the albums there is a large collection of Japanese prints, a collection which is in itself extremely significant since in England it must have been one of the first of its kind;[1] and no doubt it explains the traces of Japanese influence if not on his draughtsmanship then on a few of his decorations. Nevertheless, on his decorative work as a whole it looks as if the biggest single influence came from illuminated manuscripts; and perhaps it was from the pages of Villard de Honnecourt – consisting, it is true, chiefly of monochrome diagrams – that he borrowed the trick of including in his drawings small figures in medieval dress.

Enough, however, has been said about Burges's debts to other draughtsmen, and in any case not by any means all his lessons were learned at second hand. Because he believed that every architect should be able to draw the human figure, he made numerous studies from casts and the living model, a discipline which helps to explain his success particularly perhaps in the handling of figure sculpture. His practical approach to draughtsmanship again comes out when he rails against students who flock to Italy to make 'telling sketches, the curse of architecture'. His dislike of what he calls the 'scribble style' of drawing went hand in hand with his mistrust of picturesque effects on the drawing-board. He criticized A. W. Pugin because he 'made things look too well by his marvellous etching', and noted an 'action in all his plates which you look for in vain in the real thing'. Burges was no paper architect. 'What a pity', he is said to have remarked of a colleague, 'that he cannot build his cross-hatching', and if this twice-recorded remark is true, that colleague was none other than G. E. Street.[2]

Wherever he went Burges developed his capacity to analyse and record what he saw. Driven by an admirable curiosity, he climbed up into roofs and

[1] Elizabeth Aslin, *Nineteenth-century English Furniture* (London, 1962), p. 141.
[2] Norman Shaw, R.A., and T. G. Jackson, R.A., (eds.), *Architecture: A Profession or an Art* (London, 1892), p. 141; also R. Blomfield, A.R.A., *Architectural Drawing and Draughtsmen* (London, 1912), p. 7.

spires, he made rubbings and tracings on floors and walls, he drew countless details of masonry and joinery, sculpture and furniture – abundant evidence is to be found in the albums and published drawings. One of the albums includes careful diagrams of the different parts of a chalice, and perhaps it was by dismembering medieval treasures that he leaned how to mount the coins and the carvings of jade and ivory – his loot as a collector – in the superb metal-work made to his own designs. Photographs survive to show that several of the cabinets in his Buckingham Street rooms – cabinets which reappear at Tower House – were full of pottery and ivory caskets, enamels and other bibelots; and since he designed the cabinets himself the interests of the collector, the designer and the antiquarian must often have merged happily together.

To gather the facts which lie behind so many of his designs, to say nothing of the material for his articles, Burges must have spent many hours of his life in libraries and museums; yet he was anything but a lonely recluse, withdrawn from the world in a scholar's isolation. Fond of the theatre, friendly with artists, and devoted to animals and birds, he is unexpectedly mentioned in several memoirs. His behaviour sometimes caused amusement but he seems always to have been respected for his knowledge – the research albums, of which he was obviously rather proud, were evidently a useful source of information to his friends. He repeatedly entered for the competitions, as a rule unsuccessfully, yet curiously enough he approved of the competition system. He kept an eye on the work of his colleagues, his friends in the profession included Seddon and Aitchison, Scott and particularly Godwin, and he even refers to 'my friend **Mr Street**'; but while, as Street said, they 'practically began life together' – meaning that they both entered for the Lille competition – it is difficult to imagine anything but a critical and uneasy relationship between them since the two men were different in nearly every way. Street's books on Spanish and Italian Gothic, for instance, embody sustained and methodical histories of architecture, whereas Burges displays his erudition in short essays and papers. For the **1863** edition of Scott's *Gleanings from Westminster Abbey* Burges contributed no less than eight entries – on the Retabulum, on the Confessor's Chair and on Henry VII's Tomb among other items – but nothing on the building itself. His interests outside architecture are again apparent in the only book he ever wrote: published in 1865, *Art Applied to Industry* consists chiefly of lectures which seek to improve taste in the sphere suggested by the title.[1] Still, like everyone else he read papers at the Institute, some of which seem to have raised stormy discussions, while over a period of twenty years his articles appeared not only in *The Builder* and *The Building News* but also in *The Gentleman's Magazine*,

---

[1] Cantor Lectures delivered to the Royal Society of Arts in 1864.

VICTORIAN ARCHITECTURE

The Ecclesiologist and the *Annales Archéologiques* – I know of forty titles altogether and there may well be more. These articles, his albums of research drawings and the contents of his library[1] show the unusually wide range of his artistic interests. Blessed with a very lively mind, his was probably a most attractive personality, but at the same time his outlook and character were in many ways limited.

There is no evidence that religious convictions had much influence on his life or work. He was not deeply involved with the High Church interests which engaged Butterfield or Street, providing them with a background against which they could develop their ideas almost on the basis of a kind of commitment. Burges was neither a philosopher nor a prophet and it goes without saying that his publications are insignificant besides those of Pugin, Ruskin, and Morris, the great reformers. Nothing in Burges's character or written work can be found to correspond to Philip Webb's moral earnestness, or his profound concern over the 'rottenness in the arts'.[2] The moral problems of architecture passed him by; he was interested in appearances, in a certain kind of display, and if he could have heard Lethaby's aphorism – with the suggestion that an imposing building is in itself an 'imposition' – he would have ignored it.

Burges's buildings are often imposing and he was not afraid of bold and even crushing effects on a large scale. But this did not mean that he was equipped to meet the needs in Victorian architecture which could be catered for by buildings not only on a new, vast scale but of a new type and complexity. The flats and offices and hotels, all of them involving elaborate plans – and technical problems for the solution of which there cannot often have been helpful precedents – were designed by men such as Scott and Waterhouse, Giles and Shaw, not by Burges. His scheme for the Law Courts (Plate LXXVI) was turned down, and his Municipal Buildings at Dover – erected after his death by Pullan – were not of a size to compare with the museums, town halls and other orgulous monsters built in the public interest by men such as Waterhouse, Brodrick and Collcutt. Burges had none of Waterhouse's skill with complicated plans, and he was quite without that flair and agility which enabled Shaw to provide so many apt solutions for the varied needs of the day. While Shaw's work often points towards what lay in the architectural future, Burges, with his roots in the past, designed nothing from which the future could benefit. Again, he never designed a popular work of national significance, such as the Albert Memorial. Scott's paramount edifice is ambitious, skilfully designed and

[1] *Catalogue of Sale of his library*, 1918, V. and A. Museum.

[2] Philip Webb's *Letter Book* (MSS), kindly lent me by Mr John Brandon-Jones. The phrase comes from a letter of 1886, written by Webb to his patron on the completion of Clouds.

built with the full gloss of a highly developed professionalism; it is an accurately judged memorial to the Consort and it sums up many elements in the High Victorian ethos – but it is both slightly brash and slightly vulgar, and it embodies certain faults which Burges might have avoided.

Burges and Scott had little in common except a passion for Gothic. Scott was something of an opportunist, but in the case of the Foreign Office competition it was Scott who felt the need to justify his adoption, under duress, of another style. When for the same competition Burges prepared a set of Italianate designs (Victoria and Albert Museum) – another of his unsuccessful attempts at public architecture – he probably felt no misgivings of any kind; yet he had repeatedly stressed the need for a general acceptance among architects of one style – meaning Gothic – although he abandoned it on several other occasions. Worcester College Chapel, designed without a trace of Gothic, testifies above all to Burges's gift for eclectic synthesis, and there is no evidence that he was disturbed by the nature of several of his most prominent buildings. In spite of tremendous positive merits, Cork Cathedral and the Welsh castles must be regarded in varying degrees as archaeological shams, and Tower House was actually described as a 'model residence of the fifteenth century'. It was built by a romantic individualist who was a misfit, in many ways, in the High Victorian scene. If, among others, Butterfield and Street fulfilled themselves in the service of the Church, if Morris and Webb were concerned to establish what may be called an architectural morality, and if, in their different ways, there were men like Scott and Waterhouse and Shaw to grapple successfully with the public architecture of materialist expansion – a new architecture of cities – then it seems plain that Burges failed to identify himself with any of the major currents of High Victorian thought or practice; furthermore his work embodies no architectural advances of any kind.

Beyond a certain degree of achievement an architect's reputation seems ultimately to rest upon his sincerity and originality coupled with the extent of his influence; and Burges's sincerity is at once called in question by his shams. Webb's moral earnestness is, I believe, partly responsible for his growing reputation as an architect. The moral integrity of Butterfield and Street again is beyond doubt; they were both very original designers and they both had a widespread influence. Shaw's originality – to say nothing of his influence – more than offsets any misgivings we may have about his fluent eclecticism. It goes without saying that Burges was in many ways a very original designer, but originality does not by itself make a reputation. Few of his contemporaries could handle plain walls and simple geometric shapes with his assurance, and when it came to decorations his bright ideas, often complicated in design and expensive to execute, as a rule fell on the air: they were indeed inimitable. Thus although most of his designs were published in his lifetime, it is not surprising that he was 'more admired than followed', and his influence in England seems to have been negligible. E. W. Godwin probably relied on him for advice, for instance over the design of Castle Dromore, in Ireland, and several architects borrowed from the unexecuted designs for the Law Courts.[1] The American architect H. H. Richardson evidently admired Burges's work from a distance, for he too borrowed from the Law Courts designs, and in general saw how to adapt some of Burges's more rugged effects.[2] But even if further debts to Burges are from time to time discovered, nothing will turn him into a stylistic leader, and the limited extent of his influence alone deprives him of a reputation comparable to that of Butterfield, Street or Shaw.

It may be added that Burges, in his turn, owes little to his most influential English contemporaries. He was largely unaffected by the teaching of Ruskin, and if his handling of sculpture was occasionally 'Ruskinian' – for example when it came to the freedom of the sculptor – I doubt if he ever followed Ruskin's principles. Significant debts to Butterfield occur to my knowledge only in the early and now enlarged All Saints' church at Fleet, near Aldershot (1860–62). This church was built of brick, but even here the internal polychromy is achieved not by bricks of different colours but by paint: the effect is convincing although the method is non-constructional. I can find nothing in his work that can be traced directly to Street or Scott, Waterhouse or Shaw – he never attempted 'Queen Anne', and it is a point of interest that towards the end of his life he was preparing a caustic paper on the subject. On the other hand he was, I believe, inspired if not often directly influenced by Pugin, who had died in 1852; and he made frequent use, as can readily be proved, of the publications of Viollet-le-Duc. In fact, he relied for most of his ideas on his own researches, and it is typical of Burges that he should have avoided influences close at hand. But whatever his debts to others – more, perhaps, than are at present known to me – his work always remains personal and distinctive, easily recognized. Furthermore it was so bold and uncompromising that it did not always find ready patrons; indeed the limited extent of his practice should always be born in mind.

Thus between the designs for the Lille competition of 1855 and the enor-

[1] *Building News*, Dec. 3rd, 1869: Godwin on the subject of Burges being 'consulting architect' to Lockwood and Mawson over their design for the Bradford Town Hall; W. de l'Hôpital, *Westminster Cathedral and its Architect* (London), vol. II, p. 393: Speakman and Charlesworth borrow the entrance portion of Burges's Law Courts designs for their (unexecuted) designs for the Manchester Town Hall.

[2] H.-R. Hitchcock, *Architecture: Nineteenth and Twentieth Centuries* (London, 1958), pp. 193, 222, 267.

mous wing at Trinity College, unfinished at the time of his death in 1881, there lie a rather large number of unexecuted schemes and perhaps twenty-one or twenty-two surviving works – doubts arise over the Burges-Clutton restorations in the Salisbury Chapter House, and over a 'gallery for the Marquess of Northampton' of which I know nothing. To this count must be added the church of St Faith's, once at Stoke Newington: bombed in the war, as far as I know it is unique among Burges's buildings in having been completely destroyed. St Faith's brings the count of executed works up to twenty-two or twenty-three, and of course I am including here the restorations and additions such as those at Waltham Abbey, Gayhurst, and Worcester College Chapel. If we add also the municipal buildings at Dover, designed by Burges and built by Pullan, we may say, in round figures, that twenty-six years of architectural practice produced designs for not more than twenty-six executed commissions; and this is allowing a margin of error. It was a small body of work.

But a small practice had its advantages, and Burges could often hold his own against several of his more important contemporaries. Judged on a comparative basis his wing at Trinity College in America, for instance, is in several ways superior to Butterfield's Keble or Seddon's Aberystwyth; similarly Cardiff Castle embodies a great many splendours which were not to be found in the second Eaton Hall, by Waterhouse, or Godwin's Dromore Castle in Ireland – the former has largely been demolished, the latter is gradually becoming a ruin. Again, the Cardiff house for McConnochie, in some ways one of Burges's most satisfying buildings, has recently been described as 'one of the best medium-sized stone dwellings of the High Victorian Gothic'.[1] The space which should be devoted to these comparisons is not at present available, and the most notable characteristics of Burges's decorations will be discussed, later on, when once again we glance at the Welsh castles. Meanwhile it is perhaps worth drawing attention to one of the leading insignia both of his buildings and decorations: that is, his love of very bold geometric shapes. These compass-drawn shapes are to be seen even in an early work such as the outhouse at Gayhurst (Plate LXVIII), in the design for the campanile of Templebrady church in Ireland, and perhaps more obviously than anywhere else in the original designs for the Harrow School Speech Room. The rectangular towers at Cardiff, like the cylindrical towers at Castell Coch – considered as abstract architecture – are extremely impressive as volumes in space. Very bold, semi-circular buildings, more or less of the shape he built at Harrow, were included as part of the designs both for Trinity College and for the Law Courts; and the entrance to the Law Courts was to have been surmounted by a pair of enormous cylind-

[1] H.-R. Hitchcock, *Architecture: Nineteenth and Twentieth Centuries* (London, 1958), p. 188.

rical towers. We can understand his delight in designing churches with a rounded east end – the sweep of the apse at Cork Cathedral, for instance, is one of its most exciting features. Every church he ever designed includes a bold wheel window; and like Clutton and Godwin – both of them his friends, one of them an associate – he gave special value to openings of this kind by providing them with very broad surrounds, as a rule of stone. The shapes in his internal roofs – at Cork, at Studley Royal and in the Harrow Speech Room, also in several of the rooms in both castles and at Tower House – are again based on geometry; and taken together these roofs make up one of his outstanding contributions to the architecture of his day.

For the sake of his reputation we could wish that Burges had won more competitions and designed more buildings. But we cannot have it both ways: the limited extent of his practice probably helps to explain, above all in his decorative work, so many of the qualities we admire in it.

Burges was lucky in his rich patrons, particularly in Lord Bute and Lord Ripon; he was lucky again when the authorities at Cork gave him the opportunity to realize his ideas so completely over a long period of time. Cardiff Castle and Cork Cathedral both occupied sixteen years of his life; eight years were spent on his work for Lord Ripon at Studley Royal; and it is significant that neither Cardiff Castle nor Cork Cathedral – nor, for that matter, Tower House, after five years' work – were decoratively complete when he died. Certainly Burges knew how to take advantage of his unusual opportunities: backed very often by ample funds, and with the time to ponder his designs, he could give personal attention to work on the site more often, very likely, than was possible for men such as Scott or Waterhouse. In any case he saw to it that many of the intricate carvings destined for Cardiff, say, or Studley should be executed under close supervision in London.

It goes without saying that Burges could sustain his interest indefinitely: very rarely do we find evidence of drooping enthusiasm, a lack of vitality in his designs or inconsistency in the quality of his details. At Cardiff Castle and Castell Coch, or again at Studley Royal and Tower House – where he must have spent a fortune, although, incidentally, he left £40,000 on his death – he had the chance to pour out his ideas to the limit of his capacity; and as a designer, if not as an architect, he must have known the satisfaction of complete fulfilment.

One of the obituary writers remarked that Burges's work was 'really and in every sense his own'. Burges was not of course the only High-to-Late Victorian architect whose approach to his work was comprehensive: one thinks among others of Street and Webb, Bentley and H. H. Wilson, all of whom liked to design furniture and decorations. Yet in view of the complexity and extent of

Burges's decorative designs I have been astonished to discover how often the actual details can be traced to drawings and sketches from his own hand: precise drawings for small-scale sculpture on his chimney-pieces, and for groups of figures not only on his painted furniture, but also in his mosaics and even in his stained glass; elaborate and immensely detailed drawings for his roofs and ceilings, friezes and wall decorations; small drawings of remarkable precision and delicacy for his metal work; and large and vigorous drawings for his stencil patterns and stone furniture. These drawings are not the work of a man working to a timetable. We do not imagine him in a large office, surrounded by draughtsmen, hard pressed by his clients; and in fact Burges had few assistants. A large practice sometimes leaves its mark in a professional but rather impersonal finish suggesting an absence of affection for the work, or a lack of maturity in the ideas. Rarely in the work of Scott or Waterhouse, not always in the work of Street or Shaw, does one feel that they have pondered their effects and details, felt their way into them to the extent of leaving the stamp of their identity on every feature of their designs. This process is particularly difficult to achieve in architecture and it requires above all the luxury of time. It was a luxury that Burges, more than most, could afford.

We shall turn presently to an outline account of Burges's most important buildings. Before we do so, however, an attempt should be made to assess his achievement. He must, I believe, be regarded as an architect whose individuality and limitations made it impossible for him to contribute to the significant advances which in High and Late Victorian architecture were to be effective for the future. Nothing in his work leads to the threshold of the modern movement, he had little influence, and he was a builder of shams; and no disturbing claims will be made for him here. Moreover few even of his best buildings earn unqualified praise. The roofs at Castell Coch, for instance, although they are extremely plausible, give to the building something of the appearance of a child's toy; and at Cardiff the surrounding walls, the stable court and even the Roman gateway – all of them to my eye rather dapper and papery – fail to live up to the solid dignity of the main buildings. Cork Cathedral just falls short of real grandeur, perhaps because the external surfaces are a little too busy; and internally nothing quite reconciles one to the absence of a vault of stone. Again, it seems that Burges himself was prepared to spoil the simple geometric block of the Harrow Speech Room by the addition of towers; and certainly the external additions of a later date can only be said to weaken the original design. At Studley Royal, however, one welcomes Burges's external decorations: the criticism is that this church, like Knightshayes mansion, is in too many ways old-fashioned and derivative – but of course no such charge can be made about the decorations inside. As for Burges's wing at Trinity College, even here there are reservations, although of a different kind. The central block in Burges's wing, known as Northam Towers, was it seems added after his death; and since I have not seen the drawings for this part of the building, I cannot be sure of the extent of his responsibility for it.

Yet for all his shortcomings Burges is worthy of a great deal of respect. As the designer of at least seven outstanding buildings, including his wing at Trinity College, it seems to me that he deserves a place among the twenty foremost architects of the reign. At least six of his buildings in the British Isles will long deserve the strongest possible protection against harmful interference of any kind. These buildings are Cardiff Castle, Castell Coch, Cork Cathedral, the house for McConnochie, and Tower House – the last is included chiefly for the sake of the decorations; and as far as I know anxiety is not likely to arise over the buildings in this group except possibly in the case of the two houses. To these buildings must be added the interior decorations in Worcester College Chapel; happily they are regarded with interest and, I believe, considerable respect. Buildings which run very close in merit to those already mentioned are Skelton Church, St Michael's at Lowfield Heath – perhaps the best of Burges's small churches – and the Harrow School Speech Room. They are all indispensable examples of 'Victorian Conservanda'.

To Clutton and Burges the Lille competition of 1855 was important chiefly for reasons of prestige. Their winning entry had been warmly praised by the judges, and although the cathedral was eventually built to the designs of three Frenchmen, the unfair treatment of the English competitors brought with it a good deal of publicity. This helped to put them on the map. In the competition of 1856 for the Crimea Memorial church on the Bosphorus, Burges's designs were accorded first place, and two years later he went out to Constantinople to lay the foundation stone. There he ran into trouble with the committee, chiefly because he refused to give up the idea of stone vaulting throughout the building – 'a considerable item in the estimates' – and his scheme was again set aside. Pullan suggests that from this time onwards Burges always designed wooden roofs internally, and he was not far wrong, although a few stone vaults can be found in unimportant positions in the churches. Thus an early disappointment may to some extent have been the origin of those wonderful wooden roofs which in Cork Cathedral and Studley Royal, in the Welsh castles and in several other buildings – not by any means all of them churches – together make up one of Burges's outstanding achievements. The visit to

Constantinople increased his range of ideas and bore its most spectacular fruit, many years later, in the Arab Room at Cardiff Castle.

We must here ignore the Burges-Clutton restorations in the Salisbury Chapter House, also Burges's unexecuted design for Brisbane Cathedral which dates, according to Pullan, from 1859. His first substantial commission, dating probably from the same year, came from Lord Carrington, who required additions to an existing mansion at Gayhurst, in Buckinghamshire.[1] Here, over a period of several years, different parts of the house were redecorated according to Burges's designs; but the total expenditure of about £20,000[2] is explained by the fact that at the same time he added an entirely new kitchen, a long stable block and a circular stone outhouse. Seen from the park these additions to the old building make up a picturesque group enlivened by turrets and a bell-tower (Plate LXVIII). The outhouse, evidently designed as a privy for Lord Carrington's male servants, is capped by one of Burges's favourite conical roofs and five heavily gabled dormers. Built round a cylindrical shaft or stack, this curious structure is internally divided into five wedge-shaped compartments. At the top of the shaft sits a large, three-headed dog – Cerberus, guardian of the Styx – with three pairs of glaring red eyes exactly like billiard balls. Sketches for this dog are to be found in one of the notebooks.

Burges's most richly decorated room on the ground floor of the house includes an arrangement of narrow panels deriving, almost certainly, from the cabinet of Catherine de' Medici at Blois. Each panel is filled with specimens of flowers painted, so we are told, by a Frenchman specially brought over to do this work. Similar panelling appears in the very much later Chaucer Room at Cardiff Castle. The finest thing in the Gayhurst room is the double-decker chimney-piece, delicately carved and richly gilded, the design probably based on studies made in the François Premier wing, again at Blois. Sculpture also appears in the unpainted stone chimney-pieces in the dining-room, each with a group representing Adam and Eve. The staircase on the first floor is supported across the 'Guard Room' by a fierce, prognathous, faggot-bearing figure, again carved in stone, while above the staircase there is a heavily coffered wooden roof. Thus Burges's work at Gayhurst is a forecast in several ways of what lies ahead: not only does it include some very bold masonry, a picturesque skyline, and a touch of rather typical humour above the privy; we find in addition

[1] I am indebted to Lady Elizabeth Carlile (who with her husband occupied Gayhurst for a long period) for much information. From her I learn that a 'vast book' of drawings by Burges was in the house up to 1950. I have not yet been able to trace it. See *Country Life*, vol. XIII, 1903. On p. 87 there is a photograph of the kitchens, stables and 'spring' – i.e., presumably, the privy. See also N. Pevsner, *Buildings of England. Buckinghamshire*, p. 138.

[2] R.I.B.A. *Transactions*, 1881–2, vol. 32, p. 195. Evidence of R. Reynolds Rowe, F.S.A.

the enormous chimney pieces, a room with painted panelling, and some elaborate carpentry. The sculptor responsible for the carving was in all probability Thomas Nicholls – Cerberus is very much in his style – and Gayhurst may be the scene of the first productions of a long and fruitful partnership. From now on most of Burges's sculpture is executed by this very talented craftsman.

Nicholls soon came to public notice. He was well represented at the Exhibition of 1862 by several fine reliefs, sections of a reredos designed by Burges a year or two earlier, but shown in the sculptor's name. These reliefs were part of Burges's restorations at Waltham Abbey, a job he undertook from about 1860 onwards, but while the two central groups of sculpture were ready to be shown at the Exhibition, it seems that the remaining sections were not completed until 1875.[1] The whole reredos, now richly coloured and gilded, spreads almost from wall to wall across the east end of the Abbey. The surprising thing is that it stands up to the weight of Burges's three rather wide lancets and the single wheel window, with its heavy plate tracery, which are to be seen higher up on the same wall. But it has to be admitted that these units, magnificently bold and well designed in themselves, are uncomfortably aligned with the earlier Norman arcading; in fact the whole east wall appears as an intrusion, certainly not as a tactful restoration. One of Burges's obituaries expressed the view that he should have been given more work as a restorer; another suggested that he was unsuited to restoration because his style was too personal. The evidence at Waltham Abbey confirms the second opinion, although allowances must be made for the fact that at this time he was still a very inexperienced architect.

In all probability it was the experience gained while undertaking these restorations, whatever we may now think of them, that encouraged him to submit designs for the Cork Cathedral competition of 1863; and his success, which marks a turning point, brought him his first big job. His ideas ran far ahead of anything that could have been built for the sum available, which had been advertised as £15,000, and several unsuccessful competitors made the usual objections. But in this, as in several other jobs, Burges was lucky. The authorities at Cork came to take pride in the work as it progressed, more money was gradually raised, and the Cathedral now represents the fulfilment of nearly all his ideas for it. St Fin Barr's was begun in 1865, consecrated in 1870 and very largely completed by 1876[2] (Plate LXIX). A few features excepted, this

---

[1] R.I.B.A. Notebook for 1875, March to September. Note of payment to Nicholls of £599.

[2] For the photograph, I am indebted to Dr E. Parkinson Hill, of Waterford, who also lent me a typescript of a Diary, dated 1910, maintained by W. H. Hill. From 1870 onwards W. H. Hill superintended much of the work at Cork in Burges's absence, replacing in this job a man called Adams. The Diary is interesting but contains no revelations about the Cathedral.

Burges's drawings are preserved by the Cathedral authorities.

building probably represents Burges's most literate exercise in French Gothic. Bold and archaeologically serious, it does not achieve quite the impersonal dignity which, I suspect, partly shields Truro from the charge of sham. Cork is based on French cathedral architecture of about 1200, or perhaps a little earlier, and a contemporary said of it that it 'might easily be mistaken for a building by one of the best French architects of the 13th century, transported to its present site'. Today we should say nothing of the kind, although there is enough truth in this overstatement to justify a description of it as a sham French cathedral. Equally important, it is a cathedral in miniature.

The unexpectedly small site lies some way out of the centre of the town on gently rising ground. Approaching from the east, one's first view is of the curves of the apse and of the three splendid towers. The impression is of a mass of stone, compact and bulky, that has been forced to rise upwards as a result of lateral pressure. The most impressive aspect of this church is the west end, dominated by two of the towers and spires, a façade which includes three porches under linked gables and a typically bold wheel window, very similar to those in the transepts. The window is framed by symbols of the Evangelists carved by Nicholls – one of the largest groups of sculpture Burges ever designed; and both window and sculpture are set in a field of blue and gold mosaic. Gold mosaic – no blue this time – again provides a sparkling background for the groups of tympanum sculpture above the three porches, each with its flanking figures.

While these rich additions scarcely rob the building of its seriousness, the abundance of detail does to some extent deprive it – to use the language of the day – of 'breadth' and 'repose'. There are too many crockets and finials, too many steps to the buttresses, perhaps too many turrets: the surfaces everywhere are busy and congested, we miss above all the plain walls which enhance the value of so many of Burges's buildings. Yet for nearly everything he included he could, no doubt, have pointed to historical precedent; and when in 1873 he submitted a design for St Mary's Cathedral, Edinburgh, he re-used with comparatively few changes many of the fundamental elements of Cork, so he must still have liked the design. But if externally this church embodies an excessive display of detail, the interior shows a remarkable, large-boned simplicity. In both nave and apse the heavy arcades march conventionally in three tiers, while each bay is strongly marked by very bold shafts running from floor to roof. At the crossing the arcades stop against massive piers, square in section, which dictate the width of the broad soffits to the arches supporting the central tower. For architectural merit, in my opinion, there is nothing in this cathedral to compare with the treatment of the crossing.

Neither at Cork Cathedral nor anywhere else did Burges design a large interior comparable to that of St Augustine's at Kilburn, by Pearson, or the Great Hall in the Law Courts, by Street: the conception of these majestic vessels of space – calm, stately, and unified – was beyond him. Or perhaps it would be fairer to say that he calculated the expenditure of his patron's money with different effects in mind. To provide a wooden roof in a large stone interior is, almost inevitably, to split the interior into two parts. Street and Pearson knew the value of groining in stone, even when vaulting in stone was out of the question; and in the days of the Crimea Memorial so perhaps did Burges. But from that time onwards it looks as though he was determined to spend money not on groins and vaults in stone, but rather on the decorations – which at Cork, certainly, are beautifully designed, and carried out in magnificent materials. While it is to be doubted if the cost even of decorations like these would have equalled the cost of a roof in stone, there is no denying that the wooden roof deprives the interior of that singular, dignified unity which one longs to see: due to the contrast of colour and materials, the main body of the church seems to be made up of two parts, nave and lid. But this roof is nevertheless of particular interest for it embodies, over the altar, Burges's first experiments with the coved sections which reappear, with variations, in Lady Bute's bedroom at Castell Coch, and over the chancel at Studley Royal.

Three years had to go by after the Cork Cathedral competition before he could begin work on the site, and in the interval he redecorated Worcester College Chapel, in Oxford (Plate XCVII). The college authorities have preserved many valuable documents connected with their various building schemes, including Burges's Report and Book of Designs.[1] He was commissioned to redecorate the Chapel in 1863, and the work occupied him throughout the following year; the date 1864 appears twice on the ceiling. Burges tells us that his chief contractor was Mr Jacquet of London, and that together they spent '£3,000 in all' – a remarkably small sum, even at that date, considering the type and quality of the work. Certainly the Chapel must have pleased the

[1] My thanks are due to the Worcester College authorities, and particularly to Mr R. A. Sayce, for the opportunity of seeing many important documents. These include James Wyatt's design drawings for the Chapel and Hall; William Burges's large folio including designs for the Chapel, and two schemes for the Hall, also the Report which is full of estimates and individually dated designs; and a collection of letters relating to the alterations in the Chapel and Hall, signed by Burges, Holiday, Fisher, the Rev. Henry Daniel (of Worcester College) and others.

See also Arthur Oswald, *Country Life*, vol. LXXVII, 1935, pp. 426–31, for a description of the Chapel; and *The Times*, 1872, May 20th, p. 7, iv. A letter signed 'Paulinus' points to the Chapel decorations as the best possible reason for not adopting Burges's scheme for the re-decoration of the east end of St Paul's. For the St Paul's scheme see R. P. Pullan, *The Designs of William Burges*, 1885, (several photographs of the model); and *A Description of Mr Burges's Models for the Adornment of St Paul's* (London, 1874) (pamphlet).

authorities, since in 1877 Burges was asked to redecorate the Hall, but for reasons which cannot be discussed here the scheme this time met with less enthusiasm. In the end he prepared another set of drawings for the Hall – a severely modified version of the original scheme – and this was the basis of the decorations we see today; however, the Hall must, from now on, be ignored in this essay. The late-eighteenth-century master who originally designed both these interiors was none other than James Wyatt, a fact which is proved by the fairly recent discovery at the College of an important group of his drawings, several of them signed and bearing the date 1783.

The most notable features of Wyatt's rectangular Chapel, all of which survive, include the unusual quarter-circle curves at the corners of the room, quadrants large enough to house fairly wide niches, and the columns and pilasters against the walls which are carefully related to the beams overhead. In addition there are the fans and segments above the cornice, closely reminiscent of Heveningham Hall, in Suffolk, and a small dome in the middle of the ceiling. Wyatt introduced a shallow ante-chamber between the Chapel and the wall through which it is entered, an arrangement presumably designed to mask the fact that the entrance door, set in an earlier stone opening, lies just off the main axis of the Chapel. Burges used one side of the ante-chamber as a space in which to house an organ, but not before he had decorated the walls on both sides with designs which have their origins in Herculaneum or Pompei.

Anyone visiting the Chapel for the first time might find it difficult to believe Wyatt's original structure survives all but intact; yet Burges's structural alterations were few. He lined the walls up to the bases of the columns and pilasters with walnut panelling – walnut being the wood he chose to use throughout the Chapel – and he elaborated the ceiling with details copied from Wyatt's original designs. Burges was, no doubt, delighted to inherit the dome, and he is said to have admired the proportion of the Chapel as a whole; but he had not been called in merely to admire and touch up a late-eighteenth-century interior of a type which, in the early 1860s, was probably held in lower esteem than at any other time since it was built. To Burges, Wyatt's decorations must have appeared not only extremely dull but also entirely unsuitable. He completely transformed what he found by means of one of the most thoughtful schemes he ever devised, a scheme in which nearly every detail reminds us that we are in a Chapel, not merely a large room turned into a Chapel by the introduction of a few pieces of furniture.

Perhaps it was inevitable that Burges should have filled the niches with statues of the Evangelists: executed by Nicholls, they are enriched with gold leaf. These statues provide the scale for some of the figures elsewhere. In the

Crucifixion window above the altar, for instance, the height of the two figures which stand at the foot of the Cross is precisely matched to the height of the Evangelists in their near-by niches; and since all these figures are on exactly the same level, discrepancies of scale would have disturbed the unity of the whole wall. Perhaps this is a rare example in Victorian ecclesiastical decoration of correspondences of scale between sculptured figures and figures in stained glass.

The Chapel decorations embody a number of themes, including those of praise and thanksgiving. The text 'O Ye Priests Of The Lord, Bless Ye The Lord' appears over the altar, while part of the Te Deum is inlaid on the back of the benches. In addition, three independent pictorial sequences run horizontally round the Chapel. These are to be seen in the stained-glass windows, in the narrow frieze of paintings just above the dado, and in the lunettes above the cornice. The windows represent episodes from the life of Christ, the lunettes contain figures of the Prophets, while some of the paintings above the dado allude to the Te Deum and to the Benedicite. All these decorations were designed by Henry Holliday, who in his *Reminiscences* of 1914 recalls several interesting facts about his work for Burges, not only at Worcester College. We learn that he had helped to decorate one of Burges's early cabinets, also that he designed and painted a 'blind' window for Waltham Abbey. Then in connection with the Worcester Chapel he tells us that Burges had originally asked Millais to design the windows, but that the first specimen – representing the Annunciation – was a total failure: 'Burges ... would not have it in the Chapel at any price.' In the end – though not before Burges and Holliday had paid a tactful visit to Millais – Holiday became responsible not only for all the major paintings, but also for the windows which show distinct merit. One wonders whether it was Burges or Holiday who decided on the choice and placing of subjects, both in the windows and in the painted scenes. On this point, unfortunately, the *Reminiscences* give us no information, and we must assume that the major decisions were made by Burges. Certainly the links between the themes in the pictorial units are worked out with unusual care.

Between the altar and the Crucifixion window, for instance, appears Henry Holiday's painting of the Entombment. This is a unit in the horizontal sequence above the dado, and for once the subject is readily understood. Then in the lunette immediately above the Crucifixion window appears the Prophet Daniel; and we should remember that his escape from the lion's den is taken to prefigure the Resurrection. Thus three pictorial scenes from the independent horizontal sequences – the Entombment painting, the Crucifixion window and the Resurrection lunette – take their place above the altar so that when they are read vertically they symbolize the Passion. It may be added that the theme of the Passion is sustained on the bench ends by inlaid symbols such as the sudarium, the seamless robe and the crown of thorns.

While Holiday's windows show traces of Pre-Raphaelite influence, his paintings suggest faint but direct debts to earlier painters such as Giotto and Masaccio; but the details of most of Burges's furniture, whether of stone or of walnut, derive from High Renaissance models of about 1500. Again, the design of the mosaic floor seems to be Roman in origin, although the figures, in tesserae of stone, represent saints such as King Edward and King Edmund; and as we have seen, the painted decorations in the ante-Chapel suggest origins in Pompei or Herculaneum. Thus Burges's range in this eclectic assembly is fairly wide and may seem all the more daring in view of the context in which it appears. It may be objected that from the visual point of view Burges failed to synthesize the elements of his design into a completely harmonious unity, and if the criterion for harmony is that set by the brothers Adam or by Wyatt then no doubt the objection is valid. But we must remember that to the High Victorians harmony of this kind seemed empty and unimaginative: they were in fact reacting against it – a point to which we shall return when we discuss the decorations in the Welsh castles. With his love of story-telling and evocative detail Burges was perhaps already following an aim stated in connection with Cardiff: to provide decorations which should engage both the eye and the mind. Certainly the Chapel is full of relevant pictorial details, and in this period there can be few ecclesiastical interiors where themes are so carefully interrelated; or, for that matter, few comparable displays of what was called 'iconography' (fully described in Parker's *Handbook … To Oxford* of 1875).

Outstanding among all the Chapel decorations, it may be agreed, are those executed by Thomas Nicholls. Whereas Holiday had not the stature, say, of the painter William Dyce, Nicholls bears very favourable comparison to other men working in his own field – to the brothers O'Shea, for example, and to Earp and to Redfern. The statues of the Evangelists are however little more than competent: they lack vitality and I can see nothing in them that is personal to the sculptor. Burges included small sketches for several of these statues in one of his many studies of the Chapel, and they show clearly enough the kind of figure he had in mind. But he tells us[1] that while he supervised their execution he did not design them, and by emphasizing this fact I doubt if he was trying to escape responsibility for their appearance. I have never seen a life-size drawing by Burges for a free-standing figure, and while he could, I believe, have produced such a drawing, he must have known that beyond a few sketches,

---

[1] *The Builder*, April 30th, 1881. A review of Burges's career, with quotations.

and the necessary instructions, a sculptor should in certain kinds of work be left to himself. Nor did Burges design the creatures on the bench-ends – the swan, the boar, the tortoise and many others – more than thirty of them altogether, and all inviting a touch from the hand. But they are small in scale; no doubt Nicholls enjoyed intimate work of this kind and he rose admirably to the occasion. Several of them are spontaneously carved, most of them are accurately observed and there are signs, here and there, of very sharp characterization. Together they provide one of the high-lights of the Chapel.

Even more impressive, although in a different category, are the marble lectern and the two candelabra. Extremely refined in detail and directly inspired by Renaissance models, their formal grandeur lives up to Wyatt's columns. Burges this time provided full-size drawings in which firm black outlines show the intended silhouettes with precision. These drawings typify the designer's good sense and also his sympathetic understanding of Nicholls's ability: sufficiently informative in essentials, they are not detailed to such an extent that they would have inhibited the sculptor. I do not know what Burges was asked to provide in the way of an altar, but for the present altar furniture he can have been in no way responsible. It is the lectern, given pride of place on the mosaic floor, which now captures attention as the point of visual focus in the Chapel; and Nicholls can never have carved small figures, such as those which encircle the central drum, with greater freshness and delicacy.

The sculpture in Worcester College Chapel, most of it very successful, is the result of an intelligent, almost Ruskinian approach to a very difficult problem. It is a sad fact that not by any means all Victorian architects came to terms with a sculptor to produce such happy results. J. L. Pearson, for instance, designed a very elaborate sculptural ensemble for the east end of St Augustine's, Kilburn, but while the designs may have looked very well on paper the sculpture itself is disappointing. What went wrong? Was it a question of over-precise drawings, ill-chosen sculptors, or inadequate supervision? I cannot say. Even when immense trouble was taken in work of this kind, I imagine that results were sometimes rather different from what had been originally intended. An extreme case is the Albert Memorial (Plate LXIII), where the procedure can be briefly summarized. Scott, we know, worked by 'influence'.[1] We know, too, that in the early drawings for the Memorial the sculpture was drawn out in a 'general way' by Mr Clayton and Scott's eldest son. Soon a model of the entire Memorial was constructed, and Armstead, a sculptor Scott admired for his work at Ettington Hall, was required to make miniature models of all the sculpture – working, of course, from the Clayton-Scott (junior) drawings, and no

[1] Sir Gilbert Scott, *Personal and Professional Recollections* (London, 1879), p. 216, 266 seq.

doubt under the elder Scott's eye. Armstead's small models were then incorporated in the architectural model which unfortunately no longer survives. But photographs of Armstead's models can be seen in one of his albums (in the Royal Academy Library), and it is clear that several of the sculptors who finally executed the groups – first under the supervision of Eastlake, then of Layard – were required to work fairly closely according to Armstead's compositions. Compare, for instance, Armstead's models for Asia and America – two of the Continents at the angles of the Memorial – with the same groups in their final state by Foley and John Bell. Scott, no doubt, was keenly conscious of the focus of attention on the Memorial, and we can understand his caution; but in the end he came to doubt whether the 'central figure (Prince Albert) or a single group, as executed, is superior to the miniature models furnished by Mr Armstead'. One can scarcely be surprised at his disappointment. As a result of the method he adopted, the exact opposite of Ruskinian, some of the sculpture – in many ways excellent in its context – is personal neither to Scott, to Armstead, nor to several of the sculptors under whose name the work is recorded. One cannot imagine Burges or Street going about the provision of sculpture in this way; but then it is unlikely that either of them would have undertaken a job involving sculpture in such vast quantities. Street's Law Courts are almost deprived of figure sculpture, and I cannot help thinking that if Burges's designs for the same building had won the competition, he would have modified very drastically his ambitious ideas for its external decoration.

Nothing, in fact, could be more misleading than to think of Burges as a designer who smothered his walls with sculpture. With the exception of Cork Cathedral, where the figures in the porches were doubtless provided out of respect for historical precedent, he limited very strictly the amount of carving on the outside of all his executed buildings. In general, Burges took care to avoid any kind of carved detail which involved more than a very few repetitions – with the happy result that Nicholls can rarely have been bored; and this helps to explain why the best of his sculpture has a freshness and vitality which is rare during the Victorian period. Sometimes Burges made elaborately detailed drawings, especially for his chimney-pieces, and in the Worcester College Chapel he probably gave Nicholls more freedom than usual; no doubt the balance between total freedom and strict control depended on the job in hand. But if it is true that Nicholls was rarely bored by his work for Burges, to me it remains a mystery how he got through it and in fact it seems probable that he had assistants. Burges's notebooks include the names and addresses of several other sculptors, and we know that he employed the young Goscombe John on some of the wood-carving at Cardiff Castle;[1] yet in all Burges's later work, including of course the Welsh castles, his chief sculptor was always Thomas Nicholls. And it is worth remarking that apart from the seven large figures of the Planets on the Clock Tower at Cardiff, very little figure-sculpture – very little sculpture of any kind – is to be found on the outside either of Cardiff Castle or of Castell Coch.

These castles have been the subject of several publications, but the articles by Dr Mark Girouard, all of them beautifully illustrated, are by far the most congenial and impressive.[2] Because they are also extremely thorough and of comparatively recent date, I shall make no attempt to cover the same ground in the space at present available. We should remember that Cardiff Castle occupied Burges from 1865 until his death, though not of course exclusively, while the reconstruction of Castell Coch did not follow until ten years later, although the Report had been prepared in 1872. This said, I can only try to extend the discussion, particularly of the decorations, by raising a few points which so far as I know have not yet received attention.

Castell Coch stands on the edge of a beechwood, thick with garlic plants, above the river Taff. The cylindrical towers of this simple building leave a lasting impression of plain walls and picturesque roof-tops, but for the design of these roofs, which gave Burges a good deal of trouble, he was, I believe, in-debted more to Viollet-le-Duc than to illuminated manuscripts. The style of most sham castles of the Victorian period is distinctly national, but Burges's roofs, especially at Castell Coch, give to the building an appearance that would perhaps be less surprising in France than in Wales. In his reconstruction of the castle he made use when possible of the ancient stonework, for instance at the base of the towers. The foundations of these towers had been constructed with those fascinating transitions which in medieval building suggest a marriage between a cylinder and a pyramid. As it happens, one of Salvin's towers at Peckforton (Plate VIII) had been designed on the same system, and Salvin's walls are impressive literally stone by stone, especially at the angles. But if by comparison the masonry at Castell Coch commands very much less respect, the towers, undeniably sculptural and dramatic, are outstanding examples of Burges's love of clean, geometric shapes.

Cardiff Castle (Plate LXVII) stands on a rather dull, flat site, bordered

---

[1] M. H. Spielmann, *British Sculpture and Sculptors of To-Day* (London, 1901), p. 129. Burges's influence can, I believe, be traced in some of Goscombe John's decorative sculpture.

[2] W. G. Howell, an article on Castell Coch in *The Architectural Review*, January 1951; Professor William Rees, M.A., B.SC., *Cardiff Castle*, n.d.; Peter Floud, *Castell Coch* (M.O.W. guide, 1954, reprinted 1957); Mark Girouard, 'Cardiff Castle', *Country Life*, April 6th, 13th, 20th, 1961; and 'Castell Coch', *Country Life*, May 10th, 17th, 1962. Burges's Castell Coch Report, M.O.W., 1872.

on one side by a high road and encroached upon by the town. Burges dramatized the castle by adding to the Lodgings no less than four major towers, including the enormous Clock Tower which dominates the sky-line. In all probability he is further indebted to Viollet-le-Duc not only for the roof of this tower, but perhaps also for the idea of a sequence of rooms arranged vertically one above the other. With one exception, all the towers are surmounted by roofs with blunt and boxy outlines; thus the single delicate spire he designed to surmount the earlier octagon provides a very telling contrast. Particularly when viewed from the west the towers look like a series of enormous shafts, spaced out to set up an irregular rhythm of thumping vertical stresses. Neither front to the habitable parts of the castle embodies anything which approaches a coherent façade, and nowhere else in his external architecture did Burges permit himself a display of assertive units in such close juxtaposition. The Clock Tower at Cardiff is in my opinion finer than E. W. Pugin's tower at Scarisbrick – where, as it happens, the steeply pitched roof again suggest French origins.

Further comparisons could, as I have already suggested, be made between Cardiff Castle and Godwin's Castle Dromore in Ireland, or the second Eaton Hall by Waterhouse (Plates XVI, XXV). And even when we remember the stable block and the Roman gateway at Cardiff, we should find that Lord Bute's architectural commissions are equalled in extent by those of several other Victorian patrons; indeed, an attempt to claim outright architectural superiority for Cardiff Castle over Eaton Hall or Dromore would very properly be questioned and for a variety of reasons. Again, even when it comes to the question of decorations, there is evidence – to quote Professor Hitchcock – that Godwin could 'rival in elaboration and exceed in elegance what Burges did for Lord Bute at Cardiff'. This does not quite represent my view of the matter, although specimens of Godwin's 'Anglo-Japanese' furniture at Dromore were certainly more advanced and delicate than anything designed for Cardiff by Burges. But the fact remains that I have yet to see any High Victorian interiors from the hand, very largely, of one designer to equal either in homogeneity or completeness, in quality of execution or originality of conception the best of the interiors in the Welsh castles; and perhaps the same may be said of a few of the interiors at Tower House, and of the east end of Studley Royal. For sheer power of intoxication on the borderline between romantic historicism and romantic fantasy, Burges seems to me to stand unrivalled in his period. It was a case of total immersion in a vision of the past, and Burges identified himself so wholeheartedly with his work that in a sense the charge of sham becomes irrelevant. I would sum the matter up by saying that whereas Burges's buildings are not infrequently flawed by imperfections, while certainly as an architect he is obviously surpassed by a number of his contemporaries, his decorations occupy a position of special eminence, if not of supremacy. This view, at all events, must be my excuse for devoting more space, in this discussion of the castles, to the decorations than to the architecture.

One of the obituary writers remarked that Burges had a 'downright contempt for architectural prettiness', a truth which applies as much to the treatment of his rooms as to his buildings. His best interiors are undeniably magnificent, even grandiose, but like his architecture they are always tough and masculine. Burges was not a voluptuary, and neither, it seems safe to say, was Lord Bute. Nowhere at Cardiff do we find any hint of cushioned opulence, nothing is ever soft or yielding, rarely does Burges permit himself to be graceful. Many of the rooms are designed round one or two tremendous features, dramatic and inescapable, as a rule the chimney-piece and the ceiling. This applies, for instance, to the dining-rooms in both the castles, to Lady Bute's bedroom at Castell Coch, and again, as it happens, to the dining-room and to the library at Melbury Road. Furthermore, in several of his rooms the chimney-piece and ceiling are designed in two quite different styles. Burges will be criticized not only for the colossal scale of units of this kind but for failing to provide the links in design which would relate them to their surroundings. Large areas, even in some of the rooms which are decoratively complete, may seem too thinly decorated to support the weight of the dominating units. The sudden contrasts between flat walls and the carved decorations which project so violently from them deprive his interiors of overall coherence. Rarely did he plan his use of colour according to a scheme; and in spite of the bright colours and a liberal use of gold leaf on the ceilings and chimney-pieces, his rooms, for all their richness, can sometimes produce an effect which I have described as an onslaught.

Criticisms of Burges's bulkiness and incoherence, his crushing scale and sombre weight are no doubt valid from the point of view of eighteenth-century rules which insist on smooth transitions, harmonious relationships of scale, and stylistic unity – rules which create the type of coherence associated, for example, with the work of the brothers Adam or of Wyatt. Yet we must remember that Burges was one among many writers of his day who described the eighteenth-century as the 'Dark Ages of art', a vague but evidently potent phrase which seems to have summarized a widely shared set of opinions. Most High Victorians despised Georgian design because to them the rules of unity and coherence seemed to damp imagination, limiting the individual expression of patron and architect with results that in their eyes were above all dull and monotonous. Burges at Worcester College may have respected the scale he inherited, but we have seen how he transformed a unified interior by means of details which were both very closely distributed and stylistically incompatible. His decorations at Cardiff and elsewhere, massive as boulders in a quarry, probably represent an especially strong protest against eighteenth-century canons: certainly it is a mistake to look at High Victorian architecture and decoration, especially the work of Burges, through eighteenth-century spectacles. The episodic bumpiness of some of his interiors, no doubt distasteful to those for whom the eighteenth century represents perfection, is I believe the result not of incompetence but of a conscious aim. Burges was not interested in a gracefully coherent uniformity – quite the reverse. I believe he organized the different units in his schemes so that by abrupt contrasts of scale, and sometimes of style and materials, they should make the greatest possible dramatic impact.

Burges was not alone in his contempt for eighteenth-century rules. At Harlaxton (Plate VI) even Salvin's work already shows a few rather startling juxtapositions, although they are far less abrupt and violent than those to be seen, externally and internally in the same mansion, in the work of about 1850 by William Burn – a designer whose daring scale and imaginative exuberance suggest comparisons not only with Vanburgh but with Burges and other High Victorians. But Burn and Burges were not alone in bringing an outdoor scale indoors. Webb and Shaw, Waterhouse and Bentley, and rather later Collcutt, designed chimney-pieces and other units sometimes of enormous size: the cowled chimney-piece at Red House, for instance, makes a fairly violent contrast with its immediate surroundings, while at Dawpool and at Cragside it was not a question in certain rooms of walls being dominated by the chimney-pieces, but of chimney-pieces making up the walls – a treatment which admittedly softens the impact although the scale seems to have been without precedent.

A similar fearlessness of a large scale went hand in hand with the application of architectural proportions to other things besides chimney-pieces, for instance to specimens of movable furniture designed not only within the Morris orbit by Webb and Seddon, but by Shaw and Waterhouse, and of course by Burges himself and his imitators; and this is to say nothing of a series of by now well-known pieces of dining-room furniture such as the Chevy Chase sideboard, or again the monumental organs and the massive billiard-tables in the halls and saloons of many private houses. Conscious from 1851 onwards of a new interest in the decorative arts, several of the architects we have mentioned here were among the professional designers who sent furniture to the International and other exhibitions. No doubt the size and elaboration of the exhibits was often influenced by the spirit of competition. At Abney Hall, where a Crace-

Pugin sideboard of about 1862 confronts what I take to be Pugin decorations of an earlier date, the contrast between domestic scale and exhibition scale is obvious and perhaps significant. By 1867 one of Bruce Talbert's plates in *Gothic Forms Applied to Furniture* shows two sideboards, in one room, of such a size that the base alone in each case is at *shoulder* height of the figures in the drawing. It is, I believe, arguable that the exhibitions were partly responsible for the gradual acceptance of a colossal scale in certain items of domestic design, but not by any means all the later Victorian furniture to the new, large scale was designed for exhibition purposes. Of Burges it would be true to say that from about 1862 onwards he designed most of his decorations, including his furniture, at exhibition pitch.

Most Victorian designers were conscious both of the challenge of the past and of the fact that they could not invent a new style. Perhaps they came to exult in the drama of sheer size, and in the contrasts the new scales afforded, partly because it gave them the opportunity to re-state the past in terms that were all their own. Aside from the hotels and flats and administrative blocks, the response to the stimulus of building to a vast scale can be seen in the enormous towers by Barry and Brodrick, by Waterhouse and Collcutt, by Burges himself and by J. F. Bentley. The jump in scale by which these towers came to dominate whole districts was scarcely less violent than that which is marked by the skyscrapers of today: the Clock Tower at Cardiff was locally unpopular, perhaps because the inhabitants of a provincial town were not yet ready for the fierce contrasts already familiar in more advanced centres. Related to this love of bigness for its own sake, whether it was an expression of civic pride, of national supremacy, or of the background of tremendous wealth, went a determined assertion of individuality – including gestures which can be seen as a snub to the past. From about 1870 onwards many architects for whom Georgian monotony had become unendurable delighted to break up uniform terraces by inserting a new house, often superb in itself, but deliberately designed to contrast rather than harmonize with the other houses in the same block. Violent contrasts of style are to be seen in the houses built next door to each other by Burges and Shaw in Melbury Road, yet at the time these contrasts probably passed without comment. Thus it seems to me that when Burges in his decorations confronts us with abrupt transitions and a formidable scale he is, even if unconsciously, very much a man of his time. By 1860 the canons of Georgian taste could be ignored with approval, the inhibiting grip of archaeology had been broken down to make way, in the case of a few designers, for the imagination; and it is worth remembering that in the earlier 'sixties the chastening influence of Morris and Webb had not yet begun to exercise its full power. The

High Victorians were in a position to experiment. When it came to interior decorations, few designers exploited their opportunities more daringly than Burges.

But the value of his decorations does not of course depend merely on High Victorian nerve. Love Burges or loathe him, his rooms are packed with themes and stories, he gives us more to think about than any other designer of his period. Whether we find his humour tiresome or endearing, an agreeable relief in the midst of so much weight and erudition or the expression of the childish Billy Burges to whom Rossetti felt inclined to offer a bull's-eye, will no doubt be a matter of personal taste. What I believe cannot be denied is that he evolved new shapes, new juxtapositions and combinations of material to provide whole interiors which for all their debts to the past are different in kind, taken as a whole, from anything seen before. Where, for instance, can precedents be found for the summer smoking-room at Cardiff Castle, or for the dining-room ceiling; for Lady Bute's bedroom at Castell Coch or – to go farther afield – for the dome over the chancel at Studley Royal? Nowhere did Burges's imagination erupt with greater force than in some of his chimney-pieces, or with greater originality than in some of his ceilings (Plates LXXI, LXXII, LXXIII and LXXIV). Curiously enough, the chimney-piece in the dining-room at Cardiff Castle (Plate I) has its origins in a design for a quite different building – a private house to which we must now turn our attention.

The foundation stone of Knightshayes, in North Devon, bears the date 1869[1] (Plate XX). Commissioned by John Heathcoat Amory, M.P. (who later received a baronetcy), this was the largest private house, excluding the castles, Burges was ever called upon to design. Surrounded by trees and terraced lawns, it occupies a very beautiful setting which falls gently away on the south side towards fields and rougher ground beyond the ha-ha. It is built of rather dark red sandstone, although with dressings of lighter colour, and from most points of view appears compact and simple both in style and in outline. Comfortably embedded in the landscape, and now overgrown on the garden front by mature climbing plants, Knightshayes is a most unobtrusive building. Yet if the south elevation gives an impression of symmetry, the arrangement of windows in the recessed centre wall is worthy of a second glance, since even the 'lucarne', with its sculptured gable, is off-centre. Still more freely composed, the entrance front on the north side includes a picturesque touch in the battlements at the north-west angle.

[1] I am greatly indebted to Sir John Heathcoat Amory, Bart. (grandson of Burges's patron), and to Lady Amory, for allowing me to examine Burges's drawings, and the house itself, and also for information about it. Burges's *Book of Decorations* (1873), preserved at the house, contains nearly 60 sheets of details, not all of them in his own hand.

The interiors show many distressing if understandable changes. The drawing-room has been completely remodelled, very little of Burges's work survives in the library, while in the hall, with its simple pitched roof, the balcony is not in its original state and a gallery has entirely disappeared. None of Burges's chimney-pieces survive intact. The best sculpture is to be seen in the twelve corbel-brackets supporting the cornice in the billiard room, a series of humanized animals probably carved by Nicholls, who may also have been responsible for the very different brackets in the hall. Burges's Book of Decorations, preserved at the house, includes a number of designs which were almost certainly produced before 1873, the date inscribed on the title page. This book is of special interest because several of the many unexecuted designs to be found in it were used or adapted for later work. For instance, the figure of a woman reclining on a litter, designed originally as part of a frieze for the morning room at Knightshayes, is now to be seen on tiles in the dining-room at Tower House; while the proposed design for the drawing-room chimney-piece (p. 29, no. 23 of the Knightshayes book) was actually built, with modifications, in the dining-room at Cardiff Castle (Plate I).

That Knightshayes should now strike the beholder as an unobtrusive building may not have been the intention of the architect, and would probably surprise anyone who knew the house only from the drawing in Pullan's *Architectural Designs* (Plate 44). Burges himself may have been surprised that the colour of the stone yielded so slight a contrast with the greens and browns of nature. Pullan's drawing shows that Burges had designed two massive retaining walls in stone, arranged in tiers to bank up the south side of the platform on which the house stands. These walls would have helped to isolate the house from its surroundings, but they were never built. Perhaps in the mind of the patron – no letters between patron and architect have come to light – the desire to cut out unnecessary expense went hand in hand with a determination that the building should offer the least possible aggression to the surroundings.

Neither at Knightshayes nor anywhere else did Burges aim at the type of robust if slightly arbitrary plasticity associated, for example, with Ettington Hall, which from 1858 onwards had been remodelled by John Prichard. Burges does not enrich his surfaces with banded stonework of different colours, and he keeps external sculpture down to a minimum. There is no need to add that he was uninfluenced by the innovations in domestic architecture of Nesfield and Shaw. Knightshayes is bold and massive, but at the same time self-effacing; redeemed from dullness on the south front by the asymmetry of the fenestration, picturesque rather than plastic on the north side, this serious building is High Victorian in the type and weight of some of its details rather than in the organization of its main masses. Typical in many ways of its architect, it is a very attractive but historically unimportant country house. Its significance in Burges's work would have been greater if the proposed decorations had all been executed.

Burges had been working at Knightshayes for about eighteen months when he was called to Yorkshire to build churches at Studley Royal and at Skelton. St Mary's at Studley, in several ways more interesting than the Skelton church, was built for Lord Ripon between 1871 and 1878.[1] The plan is curiously similar to that of Pugin's St Giles at Cheadle and the position of the main units – south porch, west tower, buttresses, sacristy, and pulpit – is in each case much the same. Burges breaks away from Pugin's plan, supposing he knew it, by building his tower across the west wall, thereby reducing his nave to four bays. The entrance bay under the tower, for once vaulted in stone and rising almost to the height of the nave, is marked off from the body of the church by piers and a light screen. The choir and the chancel are distinguished as two separate areas by the decorative treatment.

If at St Mary's the main units are traditionally disposed, several details on the outside of the church show that Burges was not the man to follow custom indefinitely. Above the large east window three groups of sculpture are set within tracery against the wall, a startling but impressive composition, 'crazy' perhaps, but original – only pedants will deplore it (Plate LXX). Inside the church, above the nave, Burges repeats the king-posts and double-cove section familiar since his roof over the east end at Cork. From the end of the nave eastwards there is a marked drop in height and the choir, subdivided into two bays and lined with marble, has a painted roof of simple section following the lines of the arches. Here and in the chancel the window tracery is doubled, glazed externally, open on the inside. Burges crowns the chancel, an exact square on plan, with a smaller and flatter version, very differently decorated, of the cove-and-dome over Lady Bute's bedroom at Castell Coch; but at St Mary's the curved section of the cove or saucer-dome is continued down between the arches – and four pendentives is the result (Plate LXXIV). Below these pendentives and elsewhere in this outstanding interior, full of adroit touches, several sculptured figures are executed with precision to fit compactly into the stonework. Especially ingenious is the placing of a magnificent winged lion.

Burges was perhaps more successful in small rather than in large interiors. In the Studley chancel he not only designed an unusual combination of fluent and richly decorated shapes; on three sides the double arcading gives a veiled

[1] N. Pevsner, *Buildings of England, Yorkshire, West Riding* (1959), p. 59.

definition to the wall planes, thus adding an exciting touch of spatial elasticity. As we should expect, nearly all the decorations in this church are well designed and executed, including the mosaic floors, and the quality of Nicholls's sculpture is matched by some unusually good stained glass. St Mary's has been described as Burges's 'ecclesiastical masterpiece'; Cork Cathedral, by another authority, as his 'greatest building'. There can be little doubt that the Studley church, with the climax of the chancel inside, is the ecclesiastical masterpiece among the smaller churches.

Nothing at Knightshayes or at Studley Royal prepares us for the Harrow School Speech Room, a building which is extremely interesting even if it is not entirely successful. Several drawings by Haig of Burges's first ideas for it appeared in *The Architect* of 1872; the foundation stone was laid in 1874 and the opening ceremony performed three years later. D-shaped on plan, and built as a rigidly symmetrical block in red brick with stone dressings, it is still extremely bold in outline although it has received several alterations. Burges himself had evidently suggested the addition of a tower or towers to the arcaded straight front, thus perhaps justifying those executed in 1919 and 1925 by other hands. Standing on the road which runs between the complex of school buildings, the Speech Room occupies a site excavated out of the rising ground not far below the parish church. Burges based his plan on that of a classical theatre, arguing that on this sloping site a semi-circular arrangement of seats, rising in tiers, would reduce the cost of excavations. His main idea was to robe a classical building in Gothic dress, inside and out, but the internal decorations as they came to be executed fell short of the proposals of 1872. The present significance and varied uses of the Speech Room could scarcely have been anticipated by Burges, whose unusual and rather daring designs depended for success upon survival without changes. In theory he might have welcomed the proud accumulation of trophies and memorial tablets, in practice only Burges could have added to his own building without harm to its special merits. The Speech Room has obviously been treated with great respect, but the bold force of Burges's design has been modified on the outside by the asymmetrically placed additions, just as the homogeneity of the interior has been to some extent obscured.

The wooden roof over the main body of the auditorium is elaborately decorated, in the centre, with a cluster of small inset domes. Concentrically grouped and bordered by delicate tracery, the domes and curves were intended to echo the plan of the seating below. The roof is supported by cast-iron pillars, very tall and thin, at present with gilded capitals. In the auditorium these pillars are arranged in pairs along one of the higher rows of seats, a few yards away from the rear wall; and they follow the same curve. Springing from the capitals a system of arches and vaults, constructed of wood, links the pillars with the roof. Across the stage or platform, providing five bays, the pillars are arranged in a straight line parallel to the wall facing the audience – though these pillars were not included in the original design. Above the roof, invisible metal trusses radiate from a central drum.[1] Burges had earlier made use of cast iron in the warehouse in Upper Thames Street of about 1866, and in the now-destroyed church at Stoke Newington, but he can never have used it more boldly than he did at Harrow. Godwin tells us that Burges always hoped to build a theatre. The Speech Room is the nearest he ever came to fulfilling this ambition.

Several buildings described in the preceding paragraphs occupied Burges throughout most of the 'seventies, but in the same decade he was still very busy supervising his work for Lord Bute in South Wales. Although in 1874 *The Architect* reported that the Tower of Cardiff Castle was locally unpopular, it was prepared to describe the house for Mr McConnochie as the 'best house in the town'. Professor Hitchcock, whose judgment on this building has already been quoted, remarks also that it 'prepared the way for Burges's fine collegiate work in America'.[2] The Cardiff house is neatly planned to fit into a town site; asymmetrically composed, and with a French bias in some of the external details, it is undoubtedly one of Burges's finest buildings (Plate XIV). In 1959 its appearance more than lived up to expectations, and could be seen to correspond very closely to a drawing in one of Pullan's plates.[3] Almost the same plan was adopted for the rather smaller Tower House, built by Burges for himself from 1875 onwards, this time of brick with stone dressings but with only one large staircase. All the units and details in the Cardiff house are tightly integrated: as a whole it presents the appearance of a compactly unified mass in which the effect of compression and density, due partly to the contrasting textures in the stonework, is throughout very impressive. Similar textural contrasts are to be seen in Burges's work in America.

In 1873 an eighty-acre plot of land had been bought by the Trustees of Trinity College in Hartford, Connecticut, as the site for new College buildings.[4]

[1] Information from Mr G. M. Vine, F.R.I.C.S., F.A.I., a member of the firm of Chartered Surveyors which undertook work in the Speech Room in the 1950s. See also N. Pevsner, *Buildings of England*, *Middlesex* (1951), pp. 100, 101.

[2] H.-R. Hitchcock, *Architecture: Nineteenth and Twentieth Centuries*, p. 188.

[3] R. P. Pullan, *The Architectural Designs of William Burges*, Pl. 38.

[4] For my information about Trinity College I am indebted to the College authorities, and particularly to Professor James A. Notopoulos and Mr Wendell E. Kraft, the Assistant to the Principal (President A. C. Jacobs). Mr Kraft has supplied me with a very large collection of photographs and a photostat of Burges's *Report* of 1874, complete; also a photostat of an article in *Scribner's Monthly*, vol. XI, March 1876 (No. 5), in which the building is discussed in some detail.

On p. 612 of the *Scribner* article, there is a small but clear line-reproduction of a 'Proposed Chim-

In the same year the President of the College visited England evidently to inspect the universities, perhaps also with the intention of finding an architect. His choice fell upon William Burges, who prepared a draft scheme for an enormous complex of buildings, the intention being to group them round four very large quadrangles. This scheme was approved by the authorities, who then sent Mr F. H. Kimball, an American architect, to help Burges in London with the preparation of the working drawings.

To judge from the perspective of the whole scheme as it is reproduced in Pullan,[1] the single building executed from Burges's designs (Plate LXVI) is the equivalent of no more than one side of one of the proposed quadrangles, but the units as they came to be executed do not correspond precisely to any of the units as they were represented in the drawing. The executed building is dominated by a massive central gateway with four towers at each corner. This gateway is known as Northam Towers. Very long wings on each side of the gateway are made up of six uniform staircase blocks, based on the traditional system found in English universities, and each wing is punctuated in the middle by taller units with a pair of gables. Thus the rhythm of the entire building is ABACABA, of which C is Northam Towers. We are told that 'ground was broken' in 1875, but the two long staircase blocks were completed under Kimball's direction only in 1878; and Northam Towers was not added until 1882, that is the year after Burges's death. I have already said that without a knowledge of the drawings, which I have not seen, it is impossible to be sure, in the case of Northam Towers, of the extent of Burges's responsibility for their design.

The link between the Cardiff house and Trinity College lies not only in the contrasting textures in the stonework but also in the actual design, extremely crisp and bold, of the Gothic openings and details. The walls at Trinity are built of a brown stone cut with a 'rock face', while a light sandstone from Ohio pro-

---

ney-piece for the Dining-Hall'. The drawing represents the chimney-piece with the three angels (Plate 1), that was already built (or came to be built) in the dining-room at Cardiff Castle – one of the finest Burges ever designed. But no chimney-piece to this design was ever built at Trinity – where, to judge from photographs, the internal decorations were pleasant but rather modest, even in the Chapel.

The name of the 'resident architect' appears in the *Scribner* article as F. H. Kimball, not G. W. Keller, and Kimball was the man mentioned several times in Burges's seventeen-page *Report*. Kimball was still being quoted as 'architect of the buildings' in the minutes of a Special Meeting of the Trustees held March 2nd, 1878 (information from Mr Kraft). Perhaps Keller took over after this date. For this detail, cf. H.-R. Hitchcock; *Architecture: Nineteenth and Twentieth Centuries*, p. 188; *see also* W. W. Jordy and R. Coe (editors), *Montgomery Schuyler: American Architecture and other writings* (2 vols., Cambridge, Mass., 1961), esp. p. 122. The editors of this publication support the view that it was Kimball who went to England (and suggest that he benefited greatly from the experience of working with Burges). In note 4 (same page) they acknowledge Hitchcock's opinion but leave unresolved the question whether it was Kimball or Keller who supervised the building of Burges's wing.

[1] R. P. Pullan, *The Architectural Designs of William Burges*, Pl. 68. See also Pls. 69–71, inc. Plate 68 is reproduced to a smaller scale by Professor Hitchcock, op. cit., Pl. 88.

vides the smooth stone dressings. Perhaps it is through the contrasts of texture in stone that Burges makes us unusually conscious of the sheer weight and density of a hard material. Trinity is a tough and masculine building, and although Burges repeats the staircase blocks a dozen times, the immensely long façades show no hint of sagging or of dullness; indeed, it is the regularity of the fenestration – coupled with the fact that the 'same strings run uninterruptedly through' – that helps to give the building its considerable dignity. All but symmetrical on both façades, Burges's Trinity is formal to the point of grandeur, and it is this formality which contrasts so strikingly with other collegiate buildings of the High Victorian period – for example Seddon's University College at Aberystwyth and Butterfield's Keble at Oxford. To my knowledge no photograph of Trinity has ever appeared in the English architectural press. It deserves to be more widely known.

In 1875, as we know, the year that 'ground was broken' on the site for Trinity College, Burges began to build Tower House in Kensington, his shrine, his favourite work.[1] It was described by Lethaby – who must have been thinking of the decorations – with the words 'massive, learned, glittering, amazing'. In fact, Tower House is externally simple to the point of austerity, and it makes a poignant contrast with Shaw's house for Luke Fildes at the turn of Melbury Road: High Victorian has been superseded, not of course for the first time, by one of the several modes of Late Victorian. Perhaps it was this particular house by Shaw that aroused Burges's feelings about 'Queen Anne', but it is unlikely that we shall now discover what those feelings were. He never attempted this style, yet even at this date his mind was not entirely closed to new ideas. A visit to Greece, for instance, probably made in the earlier 'seventies, may help to explain the treatment of the piers and capitals by the Tower House entrance door. As we have seen, the plan of the house is a modified version of the house in Cardiff, a far better building, but the decorations are equal in quality and invention to those he was still designing for Lord Bute, and on these decorations, still in excellent condition, the great value of the house depends.

Burges had little use for abstract decorations, and at Tower House the walls and chimney-pieces – and indeed certain items of furniture – are as usual loaded with details which tell a story; furthermore the decorations in several rooms are worked out to illustrate a theme. In one of the bedrooms, for instance, it is the sea which provides him with most of his ideas, and this room is particularly memorable for the mermaid on the chimney-piece: carved in stone and naturalistically painted, she is one of the very few nude figures to be found

[1] R. A. Briggs, 'The Art of William Burges', R.I.B.A. *Journal*, 1916–17, vol. XXIII–XXIV, 3rd series. This article includes many details about Tower House.

anywhere among Burges's decorations. Below the mermaid on the same chimney-piece the waves in the frieze almost anticipate the wet-hair calligraphy of Art Nouveau.[1] The theme in the library is the 'dispersal of languages', and on a magnificent chimney-piece in this, Burges's favourite room, we find the celebrated dropped H. In the dining-room, however, a prevailing theme is not readily detected. Fairy-story heroes and heroines, painted on tiles high up on the walls, contend for supremacy with the signs of the zodiac on the metal ceiling, while the chimney-piece is dominated by the figure of Fame. Cast in bronze, she holds a sceptre and a crystal ball; her face and hands are carved out of ivory, and her eyes are inlaid with sapphires. Lethaby's words were carefully chosen. Most of the rooms at Tower House are worthy of description in detail, and it would be a particular pleasure to correlate Burges's drawings – of which several hundred are preserved at the R.I.B.A. – with the decorations as they came to be executed. There can be few private houses in London with anything to compare with them.

Burges as a young man repeatedly expressed his horror of what he called the 'abominable law of leasehold'. He believed that it encouraged unimaginative architecture and shoddy building, yet surprisingly enough he chose a leasehold plot for his own house. It was, as usual, very carefully built. When he died, like Street, in 1881 – that 'terrible year' as one of their friends called it – no doubt he retained his suspicions of the law of leasehold, but he may have hoped that Tower House would survive for posterity. Happily it is still with us, the structure and decorations all but complete. If for any reason it were demolished, Burges would then be represented in London only by St Anne's Buildings, where the decorations count for nothing, and by the iron-work – little more than a symbol – which is all that is left of the warehouse in Upper Thames Street.

BIBLIOGRAPHICAL NOTE

R. P. PULLAN: *The Works of the Late William Burges*, R.I.B.A., Transactions, 1881–82, vol. 32, p. 183; also the obituary, p. 17. *The Architectural Designs of William Burges* (London, 1883). *The Designs of William Burges* (London, 1885). *The House of William Burges* (London, 1885). *The Architectural Designs of William Burges*, A.R.A. (London, 1887).

E. W. GODWIN: 'The Home of an English Architect', *Art Journal*, 1886, pp. 170-3 and 301-5.

[1] N. Pevsner, *Pioneers of Modern Design*. London, edition of 1960, p. 90; the 'Mermaid' chimney-piece illustrated, p. 93.

G. E. STREET,
THE LAW COURTS
AND
THE 'SEVENTIES

JOSEPH KINNARD

IN the 'sixties Gothic had been an almost irresistible force; Palmerston may have had his triumph in the 'fifties but if anything his intervention had helped the cause of the Goths. All over England, churches, parsonages, and schools were built by architects whose knowledge of Gothic architecture was close and extensive – the sort of knowledge acquired from tinkering with old churches and building new ones, the knowledge of tracery, of mouldings, of capitals, of stonework, of all practical building matters, which no one is ever likely to have again. The architects of national reputation, working from London, were Butterfield, Scott, Pearson, Street, Burges, Bodley, William Slater, who had taken over R. C. Carpenter's work, Raphael Brandon, S. S. Teulon, and Ewan Christian, who as architect to the Ecclesiastical Commissioners restored the chancels of hundreds of churches. Another group worked from provincial centres. John Norton and Hugall worked in the Somerset and Gloucestershire area, G. F. Jones in Yorkshire, T. H. Wyatt, though from a London office, in Wiltshire, Woodyer in Surrey, Phipson in Norfolk, Chancellor in Essex, Browning, Fowler, Law and Kirk in Lincolnshire and Northamptonshire, Nicholson in Herefordshire, Hopkins and Preedy in Worcestershire, Chantrell in the Midlands, St Aubyn in Cornwall, Goddard in Leicestershire, and so on.

The significant development in the 'sixties was the confidence of the Gothic architects in designing complex secular buildings, the sort of buildings for which there were little or no medieval precedents. They demonstrated the wrongness of the notion that Gothic could only be successfully used for ecclesiastical buildings. This development, this great competence in adapting medieval forms, was most notably in evidence in the career of Alfred Waterhouse. The decade began with the building, between 1859 and 1864, of Manchester Assize Courts (Plate XXVI), which made Waterhouse the recognized master of planning large public buildings. Gothic town halls were built by Scott at Preston, 1862–7, E. W. Godwin at Northampton, 1861–4, and Congleton, 1864–6 (Plate XXIX). Butterfield built a hospital at Winchester, 1864, and Keble College, 1867–70, and of other university buildings Scott built Glasgow, 1866–71, J. P. Seddon the University of Wales – it began as an hotel – and Waterhouse Balliol's new buildings, 1867–9, and the Cambridge Union, 1865–7. St Pancras Station was built between 1867 and 1874. By the late 'sixties the likelihood was that any

223

large public building would be Gothic. Frolicsomely pinnacled rooflines were being put up all over England.

The two great buildings after the Palace of Westminster – the Law Courts and Manchester Town Hall – were the result of competitions of 1866 dominated by Gothic designs. The Town Hall (Plate XXVII) was built between 1868 and 1877 and the Law Courts between 1871 and 1882. Waterhouse's design for Manchester was selected because of the mastery of the practical matters, the plan, access, heating, ventilation, lighting; his elevations were surprisingly only ranked fourth. The site was an awkward one, 328 feet on the main, Albert Square, front, with other frontages of 388, 350 and 94 feet, and Waterhouse built right round the site leaving a centre court in which the Hall stands. All the rooms were placed along the street-fronts with the corridors to the court side. The main entrance leads into a vaulted but quite gay undercroft and to the staircases, comprising two main staircases, into one of which the building superintendent's private staircase is ingeniously corbelled, and two circular staircases for public use. These circular staircases which have rising coupled columns are a vivacious invention. The staircases lead to the main corridor, one of great dignity and spaciousness, on one side of which is the Large Hall and on the other the main rooms – the former council chamber, mayor's parlour, and so forth – along the Albert Square front. The impression the building gives inside is of spaciousness and airiness and one feels the common sense of the plan; there is no fearful expectation of getting lost in a maze of corridors. The building has an air of making sense. The enrichment, particularly on the staircases, is exuberant, and the oriels in the corridors are charming. The decoration of the main suite of rooms is lavish, solid, appropriate but not notably pleasant. The only failure is the Hall which seems heavy, overloaded, and squat. Externally it is all finely managed, and the awkward acute corner is got round with splendid confidence. The colossal tower is unfortunate, but no aspirant in a Victorian competition would have been foolish enough to omit such an expensive symbol of civic pride; still, the tower is something of a brute. All in all, it is a splendid building.

Six architects were invited to compete for the new Law Courts, but almost immediately there were difficulties, and finally, in January 1867, designs were submitted by eleven architects, who were all paid eight hundred pounds for their trouble. The architects were Abraham, Garling, Brandon, E. M. Barry, Scott, Street, Burges, Seddon, Waterhouse, Lockwood, and Deane. None of them had ever designed a building of such complex requirements – only Sir Charles Barry in the whole history of English architecture had ever done so – and not surprisingly they all failed completely to satisfy the judges. The site sloped from Carey Street to the Strand and the architects were instructed that the central hall should rise from the Strand level while the courts should be thirty-six feet higher for direct entry from the Carey Street entrance. The most difficult problem was access; it was essential that the ways of those concerned with the administration of justice and the spectators should be kept separate, and that judges, barristers, and spectators should have their own ways into courts. The impossible condition was to keep the cost down to £700,000.

The designs were exhibited in January 1867, and aroused extraordinary interest. All were Gothic except for the alternative Italian design by Garling. The architects costed their own designs; Waterhouse reckoned his would cost £1,339,328, based on the costs of Manchester Assize Courts, Scott reckoned £1,253,626, based on the costs of the Foreign Office, Lockwood reckoned £1,235,583, based on the costs of the Inns of Court Hotel. All the other estimates were close to these except for Seddon's which was £2,206,714. (When the surveyor appointed by the Treasury examined the designs he added from £200,000 to £500,000 – Scott's was increased to £1,726,494 – and only Waterhouse's estimate was found to be accurate.) When detailed consideration was given by the legal, political, and architectural adjudicators there were only five serious contenders, Barry, Scott, Waterhouse, Street, and Burges. Of these Burges was ruled out by the impossibility of his plan, for he had omitted the required central hall:

A central hall is doubtless a very attractive feature, but, however much adapted to a county assize courts, it appears to me that there are grave objections to it in the present instance; for, in the first place, it most materially diminishes the areas of light and air, and should it be circular, it has the extra disadvantage of causing sundry of the opening areas to assume an inconvenient shape. In the second place, it is a very serious addition to the expenses, if carried out on a proper scale.

He was probably right, but competitions cannot be won that way.

What Burges offered over the other architects was immense scenic superiority (Plate LXXVI). His extravaganza was French thirteenth-century Gothic of a martial sort, admirably suitable had the officials of the court been called upon to repel with bows and arrows a mass attack of furious litigants. The massive entrance through the twin round towers led to nothing but a covered way. Certainly the building would have added prodigiously to the London scene, but the lawyers had more urgent considerations in mind. Two of the plans only were satisfactory, E. M. Barry's and Waterhouse's. Both had solved the complex problems of access, but Barry's elevations were feeble and the dome rising above the records depository impossibly incongruous, and Waterhouse's

225

elevations were telling rather than distinguished. Scott addressed the adjudicators with characteristic mock-humility: 'Others may possibly have greater facility of arrangement than myself, though I have probably had as much experience in arranging large buildings as any man; but I may say that to me the labour has been such that, though I embarked on it vigorously on the very day after I agreed to join the competition, I have since been hard at work upon it, often giving to it eight hours or more a day for many days together.'

His judges agreed with his first sentence and showed little interest in the account of his labours. He was found fault with on the question of access and certainly his elevations, even by Scott standards, were disappointing. Street failed totally in his planning, for like Burges he ignored the instructions. He did include a central hall, though smaller than the one later designed, but at the wrong height, and he avoided the difficulties of access by denouncing them; 'I observe, in the instructions to architects, a request that the gallery of each court should be separately reached from the street. This appears to me to be an impossible arrangement without vast loss of space and great expense, and therefore an impossible arrangement in so restricted a site as that with which we are dealing.' That high-handed rebuff must have annoyed the judges, but the elevations (Plate LXXV) he offered were, Burges apart, so immensely more resourceful than the others that Street became one of the favourites. The particular attraction of Street's designs was their bold simplicity; there was a minimum of Gothic detail, and that detail in the salient places, and no nonsense of imposed symmetry along the 500-feet Strand front. The cornices were almost unbroken, the upper two storeys of windows combined to avoid the impression of endless repetition of small windows, the towers, except for the record tower at the west, simple in silhouette. There was the distinction there that Waterhouse lacked and nothing of the fussiness that marred the Scott and Barry elevations.

The result was declared in July of 1867 when the judges recommended that Barry and Street should act jointly. This brought an immediate protest from Scott to the effect that he had entered the singles competition and found himself playing against a doubles combination. Scott thought the combined merits of his plan and elevations exceeded those of others: 'Mr Waterhouse was perhaps the closest rival, but Mr Street had but a poor plan, while his architecture was unworthy of his talent, and had evidently, been much hurried; while Mr Burges, though his architecture exceeded in merit that of any other competitor, was nevertheless eccentric and wild in his treatment of it, and his plan was nothing.'

The Attorney-General upheld Scott's objection and it was not until June 1868 that the matter was settled. The decision was the right one, though how it was arrived at ('influential friends' were hinted at in the press) is not known. Street was given the Law Courts and Barry the rebuilding of the National Gallery – his coarse designs for this were fortunately never carried out. Barry read the decision in a newspaper in his club, and he never forgave Street whom he blamed for the snub; Street certainly had not acted with delicacy of feeling.

The competition had abundantly displayed the variety of the Gothic Revival at its height. Two of the masters had not been among the competitors – Butterfield because he declined to enter competitions, and Pearson because he had not yet reached a position of sufficient note – but still, with the designs of Burges, Street, and Waterhouse, there was distinction, copiousness of invention, and learning.

❖

The decision to appoint Street must have been particularly galling to Scott, for the chosen man was thirteen years his junior, and had never designed any large civic building. But Street had never been an admirer of Scott's and had confessed his belief that All Saints, Margaret Street, was the greatest modern church. He belonged, as an admirer of Butterfield and a High Churchman, to the Athanasian stream of the Gothic Revival and it was one of the ironies of the architecture of the times that the doctrinaire and traditional, the liturgically minded and Tory, should have developed Gothic to suit Victorian needs while the liberals and moderates should have clung to imitation medieval. Street was a man of great powers of mind – the rapidity of assimiliation for his books on Italian and Spanish architecture is testimony to his academic gifts – and equal energy.

Up early, in late; getting meals piecemeal and at all sorts of hours; driving forty miles across country to intercept a train; fitting in the visits to different places like a complicated puzzle – so many minutes here, so many there; so many letters, or specifications, or reports to be written in transit. Letter-writing in trains was constant. 'I have written nineteen letters between Bletchley and Moreton,' he writes – in the train, of course. Not infrequently he wrote his letters in cabs.[1]

His industry was matched by his severity and self-confidence; he could hardly have been a likable man. Norman Shaw, who succeeded Philip Webb in his office – the fact that these two, as well as William Morris, chose to work for him is indicative of the admiration of the younger men for his work – wrote:

[1] A. E. Street, *Memoir of George Edmund Street, R.A., 1824–1881* (John Murray, 1888).

When a new work appeared, his custom was to draw it out in pencil in his own room – plans, elevations, and sections, even putting in the margin lines and places where he wished the title to go; nothing was sketched in, it was *drawn*, and exactly as he wished it to be, so that really there was little to do, except to ink in his drawings, and tint and complete them. The rapidity and precision with which he drew were marvellous. I have never seen any one, not merely to equal, but to approach him, and he was as accurate as he was rapid ... I well remember a little *tour de force* that fairly took our breath away. He told us one morning that he was just off to measure an old church – I think in Buckinghamshire – and he left by the ten o'clock train. About half-past four he came back and into the office for some drawing paper; he then retired into his own room, reappearing in about an hour's time with the whole church carefully drawn to scale, with his proposed additions to it, margin lines and title as usual, all ready to ink in and finish.

Shaw ended on a note perhaps less eulogistic than first seems.

He was the beau-ideal of a perfect enthusiast. He believed in his own work, and in what he was doing at the time, absolutely; and the charm of his work is that when looking at it you may be certain that it is entirely his own, and this applies to the smallest detail as to the general conception. I am certain that during the whole time I was with him I never designed one single moulding.

In his biography, Street's son added a list of works, incomplete and not entirely accurate, showing that there were some 260 original works and some 460 restorations and additions – and every moulding from the master's hand. The churches were scattered over the country, but more numerously in the Oxford, Buckinghamshire, Berkshire areas, with an outcrop in Yorkshire where he designed, like Pearson, for Sir Tatton Sykes. Along with the churches were schools and parsonages, unostentatious, solid, and inexpensive. Not surprisingly the buildings varied in quality and many of them, often cheap churches, are of little note. But there is never any nonsense about a Street church, and never much prettiness. He had learned from Butterfield the art of elimination; he too could build boldly in brick, could leave plain surfaces tellingly alone, could do without crockets and trefoils. Eastlake, in what was implied criticism of Scott Gothic, very accurately described his essential merit.

Mr Street was one of the first architects of the Revival who showed how effective Gothic architecture might be made where it simply depends for effect on artistic proportion. In this respect he brought about a great and useful reformation in the practice of his art. If Pugin and his followers could decorate their walls with carved panels, fill their windows with tracery, crown their buttresses with crocketed pinnacles, and enrich their porches with canopied niches, they made a showy building. But shorn of such details it cut a sorry figure. Now, if Mr Street were limited to the arrangement of four walls, a roof, a couple of windows, a door, and a chimney shaft, on the distinct understanding that none of these features was to be ornamented in the slightest degree, we may be quite sure that he would group them in such a fashion as to make them picturesque. Nothing can possibly be simpler than his works at Cuddesdon and East Grinstead – the first a college, the latter a convent. They had literally no architectural character beyond what may be secured by stout masonry, a steep roof, and a few dormer windows. But there is a genuine *cachet* on each design which is impossible to mistake. They are the production of an artist hand.[1]

This was perhaps a little unjust to Pugin and was giving something to Street that was properly Butterfield's, but the development was as he described it. The range of churches was great, from the elaborately polychromatic St James the Less, Thorndike Street, to the great barn of Oakengates, in Shropshire, to the powerfully accented and forceful St Philip and St James, Oxford. Considering the number of churches he designed and the speed with which he did so it can hardly be surprising that there are a proportion of dull and undistinguished ones, but his reputation for designing a one-style church, 'vigorous', is certainly unmerited. The manner was hard, sometimes strident, and Street would perhaps have thought grace and suavity frivolous qualities, but it was not obtrusively belligerent as was much of Butterfield's later work. The muscles of his buildings may have been obvious, but there was no fist-shaking.

When the candidates for the new Courts came to be selected and it was understood that the designs were to be Gothic, Street's name must have been unhesitatingly put forward. Scott was of course the popular practitioner, but it could hardly have been unknown to the Government advisers that he ranked in professional circles as at best a middle-brow. Butterfield could not be chosen because he refused to enter competitions, Pearson was too little known, Burges was perhaps the architects' choice, Waterhouse's experience of designing large buildings made him an inevitable choice. Street had a public reputation second only to Scott's and a professional reputation far superior to his.

As soon as Street was appointed architect, the farce of the new Embankment site, next to Somerset House, began. The result was that not until 1870 did

[1] Charles L. Eastlake, *A History of the Gothic Revival* (Longmans, Green and Co., 1872).

he have ready the final scheme for the Strand-Carey Street site, and not until 1871 that tenders for the foundations were sought. The events of 1871 were to have a profound effect on English architecture. The revised plan was quite different from the one with which Street had won the competition. To all intents and purposes he had scrapped his own plan and taken Waterhouse's but oriented it north–south instead of east–west. He provided the required separate access from the streets for spectators and enlarged the hall. All the elevations had consequently to be recast and in fact showed hardly any resemblance to the originals. As soon as the elevations for the Strand front were exhibited the outcry was raised. The campaign against the building was led by the architectural historian James Fergusson, and given abundant space in *The Times*. Most of those who attacked the design had a very inadequate idea of what was involved, partly because they were judging on the basis of a line illustration in the building papers, which was more a diagram than anything else and which accentuated features that would be unnoticeable in the completed building and partly because they overlooked the fact of the length (over 500 feet) of the front and the fact that it would not, in a narrow street, be seen instantaneously as a front – the condition, in short, of Street's design. Fergusson had two objections, one general and one particular. His objection was to Victorian Gothic; he thought the age should have its own expression and that thirteenth-century style was a confession of failure. He then objected to the design in detail; he thought the front not grand enough, the whole building too ecclesiastical, and above all disliked the hall, which, seemingly from an inability to read a plan, he thought would be unlighted, dark and useless. Objections of all sorts were raised, some of them only malicious. Scott and E. M. Barry at least must have enjoyed the correspondence. Obviously Street, the hero of the young, had his supporters and E. W. Godwin defended the designs at length in *The Architect*. He showed that *The Times* advocacy for a building on the lines of the town halls of Brussels, Bruges, Louvain, Ghent and the Cloth Hall of Ypres was inappropriate for a building of such complex purpose:

> The eastern part of the Strand front looks just what it is – five storeys of offices *attached* to the Law Courts. No doubt the *Times* would like to see the windows in a frontage of 507 feet all of uniform shape and size. This possibly is the only idea of architectural unity which our amateurs possess – closet and council chamber, court and corridor, all lit by a regulation pattern window.

As to the fussiness and over-ornateness, he was able convincingly to disabuse the critics:

In the whole of the Strand front there are not 700 superficial feet of tracery including the windows of the gable and the great hall; that is to say, the quantity of tracery in this 500-feet frontage is less than many a single church window, is less than in the comparatively small frontage of the Manchester Assize Courts, and considerably less than that in the great halls at Ypres and Louvain etc.

This able defence and others did little good; the Law Courts was an unpopular building before it was started.

The Courts were not opened until 1882, after the architect's death. Thirty-five million bricks had been used and a million cubic feet of stone. There were eleven miles of pipes for heating. And Street designed nearly everything. Only someone of his ferocious industry could have accomplished the work. One of his assistants at the time of the Law Courts, Augustus W. Tanner, recalled:[1]

The fastest piece of work we ever remember him to have accomplished was on one occasion when he covered fourteen sheets of double elephant paper with a mass of beautifully drawn full-size mason's mouldings, with in addition, on nearly every sheet, explanatory portions of the building, drawn to a scale of inch or half-inch to the foot, and all within a space of two hours. All the details were written in and referenced complete, and for all practical purposes might have been given to the builder at once; but he always allowed his subordinates the privilege – and it was a privilege very highly esteemed – to tint and ink these drawings in, and carefully finish them as it were. After such an occasion Mr Street would walk out of his office and away, leaving his clerks to walk into his room, and with wonder and astonishment survey the work he left behind him. He used a black ebony engineers' T-square, and when drawing the rattling of this square was incessant ... A consummate master of his art beyond all his contemporaries, Mr Street was also a thorough man of business. His calculations were rapid and exact, his memory never failed him ... On the Works he was nimble and fearless; all the workmen knew him, and he knew them. Ladders and paths which many another gentleman feared to take, he would traverse with ease and comfort. Thus he was well acquainted with every portion of the vast pile as the work proceeded.

The incredible labour went on almost until his death. He visited the Courts for the last time on November 17th, 1881, three weeks before the hall was cleared of scaffolding. He died on December 18th of that year.

[1] *British Architect*, December 1st, 1882.

The Law Courts remain the major Gothic Revival building after the Houses of Parliament, but these two buildings could hardly be more different. In Barry's masterpiece the abundant detail was repetitively laid on with hardly any variations; in the event the result was charming. Street's detail was not of this mechanical sort, but was as closely related to the structure as the embellishment of any thirteenth-century cathedral. The main Strand front is a design of the highest ingenuity. It consists of two almost symmetrical overlapping groups. The first to the east, is centred on a gabled entrance on either side of which are gabled sections with tourelles at the angles and beyond these the ordinary faces of the building.

The symmetry here is not in fact exact, although this is not at first noticeable; the tourelle blocks are of different widths and their window pattern different and the end blocks, too, are of different length. The windows of the two lower storeys, screened by the arcade, are absolutely plain and the windows of the three storeys above the lower two floors are vertically combined with smaller windows for the top storey – for the tourelle blocks, where the emphasis is vertical, the pattern is reversed so that the upper storey windows are combined. This quiet piece of ingenuity is entirely successful. The western tourelle block of this composition is also the east feature of the second symmetrical composition centred on the main entrance to the great hall (Plate LXXVIII). This group is symmetrical except at the ground floor. Wherever seen, the front has an apparent total symmetry, sufficient at least for a monumental façade, and two real symmetrical compositions. The completeness and consistency of the front is furthered by the arcade, the continuous four-feet-deep string course, and the regularly placed tourelles. The total effect is of richness, but there is in fact remarkably little ornamentation. The design is one of intellectual subtlety, boldness and full of resource. An imposed symmetrical façade would have been, because of the site, a failure – it took immense skill to get the best of both worlds as Street here does.

The quadrangle, with the office block to the east, is suitably restrained in brick and stone; its central features are perhaps unnecessarily emphatic, but it is impossible to receive the full effect now that the centre is covered with shacks called Queen's Bench Courts 9 and 10. The main west front, massively and impressively in stone, has such a combination of rich detail and plain ashlar walling that it seems a Gothic version of Cockerell. Here again there is an ingenious combination of suggested symmetry and regularity and the variety and asymmetry required by the building. The façade, broken now by the bridge, is dignified, solid and varied; the combining of the two top storeys of windows happily solves the problem of comparatively small windows on a long frontage. The

Carey Street fronts[1] are lighter in tone; the bands of brick and stone seem almost gay. Everywhere there are details of note – basement windows on Bell Yard of Hawksmoorean force in simplicity, the beautifully proportioned arch on the Strand front at the west end, the chimneys, and the bold details of the windows, sensible plate glass and sash affairs.

Internally the building is dominated by the great hall (Plate LXXVII), 230 feet long, 48 feet wide and 82 feet high, a room of complete assurance and grandeur with some thoroughly Victorian quirks in the lancets of the north end. The one obvious failure, and this applies throughout the building, is the sculpture, which is dull, often dreary and poorly executed; the capitals in the corridors and elsewhere are extraordinarily feeble and dispiriting – dead leaf rather than stiff leaf. It does seem here that Street's insistence on designing everything himself had exhausted him. 'I am certain that during the whole time I was with him I never designed one single moulding.' The result was a lack of vivacity and Scott's 'Mr Street works by drawing, I by influence' has, on the evidence here, something to be said for it. The hall functions poorly, but it is magnificent and worth a lot of inconvenience. That it is grossly extravagant to its use was not Street's fault, for the instructions as to height had been laid down in the competition. There is little extravagance in the rest of the building. The courts are well lighted – Street took immense pains in detailing the charmless panelling – and the corridors simple without being bare. There are window mouldings of remarkable directness and originality, and the staircases are effective and well lighted without being thrilling

There can be no doubt as to Street's immense ability as a designer. The complex, intricate, building is grand, subtle and learned, but it is also cold and unengaging. It is not a building anyone, however much he admires it, could feel affection towards. There is something barren about it and it seems, because of its tremendous completeness and competence, to call into question the whole endeavour of the Gothic Revival. It does not lack grandeur – it makes Manchester Town Hall look comparatively brash – but it does lack warmth and grace. That Street was more resourceful, bolder, more fastidious and more learned in Gothic than Barry would probably not be questioned – but who would simply 'like' the Law Courts as much as the Houses of Parliament? The Law Courts are not engaging and perhaps never will be. Butterfield's work is not engaging, but engagingness is only one of the pleasures of architecture. To Street's younger contemporaries the Law Courts were like a magnificent mausoleum to the Gothic Revival. The best Victorian architectural journalist, H. Heathcote Statham, described it as being 'full of unlighted or ill-lighted corridors', and concluded:

[1] That Philip Webb had anything to do with these, as has often been said, is most unlikely; he had left Street's office in 1859.

The style is an unwieldy resuscitation of early Medieval architecture, the only decided merit is its monumental largeness and solidity of detail. But it has for a long time past palled on the Medievalist, and the whole building, as an architect once observed to me, is 'the grave of modern Gothic' – a costly and inconvenient anachronism.[1]

To the lawyers it soon became a traditional joke, a joke that seems still not to have lost its savour. Baron Huddleston said that among its beauties three might be singled out; the Courts were constructed so that counsel could not hear the judge, the judge could not hear the witness, and the jury could hear neither. When he was asked for advice on the proposed Birmingham courts he said: 'Go to the New Courts in London, and avoid everything that you see there; and then you may be in the way of getting something like good Courts.'

While the Courts were being built there had been a sudden and complete change of taste. There had been an awakened interest in the social arts. Earnestness was out of date. The building papers began to illustrate town houses rather than churches, and the architect of the age was Norman Shaw. In painting, Leighton was setting classic academic standards and Whistler had introduced the latest French taste to a reluctant England. In the novel, the banter of the idle rich appeared in *Daniel Deronda*. In the shops appeared photographs of society and near-professional beauties. The suave, the sophisticated, the delicate, the chic – these were qualities not in the emotional range of Butterfield and Street. Suddenly their buildings seemed too earnest, too strong, too provincial, too gloomy, too religious. They seemed primitively harsh and insistent. The reaction against Gothic quickly spread and affected the younger architects – their Gothic lacked the toughness and vitality of Street's, or they deserted to the Shaw school. Public buildings were clothed in Jacobean garments or full Classic regalia; if the tailor of the former manner was H. T. Hare and of the latter John Belcher the results were admirable. Only a very backward committee would choose a Gothic design after the Law Courts. The reaction, however just, obscured the merits of many notable buildings, not least the Law Courts. The Courts did not deserve the insults of the time; they remain a great work of uninviting architecture – but within is one of the glories of English architecture, the Hall, the perfect embodiment in stone of the majesty of the law.

[1] H. Heathcote Statham, *Modern Architecture* (Chapman and Hall, 1897).

RICHARD
NORMAN SHAW

NIKOLAUS PEVSNER

Richard Norman Shaw was born at Edinburgh in 1831. His father was an Irish Protestant, 'with a Huguenot strain', says E. S. Prior in the *Dictionary of National Biography*. His mother was Scottish. He received his schooling first at Edinburgh, then at Newcastle, and about 1846 entered the office of William Burn to become an architect. Burn (1789–1870) was an extremely competent man, Scottish too, a specialist in country-house work, often additions rather than new buildings, tactful and unostentatious – so much so, in fact, that he never had his designs illustrated in the technical journals. In 1852 Shaw won the Royal Academy Silver Medal, in 1853 the Gold Medal and Travelling Scholarship. The results of his travels to Italy, France, and also such picturesque places as Prague and Lübeck were published in 1858 under the title *Architectural Sketches from the Continent*, a usual thing to do in the mid-Victorian decades, as it established the author as a scholar and an artist and at the same time as a potentially resourceful practitioner. G. E. Street's *Brick and Marble Architecture* and his *Some Account of Gothic Architecture in Spain* are useful to this day. They came out in 1855 and 1865, but Street had travelled in 1850, 1853, 1854, 1861, 1862, 1863. It was Street whose office Norman Shaw joined in the year that the *Architectural Sketches* came out. Street, it need hardly be said, was one of the most serious, truthful and conscientious architects of the Gothic Revival. Shaw got the job of chief draughtsman in succession to Philip Webb. Not a year after Webb had left Street, he designed Red House for William Morris, who in his turn, when he had made up his mind to be an architect had also worked under Street. That was in 1856, before Street had moved from Oxford to London. Shaw's earliest published work, a desk-cum-bookcase, illustrated in *The Builder* in 1861 and recently acquired by the Victoria and Albert Museum, is still wholly of the Gothic Revival, Early English, with allusions to shrines, and highly polished colonnettes 'closely resembling marble', as *The Builder* writes. At that time, E. S. Prior says in the biographical entry already referred to, Butterfield was his chief admiration, Viollet-le-Duc his classic of Gothic construction.

Then, in 1862 or 1863, he started practice on his own, at 30 Argyll Street, off Regent Street, and in partnership with William Eden Nesfield. The partnership lasted until 1868 and must be looked at a little more closely, as Sir Reginald

Blomfield's book on Shaw[1] – the only book we have on him – contributes little to clarify it, and as it was in the later 'sixties that the style emerged which inspired Shaw's mature mastery of the 'seventies. Webb was born in the same year as Shaw, Nesfield was four years younger. His father had been a military man, major before he retired, then a painter in water-colours, then the leading formal gardener of the day. The son was a brilliant draughtsman too. He learnt the skill from J. D. Harding. In 1851 Nesfield was articled to Burn and there made friends with Shaw. Shaw on his journey to France in 1854 was accompanied by young Nesfield who had by then moved into the office of Anthony Salvin, a less scrupulous and more inventive architect, who was his uncle. He travelled on the Continent again in 1857 and 1858 (or 1859) and, seeing the success of Shaw's *Sketches*, brought out his as a book in 1862. He called it *Specimens of Medieval Architecture in France and Italy*. Like Shaw he was a convinced medievalist. Together they had measured and drawn not only buildings of the medieval centuries but also of medievalism: Pugin's Houses of Parliament and Pugin's St Augustine, Ramsgate, and in addition they had, while in France, been allowed by the great Viollet-le-Duc to trace some of his drawings.

So, in the years of the partnership both Shaw and Nesfield went on producing Gothic work. Under the joint name of the firm, drawings are signed for the churches of Farnham Royal (1866 etc.) and Kings Walden (1868) and for the English Episcopal Church at Lyons (1868). On the other hand, the beautiful church at Bingley in Yorkshire, of 1864 etc., is Shaw's design, the wing to Coombe Abbey in Warwickshire, of 1862 etc., now demolished, is Nesfield's, though in certain details very similar to Shaw's desk of 1861, and Cloverley Hall in Shropshire, of 1862 etc., now, alas, also demolished, is by Nesfield, though it was published in *The Builder* as by Nesfield & Shaw (Plate XV). However, the surviving drawings are by Nesfield, and this is confirmed by C. L. Eastlake's *A History of the Gothic Revival*, which came out in 1873 when the events were still fresh in his and others' memories. Eastlake wrote this of Cloverley Hall:

> To describe a modern building by the general remark that its style can be properly referred to no precise period in the history of styles, would, not many years ago, have been equivalent to pronouncing its condemnation, and even at the present time there are but few designers who can depart from recognized canons of taste without arriving at a result more original than satisfactory.[2] But in this admirable work Mr Nesfield has succeeded in realizing the true spirit of old-world art, without hampering himself by those

---

[1] *Richard Norman Shaw*, R.A., *Architect, 1831–1912* (Batsford, London, 1940).

[2] This remark, no doubt, was meant to dispose of the worst mixtures of the Free or Mixed Renaissance and, within the Gothic style, of, say, Thomas Harris.

nice considerations of date and stereotyped conditions of form which in the last generation were sometimes valued more highly than the display of inventive power.[1]

Nesfield's inventive power showed itself in other ways as well. Among his earliest work is a lodge in Regent's Park, dated 1864, and representing a pretty, highly picturesque Wealden style, with half-timbering and tile-hanging. Two years later a lodge at Kew Gardens is inspired by the Anglo-Dutch of the mid-seventeenth century, and more specifically the Dutch House at Kew. The brick-work, the broad pilasters, the hipped roof were a complete innovation, and Nesfield seems almost immediately to have translated this style from the smaller to the larger scale. The exact dating of Kinmel Park, Abergele, is still undecided. The surviving drawings are all of 1871–4, but they are details as demanded only when a building is under construction. J. M. Brydon in the *Architectural Review*, in 1897, says the designs were begun in 1866, but in *The Builder*, in 1888, he calls them begun 'twenty years ago'. So *c*. 1866–8 is the safest guess. Now Kinmel Park (Plate XXII) is entirely in what was soon to be called the Queen Anne style, i.e. a mixture of William and Mary with Louis XIII motifs.[2] Its symmetry, its restraint in decoration, its refined detail are unique at the time and point far forward.

Now as it is precisely this so-called Queen Anne style that Shaw is remembered for, it may be just as well to ask whether he might not have had a hand in these designs of his younger partner. After all, in 1866 Shaw was at least twenty-five, Nesfield only twenty-one. But little else than the argument just adduced is in favour of an attribution to Shaw. For one thing the partnership was called Nesfield & Shaw, not Shaw & Nesfield, though that may be due to Nesfield being the wealthy, Shaw the poorer partner. Nesfield had been to Eton. Secondly, Brydon tells us in 1888, when Shaw was very much alive, that the partnership was 'purely nominal. They never paid any attention to each other's works and never did a joint work.' Thirdly, to account for the seeming conspiracy of silence against Nesfield's historical importance, it must be remembered that Nesfield was a very retiring character, hostile to all publicity, or what he called advertising. So if *The Builder* in its obituary notice after Nesfield's death, writes, 'It is an open point whether it is to Mr Nesfield or Mr Norman Shaw that we are most indebted for the great advance which the last twenty years have made in domestic art', we can perhaps now regard that point as closed, and Sir Reginald Blomfield's remark that in the partnership 'Nesfield

[1] P. 340. Cloverley Hall cost £60,000 and was 450ft. by 440 ft. in size. Nesfield must have been a very well-connected young man.

[2] And, as a matter of fact, just a touch of *japonaiserie* in the lotus-flower friezes which had already appeared at Coombe Abbey and Cloverley Hall – very early cases and memorable as such.

talked about the work and Shaw did it' (p. 17) as unjustified. Another point, however, remains open, that of the sources of Nesfield's tile-hanging and Nesfield's 'Queen Anne'. George Devey (1820–86), it seems, has quite a good claim. Unfortunately Devey was also one of those who refused to have their houses publicized. In *The Building News* for 1886, Percy G. Stone, a pupil – Voysey was another – calls Devey merely 'one of the first revivalists of a better state of things', but Walter Godfrey, writing in the *Architectural Review*, volume XXI, in 1907, unfortunately with far too little documentation, insists that the Dutch brick gables at Betteshanger, near Dover, are of 1856. The big bow-window with many mullions and several transoms at St Albans' Court in Kent is dated 1864 ('peractum') and that certainly precedes Nesfield's and by an even longer time Shaw's uses of this motif.

Another unquestionable source for Nesfield as well as Shaw is Philip Webb. Though he was not older than Shaw, he had in William Morris's Red House, at Bexley Heath, already mixed Gothic arches and profiles with Queen Anne windows, and that was in 1859 (Plate XCI). Finally one more building has recently been mentioned in connection with the introduction of Queen Anne, J. J. Stevenson's Red House, in the Bayswater Road. That, however, dates from 1870 and so does not precede Nesfield even if it precedes Shaw.

For Shaw, at last to return to him, still designed Leys Wood, near Groombridge, in 1868 in a half-timber-gabled, tile-hung, Old English, Sussex style, eminently picturesque and inventive and with a great theatrical virtuosity (Plate LXXXVI). There is unlimited promise at Leys Wood, but of the spirit of Webb there is nothing, nor of that of Kinmel Park.[1] Four years later all that has changed, and Shaw's Queen Anne has arrived, and it is a Queen Anne at once very different from Nesfield's, let alone Stevenson's. The key buildings are New Zealand Chambers in Leadenhall Street, designed in 1872 (or, as E. S. Prior says in the *Dictionary of National Biography*, 1871), completed in 1874 and destroyed in the war, and Lowther Lodge in Kensington Gore, now the Royal Geographical Society, which dates from 1873. New Zealand Chambers (Plate LXXIX) was a terrace house of no more than three bays, symmetrical except for the charming touch of an oval window pushing the heavily pedimented portal slightly to the left. To the left and right were large office windows, with Georgian glazing bars, but no period motifs at all otherwise, just large windows to let as much light as possible into the dark ground floor. Above, the first- and second-floor windows are vertically connected into oriels, and the motif of the glazing is what became one of Shaw's favourites, the Ipswich motif, i.e. the motif of Sparrowe's House, at Ipswich, of about 1670, glazing with three transoms, except that for

[1] Yet Leys Wood was published in 1868 as by Nesfield & Shaw.

the double-width middle light the bottom transom is left out and replaced by an arch.[1] It is a fanciful motif, and the façade of New Zealand Chambers indeed introduced into the City a touch of sweet fancy, an elegance of handling and a spirit of novelty in total contrast to the ostentatious ponderousness all round. Lowther Lodge is by its pilasters in several Orders and its Dutch gables more dependent on Nesfield and even perhaps Stevenson, but Shaw had remained faithful to the picturesque asymmetry of Leys Wood – the house should be considered in the state in which it was before the east wing was added – and that distinguishes Lowther Lodge at once from Kinmel Park.[2]

Even so, that Shaw was inspired to this belated change of style by watching Nesfield can hardly be questioned. It must after all be remembered that the quiet and perhaps gradual cessation of the partnership did not mean a weakening of the ties between the two friends. They continued sharing their offices at 30 Argyll Street until 1876, when Nesfield moved to 19 Margaret Street and Shaw to 29 Bloomsbury Square. Also Shaw did not give up his Wealden style for Queen Anne. He carried on with both of them (see e.g. Wispers, Midhurst, 1875, and Merrist Wood, Guildford, 1877), and he also carried on with the Elizabethan and Jacobean type of house with its large, many-transomed bay window such as Devey had done (Adcote, 1877, Flete, 1878, Dawpool, 1882). This attitude distinguishes him from Webb, whose architectural expression is more single-minded and idiosyncratic, besides being more forceful. Shaw said of Webb, so Lethaby tells us:[3] 'A very able man indeed, but with a strong liking for the ugly.' Webb wrote of Queen Anne, no doubt meaning Shaw, in a letter of 1886, 'the dilettante-picturesque of the so-called Queen Anne style', and called it 'exceedingly artificial', and William Morris, Webb's friend and client, joined in by writing in an article in 1888 of Shaw's 'elegantly fantastic Queen Anne houses at Chelsea', listing them among the examples of a revival of architecture by means of 'a quite self-conscious and very laborious eclecticism'.[4] Bodley's work at Magdalen College, Oxford, is bracketed with Shaw and also Robson's schools for the newly-created London School Board, work inspired by the Shaw of Lowther Lodge, or perhaps more the Stevenson of Red House, since Stevenson himself worked for the School Board.[5] Shaw's first house in Chelsea was Cheyne House,

[1] The motif appears also on Devey's Betteshanger, but it is by no means clear whether it belongs to the work of 1856, or to the extensive later works. Nesfield used the Ipswich window in 1878 at Loughton Hall, Essex.

[2] Or Nesfield's equally classical Bodrhyddan, Flintshire, of 1872–3 which is also perfectly symmetrical.

[3] *Philip Webb* (O.U.P., 1935), p. 75.

[4] *Collected Works*, XXII, p. 329, from the *Fortnightly Review*, May 1888.

[5] See H.-R. Hitchcock, *Architecture: Nineteenth and Twentieth Centuries*, Pelican History of Art, 1958, p. 212. Also D. Gregory Jones in the *Architectural Review*, CXXI, 1958.

of 1875–6, followed by Swan House, of 1876–7 (Fig. 1). Both are in Chelsea Embankment facing the Thames. Both are characterized by the use of exceedingly long, narrow, segment arched windows, and this is indeed a Queen Anne motif. Shaw may have taken it from Church Row, Hampstead, in whose immediate neighbourhood he had just built himself a house. Cheyne House and Swan House have symmetrical façades too,[1] that of Cheyne House very restrained,

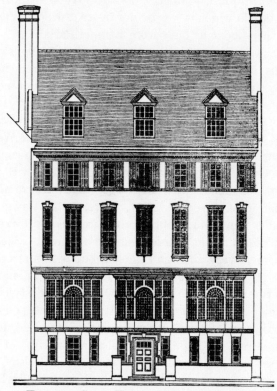

FIG. 1.   *Swan House, Chelsea, London*

that of Swan House with the delightfully enterprising motif of three Ipswich oriels squeezed in above a low ground floor and carrying a superstructure which would be too heavy for them, if it were not for the visual lightening by virtue of the equally excessively attenuated little oriels. Here is an originality, a fertility of invention and combination, and an elegance completely new at the time and within our inadequate categories, emphatically post-Victorian. That is Shaw's greatness in the English nineteenth century. Like Morris in his designs for tex-

[1] Though the plan of the whole of Cheyne House is asymmetrical.

tiles, like Webb in his buildings, he defeated the grossness of the High Victorian and reintroduced delicacy, sensitivity and a nice sense of composition and proportion.

For composition the finest example is his own house (Plate LXXXII) in Ellerdale Road, Hampstead, already referred to, and designed in 1875 – where a big three-storeyed and gabled Ipswich oriel is balanced by a normal canted bay-window, and the fenestration in between is syncopated so as to express the staircase against the rooms. Heights and widths of the windows vary seemingly arbitrarily, but in fact with great subtlety.

Now this was Shaw's stylistic position when the last quarter of the century set in. Adcote in stone, with Elizabethan windows, Merrist Wood, partly half-timbered and partly tile-hung, both date from 1877, and both exhibit in terms of their chosen styles Shaw's unfailing virtuosity in picturesque composition – what E. S. Prior called his 'stylistic scenery' – especially in the relations of large, many-transomed windows to tiny openings. It seems easier, when one looks at it, than it really is. Nor did Shaw consider his style, or styles or manner settled. On the contrary, two more changes were to come, the first of them represented by No. 170 Queen's Gate, of 1888, and Bryanston, of 1890. Bryanston (Plate XIX), curiously enough, though designed over thirty years after Nesfield's Kinmel Park, comes nearest to it in formal composition and relation of brick-walling to windows. Number 170 Queen's Gate (Plate LXXXIV) is, except for the pedimented doorway and the central dormer window, unornamented through-out, a three-storeyed block of nine bays, of brick with stone quoins – Wrenish in style and similar, for example, to the tall rows of chambers in the Temple.

From here there runs a direct way to the English domestic neo-Georgian of 1910 and after. And if Shaw in his later years is responsible for this English substitute for modern architecture, he is also responsible for the more reprehen-sible Baroque Edwardian-Imperial-Palladianism of official architecture. For Shaw in his sixtieth year designed Chesters in Northumberland with grand con-cave façades, giant detached columns and windows with the rusticated surrounds of alternating sizes that Gibbs was so fond of. Chesters is Sir Reginald Blomfield's favourite of all Shaw's works. No wonder, as it is from there that Blomfield's own style proceeded.

Shaw's most Baroque is also his last work: the Piccadilly Hotel, of 1905, and the unexecuted designs for the Regent Street Quadrant. One cannot help feeling uncomfortable in front of these displays of Shaw's undiminished power. Not only because the responsibility rests with him for breaking Nash's scale of pro-portions and his skyline, nor only because here the most original of British Victorian architects suddenly recedes into a line with the Belchers and Mountfords, but also because after the delicacy of Shaw's work of the 'seventies all this seems so massive, so showy, so vulgar. Historically speaking, too, these last works of Shaw are not of anything like the same importance as the earlier ones. Sir Reginald Blomfield, of course, did not share this view of the development. He writes:

> Street ... held with Pugin, not only that Gothic was the only Christian art, but that it was the only possible architecture ... It took Shaw many years to recover from this unfortunate early start; all his life was spent in working his way from it, to the monumental Classic, the goal of his ambition, which he never quite reached.

Shaw's position in English architecture is certainly not that, nor is it as simple anyway. His evolution and achievement must be seen in relation to the Victorian age *in toto*. It was the age of historicism in architecture. For the first, the pre-Victorian, generation there was no problem in this. You built Classical or Gothic as your client wished you to, or as the job seemed to require, and you were not too much worried about accuracy of details. Then came a widening of the sources on the one hand – Italian Renaissance, Elizabethan, French Renaissance – and, on the other, the new claims to archaeological exactitude. The former appealed to the more adventurous, the latter to the more responsible architects.

While Shaw was developing his own style between 1868 and 1875, among the new and spectacular buildings he saw go up were Scott's Gothic St Pancras Station (begun in 1865) and his Italian Goverment Offices, in Whitehall (1862–75), Street's Gothic Law Courts (1871–82) and Waterhouse's Gothic Manchester Town Hall (1868–77) and Romanesque Natural History Museum (1873–80). He cannot have been in sympathy with any of them, in the first place because up to his fifty-fifth year he was a domestic architect almost entirely and kept away from large-scale official or commercial building.

Yet he was also a historicist, as ultimately Webb and Morris were, too. He added to the then accepted styles two new ones, even if – as we have seen – the original initiative was not his – the Anglo-Dutch style of Kew Palace and Ipswich, and the William and Mary to Queen Anne. The influence of these innovations was great. Shaw's Dutch is the chief source of Ernest George's style of the Cadogan district, and of Harrington and Collingham Gardens, the most popular West End style of the late 'eighties. Shaw's Queen Anne inspired Mackmurdo, Shaw's country-house felicities Voysey, Baillie Scott, even Mackintosh, and far more of the architects of about 1900 than can here be named. A few more examples may be permitted to prove this point. Bedford Park (Plate

LXXXIII) is the first, that earliest of all garden suburbs, begun 1876 – Shaw's drawings for the church are dated 1878, for the inn and store 1880. Look at the inn and store and you would hardly believe that this is separated by nearly thirty years from the Hampstead Garden Suburb. Or go to Swan House and you will recognize at once the source of Voysey's tiny oriels on 14–16 Hans Road. Go to Adcote, and there is the source of Voysey's bay-windows at Wancote and and Broadleys (Plate XCVI), and Mackintosh's windows on the Glasgow School of Art. And so on.

Shaw was tall, thin and distinguished-looking, so Blomfield tells us, quick of mind, easily amused, suave and persuasive with his clients, and, as Lethaby adds, generous to his clerks. His office, as a school, was with all its variety of personalities no doubt the strongest force in English architecture between 1890 and 1910. There was Lethaby, theorist, prominent member of the Arts and Crafts Movement, a scholarly historian of medieval architecture and first head of the most progressive of European art schools, the London Central School. Then there was Prior, Slade Professor in Cambridge and author of the best books in English on Gothic art, and T. G. Jackson, the belated medievalist who was engaged on so many Oxford Colleges, and Sir Reginald Blomfield, and Horsley, and Macartney, first editor of the *Architectural Review*, and Ernest Newton, initiator of twentieth-

FIG. 2. *42 Netherhall Gardens, London*

century neo-Georgian. Lethaby built little, and what he built is without exception outstanding in quality and character. His first job, Avon Tyrell in the New Forest, was passed on to him by Shaw to whom it had been offered. His aesthetic and moral sympathies were more with Webb and Morris than with Shaw. Prior, on the other hand, was an architect of such *outré* originality that it makes Shaw's own originality appear quite sedate. His play with found materials, reminds one occasionally of Gaudí, his delight in unexpected plan patterns of Lutyens. Jackson took over from the Shaw of the Jacobean and later seventeenth-century stone houses; Newton, as we have seen, from 170 Queen's Gate. However differently they developed, they received their initial stimulus from Shaw, and that alone secures him a seat of honour in the Valhalla of the Victorians.

BIBLIOGRAPHICAL NOTE

This paper was originally written as a review of Sir Reginald Blomfield's book in 1940–1. It appeared in the *Architectural Review*, LXXXIX, 1941. Much had to be done to adjust it to independent publication and bring it up to date in the light of the research of others, especially Mr John Brandon-Jones, and my own maturer knowledge. Mr Brandon-Jones's paper on *The Work of Philip Webb and Norman Shaw* came out in the *Architectural Association Journal* in July–August, 1955. Of nineteenth-century literature the following was used (apart from Eastlake's *Gothic Revival* – see above): for Nesfield, *The Builder*, LIV, 1888, pp. 225, 244 and 269, *Journal of the R.I.B.A.*, 3rd ser., II, 1895 (by Phené Spiers), and *Architectural Review* I, 1896–7 (by J. M. Brydon), and II, 1897 (by Bulkeley Cresswell); on Shaw (apart from Blomfield's book), the *Dictionary of National Biography* (E. S. Prior) and a volume of bound illustrations at the R.I.B.A. called *Illustrations of the Works of R. Norman Shaw*. Drawings by Nesfield are at the R.I.B.A. (U 6) and the Victoria and Albert Museum (DD 7), by Shaw at the R.I.B.A. (V 10–12) and the V. & A. (DD 11).

POSTSCRIPT

After this paper had been completed two bits have come to light which ought to be added. Cockerell, so Mr. Dodd tells me, refers to Norman Shaw as 'quite by far the best pupil I have had' – i.e. at Cockerell's Royal Academy lectures, and Simeon Solomon, the painter, refers to Nesfield in a letter to Swinburne (dated 1869 in the new Yale edition of the letters, Vol. II, pp. 32-3) as 'one of our best architects, a man of great knowledge, invention and consummate amiability'. He is, Solomon adds, 'a fat, jolly hearty fellow, genuinely good natured, very fond of smoking and, I grieve to say, of women'.

PHILIP WEBB

JOHN BRANDON-JONES

Ⅰɴ ᴊᴀɴᴜᴀʀʏ, 1856, William Morris, having passed in the Final Schools at Oxford, articled himself as a pupil in the office of George Edmund Street. It was there that he first met Philip Webb, who, as Street's senior assistant, undertook the task of introducing him to the practical aspects of architecture and building.

Webb, then twenty-five, was only three years older than Morris. The son of an Oxford doctor, he had been apprenticed to John Billing, of Reading. After a short period with Bidlake and Lovatt, in Wolverhampton, he had come back to his native town to work for Street, who had just completed the Theological College at Cuddesdon, and was building churches at Bournemouth and Boyne Hill. Webb disliked the industrial Midlands and was delighted to come home to the university city he loved, and to work under a master he respected. On his return to Oxford, Webb was paid at the rate of one pound per week, only half the salary he had been receiving in Wolverhampton, but Street found in him an unusually capable and trustworthy assistant, and at the end of one year doubled his salary and promoted him to the position of 'chief clerk'.

During the spring and summer of 1856, Webb and Morris became fast friends, for in addition to architecture they had many interests in common. Both enjoyed outdoor activities, walking, riding, swimming and rowing together, and exploring France as well as England in search of masterpieces of ancient architecture. Webb taught Morris the elements of building construction, Morris in turn introduced his new friend to Burne-Jones and Faulkner and some years later to Socialism, for notwithstanding Webb's quiet and retiring nature, the enthusiastic Morris was able to drag him from his drawing-board to speak at political meetings, and for several years it was Webb's task as treasurer to collect subscriptions and balance the accounts of the Socialist League. Even before his meeting with Morris, Webb had become interested in Ruskin, for in 1855 he noted the purchase of *The Stones of Venice* for £3 10s., a considerable expenditure for a man whose total income was little over fifty pounds a year.

When Street moved his headquarters to London, in August, 1856, Webb and Morris migrated with him. Soon afterwards Morris, under the influence of Rossetti, gave up his architectural career for painting, but the close friendship between the two young men continued throughout their lives. Webb remained in charge of Street's office, where he was joined by Norman Shaw, who succeeded him as 'chief clerk' in 1859. Each of these two outstanding architects had a life-long respect for the other's talents and they remained on friendly terms, although their ways diverged in later life.

Shaw, as his practice grew, collected around him a remarkable band of pupils and assistants in which were included at one time or another nearly all the most promising young architects of the succeeding generation. Webb, on the other hand, always preferred to work alone. Shaw followed Street as an active and faithful member of the Royal Academy; but Webb, in spite of Street's efforts to bring him into the fold, refused to allow his name to be put forward for the R.A., nor did he become a member of any professional association. He contented himself with membership of the Royal Sanitary Institute and of the Society for the Protection of Ancient Buildings.

In London Webb worked with Street on competition drawings for Lille Cathedral and for the Government Offices in Whitehall, and it was during his time in the office that Street built St James the Less, Westminster, and St Paul's, Herne Hill. Street's work was interesting and up to a point successful, but to Webb it became more and more artificial. He began to feel that it was absurd for a nineteenth-century architect to try to act the part of a thirteenth-century master-mason. He saw that however brilliant the performance it could never be the real thing, and when Morris announced his forthcoming marriage and his intention to build a house for himself, Webb was ready to leave Street to work with him on the designs for Red House (Plate XCI, Figs. 3, 4).

The building they produced is noteworthy as the first work of what was later to become a remarkable team, but it was not so revolutionary as has sometimes been suggested; in fact it was only a short step forward from the vicarage houses

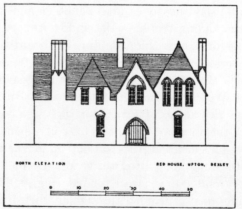

FIG. 3.   *Red House, Bexley Heath, Kent*

250

on which Webb had been working under Street, and those details that did not derive from Street's practice were based on precedents set by Butterfield, whose work Webb had studied and sketched. More revolutionary than any of the architectural features was the raising of the kitchen from its customary position in the basement, and the provision of windows allowing the servants to overlook the garden. While Red House was still building, Webb designed a house at Fairmile, near Cobham, now known as Benfleet Hall. The client was Spencer Stanhope, one of the group of young artists who had joined with Rossetti and Morris in decorating the Oxford Union. This little known house has since been enlarged, but it still has great interest as showing Webb's second thoughts on some of the less satisfactory details of Red House.

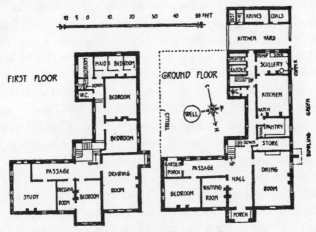

FIG. 4. *Red House – plan*

In 1862 Webb designed, for Colonel Gillum, a row of shops in Worship Street, near Finsbury Square. These buildings, which still exist, have a distinctly Gothic flavour and in the high-pitched roof are large dormers with a very wide overhang to the front eaves in the manner so common in the north of France. They obviously owe something to observations made by Webb and Morris on their French journeys. The Worship Street scheme was the only work that Webb allowed to appear in a contemporary architectural paper, *The Builder*. He refused a request from Eastlake, who wished to describe his work in *A History of the Gothic Revival*, giving two reasons, firstly that he made it a rule not to make unnecessarily public any work he designed, and secondly that he did not consider that his work could properly come under the category of Gothic Revival. No further illustrations were permitted by him until after his retirement in 1900 when, under pressure from friends led by Lethaby and Cockerell, he allowed *Country*

Life to publish photographs of Red House and several later buildings, including Clouds.

Webb's first major work was the great house at Arisaig, beyond Fort William, begun in 1863. It was built in a simplified Gothic manner, well adapted to the peculiar qualities of the two sorts of local stone. The bulk of the walling is of a granite-like stone, full of colour and sparkle; it can be split roughly to shape, but as it is unsuitable for dressing, all the quoins and window lintels and arches are made from a hard brown whinstone. The use of the two materials was most effective and the house was well sited on a hill-side overlooking Loch Nan Uamh. Unfortunately it was badly damaged by fire in 1935 and rebuilding on a reduced scale has produced a somewhat unsatisfactory result. Many years later, in a letter to George Jack, Webb said that the house at Arisaig was 'a product of his ignorance', but that there were some good points to the stable. This stable has survived, and it is a remarkable building, a single roof of cathedral scale covers coach- and cart-houses as well as horse-boxes and cow-byres. The entrance to the yard is by a great gateway with a pigeon loft above, and opposite to the stable Webb built a pair of houses for the factor and the coachman on the foundations of a farm-house destroyed by the red-coats who arrived just too late to intercept Prince Charlie on his flight to Skye. In this group of buildings Webb relied on practical planning and a common-sense use of material, with the result that they are completely 'dateless'; the only consciously architectural feature is the bold, ogee drip-moulding in the gable above the door to the stable loft.

While Webb was working on these commissions, Morris had been furnishing Red House and as a result of his experience had started his business as a decorator. Webb had of course been concerned in the designing of the Red House furniture and it was natural that he should become a partner in the firm. Taking second place only to Morris himself, he was responsible for most of the early furniture designs and for the setting-out and fitting-up of the stained glass. Webb designed several of the firm's heraldic windows and drew the birds and animals in a number of Morris patterns for wall-papers and fabrics. He worked so closely with Morris that in many cases it is hard to separate their responsibility for design and execution of their joint productions. Even after the reconstruction of Morris and Company in 1875 Webb continued to make an important contribution as a designer and consultant, although he was no longer a partner.

In 1868 Colonel Gillum asked Webb to design a house at East Barnet, since destroyed to make way for a building estate, and in the same year he built solicitors' offices on the north side of Lincoln's Inn Fields which still survive, although the interesting top-lit central stair has been removed and replaced by a lift. By far the most important work in hand at this time was No. 1 Palace Green,

Kensington, for the Hon. George Howard, later Earl of Carlisle. Webb had intended that the house should be faced entirely in red brick, but this was not considered good enough by the Commissioners of Woods and Forests, who insisted that it should be enriched with stone cornices and carvings in place of the robust moulded brickwork shown on the original design. The result of this official intervention is a rather disturbing lack of unity in the elevations as they stand today. The interior decoration of the house was of unusual interest, for the architect collaborated with Morris from the start and Burne-Jones and Walter Crane were among the artists employed on the decorations. Some of the Burne-Jones paintings can be seen in the Birmingham Art Gallery, but as the house has recently been divided into flats very little now remains of this once splendid interior.

The Howards proved good clients and in later years Webb was responsible for various works on the family estate at Naworth, including the house called Four Gables, originally intended for Lord Carlisle's agent at Brampton. It was through the influence of George Howard that Webb was invited to design the parish church at Brampton, in 1875, and here again he had the assistance of Morris and Burne-Jones, who made the cartoons for a fine series of windows. As it turned out, Brampton was the only church completed to Webb's design. Plans for other churches were made, but for one reason or another all were abandoned, and his ideas on ecclesiastical architecture can only be deduced from the surviving drawings and sketches. Among the most interesting is a small scale-drawing in the R.I.B.A. collection which shows in considerable detail Webb's conception of a cathedral, apparently inspired by the conditions for the first Liverpool competition held in 1884. Webb never completed the drawings, but his sketch plan shows a great circular central space nearly ninety feet in diameter, roofed with an ingenious Gothic vault. As always, he had the whole structure in his mind and was therefore able to indicate all the essentials of the scheme on a single sheet of paper. In addition to a half-plan giving the leading dimensions, there are sections and minute perspective drawings covering every important point both interior and exterior. It is unfortunate that Webb was never given the opportunity to develop a building of this scale, for he was perhaps the only man of his generation who could have rivalled the work of his friend Bentley at Westminster.

In the early 'seventies Joldwynds, near Dorking, was built for Sir William Bowman. Here as in all his larger houses Webb's plan was based on a two-storey central hall with gallery access to the bedrooms. This theme had been handled informally at Arisaig, but in the later houses Webb seems to have started off with a formal arrangement from which he departed only as necessity suggested. Three out of the four elevations of Joldwynds were symmetrical, as was the main block at Rounton Grange, designed for Sir Lowthian Bell in 1872. Joldwynds was built according to the local tradition, in brickwork with tile-hanging to the upper walls and gables, while at Rounton in Yorkshire the walling was of sandstone and the roof of native pantiles. Rounton (Plate XC) was a solid-looking masonry tower, four storeys in height with a pyramidal roof over each corner. With its ochre walls and orange-red tiling set among green lawns and forest trees, the house looked far more friendly in fact than in photographs.

At this time Webb's details had still a distinctly Gothic element, but his work was certainly not medievalist or archaeological. Even when he used a pointed arch or an ogee drip moulding the window beneath it was usually a sensible large-scale sash. The interior of Rounton was once again a work of collaboration, Webb himself designed much of the furniture including the vast oak sideboard and the serving table in the dining-room, Morris painted the ceiling of this room with his own hand, and Burne-Jones supplied cartoons from which the ladies of the household worked an embroidered hanging for the frieze. Other rooms were furnished by Morris and hung with his wall-papers and fabrics. Both Joldwynds and Rounton Grange have been destroyed by subsequent owners unable to live up to them. Fortunately Rounton was well recorded in a series of photographs by *Country Life*, but of Jolwynds there is no comprehensive record, although the contract drawings are now in the Victoria and Albert Print Room, and a set of progress photographs showing the buildings under construction has survived. It was characteristic of Webb that although he refused to sit for a portrait photograph, he had records made of the progress of a number of his buildings.

The Bell family, like the Howards, proved faithful supporters. Webb designed houses for several members of the family. He was employed as consultant for industrial buildings in their ironworks, and in 1890 as architect for Bell Brothers' offices in Zetland Road, Middlesbrough (Plate LXXXV). One of the most surprising and influential of Webb's houses was Smeaton Manor, built for Sir Lowthian's son-in-law, Major Godman, in 1877 (Plate LXXXIX, Fig. 5). A sym-

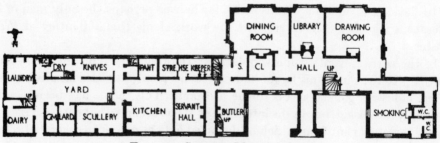

FIG. 5. *Smeaton Manor – plan*

metrical red-brick building with white painted sashes of Georgian proportions, its photograph might have been passed over without comment in a collection of illustrations of Garden City houses of the 1920s, yet it was built more than ten years before Norman Shaw's 170 Queen's Gate set the fashion for the English Renaissance revival, and thirty years before Edwin Lutyens built comparable houses at Great Shelford and at Chussex, Walton Heath. Those who think of Webb only as the architect of Red House and No. 1 Palace Green may be puzzled by Lutyens's admiration for him, but it was from buildings like Smeaton and Coneyhurst, near Ewhurst, that the younger generation learned to respect Webb for the freshness and common sense of his approach to building.

There was nothing medieval about Smeaton, nor was the house strictly neo-Georgian, but Webb was willing to learn from architects and builders of any period. Many of the details echo the work of older bricklayers in the near-by village, just as the stonework at Arisaig or Rounton followed the traditions of earlier masons and in later years Sussex stone was happily combined with local brick and tile-hanging at Standen. Notwithstanding his respect for the old and tried methods of construction, Webb's own unmistakable touch can be observed in every one of his buildings. He looked and learned and digested what he saw, but he never copied. Webb was also moving away from the Gothic in the interior of Smeaton Manor for, although there is still a touch of the old romanticism in the staircase winding somewhat perilously around a massive oak post, the main rooms of the house have white painted panelling and simple fire-places rather like those of an eighteenth-century country builder. Webb was now turning from the magnificent but typically Victorian elaboration of Rounton towards the lighter touch that was characteristic of his later work at Ewhurst or Standen. Smeaton Manor remained in its original condition until the death of Air-Commodore Godman, son of the original owner, but within the last few years the house has changed hands and has suffered drastic alterations – particularly unfortunate is the destruction of the unusual projecting porch and the substitution of a poorly-detailed stone surround to the front door.

In 1878 Webb designed New Place, at Welwyn, a comparatively modest house, for his doctor brother, but his main work between 1877 and 1886 was the building of Clouds, near East Knoyle, for the Hon. Percy Wyndham. To Clouds Webb devoted almost his whole attention for nearly five years and during that period he refused several other attractive commissions. This splendid house was not only the major work of one of our greatest architects; it was at the same time a social historical document of considerable importance and it is tragic that it has now been partially demolished and mutilated almost beyond recognition. Clouds was the ideal answer to a very special problem. It was designed as a setting for house parties in the days when the government of England depended to a great extent upon arrangements made at these elaborately informal meetings where Cabinet decisions were anticipated and society weddings arranged. Mrs Wyndham was one of the great hostesses of her day, and in her house one might meet the Balfours, the Curzons, the Londonderrys or the Tennants; among her friends she numbered Wilfred S. Blunt and Oliver Lodge, as well as the artists Leighton, Watts, Prinsep, Burne-Jones and Morris.

Webb first visited the Clouds estate in December, 1876. He walked over the site with Mr and Mrs Wyndham and took notes of their requirements, then in a letter, dated December 28th, 1876, stated his terms of employment:

> That all drawings whether of works done or only proposed should be my property (this not to exclude my providing you with all the necessary plans etc. for your future use after the work was done). That my payment should be at the rate of five per cent on the cost of all works done under my direction and further payment of all travelling expenses for myself and assistants. That if plans in whole and in detail are prepared by me ready to be laid before contractors and the works should not be carried out, two and a half per cent on my estimated cost of the execution of the works be paid to me. That if only preliminary sketches and plans be made, one and a quarter per cent on my estimated cost be paid me for the same.

These arrangements were agreed and after various consultations and further visits to the site Webb announced in a letter of January 29th, 1877, that he was ready to show his preliminary sketches.

The work went on and in April Webb sent a long letter discussing the siting of the house and the preservation of various trees. In this letter he wrote:

> In conversation with Mrs Wyndham I gathered that she was not quite content with the ground plan scheme for the house; now as it is very important that she should be quite satisfied as to the objects to be gained I should be glad if she would again closely consider the matter since my explanation. The point I've aimed at in the Hall is to get North and South light and view – in the Dining Room North view and East light – in the staircases to serve the more private and the more public rooms and in the offices to screen the East garden – nothing I saw on my last visit made me wish for another kind of plan, but as I am not to live in the house and you and Mrs Wyndham will, I should like to have your expression of opinion again before anything further is done.

In June Webb was collecting and considering samples of the local stone and brick, meanwhile an alternative plan was prepared. In August Webb wrote:

> Since I last saw you I have closely considered this last scheme and strongly advise your consideration of it, as much better meeting the peculiar site than the first plan and that it gives easily and well some of the particular arrangements which you and Mrs Wyndham expressed a wish for and which in the other plan could not be obtained.

Webb could picture Mrs Wyndham receiving guests in the Great Hall and he would, in the same spirit, consider a stable from the point of view of the horse. His imagination enabled him to visualize the practical problems of cook and scullery maid as vividly as he foresaw the effects of mass, volume and ornament involved in the aesthetic side of a design. Whether he was thinking of the mistress, the servants or the animals he was equally determined to spare no effort in providing accommodation to suit the needs of the inhabitants, but on any question of design as opposed to convenience he was despotic and would make no concession to please a client at the expense of his conscience.

The early designs for Clouds were planned round an open courtyard, but, as so often happens, it became apparent that the cost was getting out of hand. Webb considered possible reductions, but advised Mr Wyndham that it would be unwise to make the court less than about sixty-five feet square and in March, 1878, he wrote to his client warning him against too great a hurry:

> I must beg you not to be too sure as to when we shall be able to begin, for the amount of work before me is very great though I have been refusing further work elsewhere ... I must beg you also to remember that I shall have to add twenty to twenty-five per cent to my estimate if a first-rate London Builder is employed.

Later in the year negotiations were entered into with a contractor, George Smith, of London, and in the spring of 1879 bills of quantities were ready for pricing. The tender was received in May, but unfortunately it exceeded the estimate by more than £5,000, and as it proved impossible to agree to the necessary reductions Mr Wyndham decided to defer the whole project.

Webb then set to work again, abandoning the courtyard and reverting to his favourite plan with rooms grouped round a central top-lit hall. This third and final design was much more compact than its predecessors. Axial in its basic lines, it was in fact almost Classical, and it is interesting to find that at about this time Webb was studying *Vitruvius Britannicus* in the library of the Victoria and Albert Museum, where he made notes of Vanbrugh's work and copied the plan of King's Weston.

Tracings of the new scheme were submitted to Mr Wyndham in November, 1879, and by this time Webb hoped that the house with its offices and stables could be completed within the limit of £75,000. In June, 1880, the quantity surveyor began to measure the new drawings, but it was not until May, 1881, that the complete bills, including the stables, were in the hands of the contractor. Once again the price was too high, this time by £4,300, however, after due consideration Mr Wyndham decided to accept the tender; but owing to the sudden death of the head of the firm, George Smith and Company found themselves unable to enter into a contract and poor Webb was faced with the task of finding another builder and negotiating a fresh tender. He applied to G. E. Street and other friends for advice, and followed up their suggestions by personal inspection of builders' yards in Blandford, Bristol, Frome, Tewkesbury and Gloucester. In the end a satisfactory price was agreed with Albert Estcourt, of Gloucester, who had worked for Burges and was also recommended by T. G. Jackson. The contract was signed on November 4th, 1881, after nearly five years' preparatory work, but there was still a vast amount of drawing to be done, sub-contracts to be arranged, materials and workmanship to be checked and supervised and accounts settled. It was not until January 6th, 1887, that Webb was able to send Mr Estcourt his final certificate. Only two years later on January 6th, 1889, the greater part of the house was gutted by fire, but the interior was carefully restored under Webb's direction (Plate LXXXVIII, Figs. 6, 7).

The decorative work at Clouds was far removed from the somewhat gloomy richness of Webb's early interiors. He no longer relied upon painted decoration of the kind executed by Morris and Burne-Jones at Palace Green or Rounton Grange. In the Great Hall (Plate LXXXVII) the elements of construction formed the basis of the design. Unstained roof-timbers and gallery panelling were supported on Purbeck Marble shafts and combined with elegant white painted joinery and door-casings. Colour was introduced in limited quantities by the use of Morris tapestry and carpets. The drawing-room was all white with a delicately-modelled ceiling and frieze in plaster, the dining-room was also given a fine plaster ceiling, but the walls were panelled in oak and there was an antique marbled fire-place of Italian design.

The plaster decorations for all the main rooms were executed from meticulous detail drawings made by Webb himself. These designs were neither Classic nor Gothic but had something of the crisp freshness of early Renaissance or Byzantine carving. Webb made the drawings for much of his work on a little board he carried with him while travelling in Italy, during the winter of 1884–5.

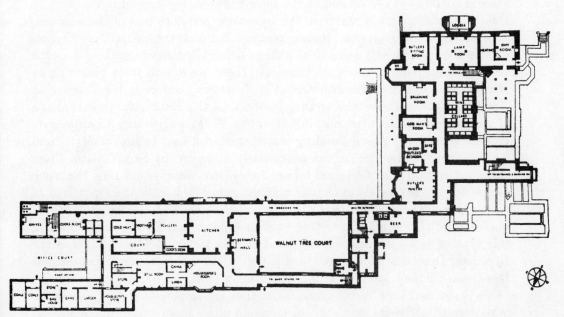

FIG. 6. *Clouds House – plan of lower ground floor*

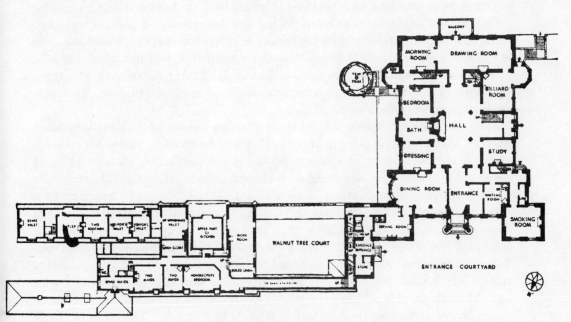

FIG. 7. *Clouds House – plan of ground floor*

259

He was thinking of Clouds and at the same time soaking himself in the work of the Italian master-craftsmen from the Byzantine period to that of Brunelleschi.

Notebooks used on this Italian journey indicate the breadth of Webb's interests, on one page is a sketch of a horse-driven Roman corn-mill and on the next a rough plan of the Villa Madama. There are details from buildings by Michelangelo and Brunelleschi, from the Colosseum and from the Duomo, at Torcello. Unlike Morris who stoutly maintained the Ruskinian view that the Renaissance had produced nothing of value, Webb was willing to appreciate grace and straightforward building craftsmanship wherever he found it, and while staying in Florence he was particularly attracted by San Miniato. From this time onwards he often used formal foliage decorations that echo the black and white marble panels of that famous church. Webb used these patterns in ways of his own. Avoiding direct copying, he translated from the Italian coloured marbles into plaster relief or fretted work in English oak. Excellent examples of this type of detail can be seen in one of Webb's last works, the Chapel of the Rochester Deaconess House, at 113 North Side, Clapham Common, designed for Deaconess Gilmore, sister of William Morris, in 1896.

Lethaby said that Webb would insist that flat ornament should usually be 'a pattern which would turn the white ground into a mosaic pattern effective at a distance' – the spaces as well as the forms must come right. Webb could not take refuge in bareness and baldness. He felt that to do this might be calling attention and might seem affected posing and advertising. A building was not to be noticeable by reason of its bareness nor by its elaboration. Sound building is the first necessity, and restraint is entirely right if it does not pass over into affectation. Webb had no more use for 'Evasionist Art' or a 'Negationist Style'. His mind was set on forming a natural mode of modern building. 'Common sense is our only ware,' he would say.

It is difficult to explain in words, or even by means of illustrations, what makes a Webb building more impressive than one designed by any of his contemporaries. He was working at a time when the vogue was for the 'Picturesque' and many of his fellows were concerned with the appearance rather than the structure of their designs. Even Norman Shaw was not ashamed to apply boarding to a brick or concrete wall to simulate half-timber framing; his perspective drawings were exquisite, but the buildings they represented were sometimes far from solid and the materials often lacking in quality. Webb's studies of beasts and flowers and ancient buildings prove that he too was a magnificent draughtsman, but he never made an Academy perspective. His architectural drawings were calculated to provide all the necessary information for the builder and nothing more. Every detail was thought out as a thing to be made. The ways in which pieces of wood or metal or stone were to be fashioned or fitted together were clearly shown and often a plan and section would be further explained by a small but accurate perspective drawing.

The conscientious study of every minute detail of design and construction gave to Webb's finished work a feeling of reality and solidity that contrasted with the scenic effects achieved by his rivals. This quality must have been apparent even when the buildings were new. It is even more obvious now, when they have been mellowed and matured by time and weather, while so many contemporary works have become shabby or fallen to pieces.

Webb's designs did not come easily. Not every building was so complicated or took so long to design as Clouds, but even his minor works, gardeners' cottages or repairs to old buildings, received a degree of attention that was rare in his time and is even rarer today. He obstinately refused to be rushed. He studied every possibility and would reject and reject again, and simplify and eliminate until he achieved the effect he wanted. George Jack remarked that his master was apt to be 'fidgety' about details of design, and Webb was certainly as anxious about technical matters as he was about mouldings or carved ornament. Drainage and damp-proof courses as well as chimney flues and under-floor ventilation were matters of concern.

In all his buildings Webb shows his strong feeling for the nature of his materials. He did not make a drawing of an elevation or a detail and then decide on the material. He would methodically investigate the materials available and examine the uses made of each by earlier builders. Then he would base his own design on the results of his study of the qualities and possibilities of a particular stone or brick. The profiles of his cornices and sills, for example, were varied to suit the northern sandstones or the limestones of the south.When he used a brick of a comparatively even colour, as at Smeaton, he relied on the arrangement of recessed or projecting bricks to give relief, while at Standen the varied colour of the bricks themselves allowed for surface pattern-making by the use of alternations of light and dark bricks in the walling and a concentration of the brighter reds around door and window openings. The same appreciation of scale in relation to the quality of material can be observed in Webb's furniture designs for oak or mahogany, and in his metal work and fittings in iron, copper or glass.

Webb, as a young man, was strongly attracted by the severity of the church at Mantes, and a love of simplicity on a grand scale remained with him throughout his life. He had learned much from Ruskin, but he came to the conclusion that the proposition that a building was not architecture without sculpture and painting was a misleading fallacy. In 1905 he wrote of Westminster Cathedral:

I looked in for an hour on Bentley's Church. It touched me sharply, he being gone, that I could not tell him what had come over me while looking at the outcome of this last living force of his life's efforts.

Webb was impressed by 'the effectiveness *without* the "overlay" of the strong-hearted Bentley's interior' and asked, 'Can we in these days call for it to be white-washed and left as it is? – which I should rejoice in seeing.'

Yet, although he was continually drawn towards the gaunt and primitive, Webb had an instinctive appreciation of urbanity and elegance. 'Professor Cockerell's gallery building at Oxford', he wrote, 'expresses what I mean by imagination with graceful simplicity.' In his own work, Webb found it difficult to balance the two aspects of his architectural vision.

An architect working within an accepted convention, ancient or modern, starts with a number of questions already answered; and because of this background he can produce a highly sophisticated design. But Webb by cutting himself off from the styles in a historical sense also to some extent cut himself off from style in the sense of elegance. His single-minded attempt to found his designs upon a logical study of the conditions of life and the nature of materials produced results that shocked, and still shock, those whose critical faculties have been trained and conditioned to the acceptance of a style as a basis for design.

Webb's work was equally unacceptable to orthodox supporters of the Classic and of the Gothic, and today it may be as puzzling to a generation accustomed to the conventional modern style as it was to his contemporaries. His careful studies and expert supervision resulted in a high degree of craftsmanship, but his buildings often lack the unity that can be expected of work conceived in a style. It was the unusual combination of an extremely fine finish with a completely unconventional approach that made Webb's work unique.

Webb was a hard master and the rigorous and uncompromising standards he laid down for himself and his clients could only be maintained at the cost of a considerable personal sacrifice. His private means amounted to no more than £4 per annum, his share of the rent of property owned jointly with his sister and brothers, he had to live on what he earned. In hard times, especially during the first years of practice, he and his brothers frequently made loans to one another, depending upon which of them happened to be in funds. During his forty years in practice, from 1860 to 1900, Webb's income averaged about £380 a year after paying his office expenses and clerks' wages.

The expenses of the practice were small. The yearly rent of the office and living-rooms in Gray's Inn was £60, and for most of the time he was paying between £250 and £350 in salaries for two assistants. As he never had to carry the overheads of a big office he could afford to accept the work he liked and to take his time over it. During the first year that he was working on the design for Clouds he was out of pocket after paying his draughtsmen, and over the whole period from 1880 to 1888, while he was putting almost his whole energies into the one job, his net income was less than £320 a year. But, because he knew that he was giving more than he was getting, he could treat his clients as his equals and give on his own terms – a very important matter to a man of his independent spirit.

In addition to his architectural practice Webb continued his close association with William Morris, and his importance as the grey eminence of Morris and Company can hardly be overrated. For many years Webb and Morris had a standing arrangement to breakfast with Burne-Jones on a Sunday morning, and at these meetings the three would discuss work in progress and plans for the future.

Webb and his protegés, George Jack and W. R. Lethaby, were responsible for the architectural side of practically all the decorative work carried out by Morris and Company until the end of the century, and it was to Webb that Morris's manager, Warrington Taylor, turned when the affairs of the firm showed signs of getting out of hand.

In 1867 Taylor wrote to Webb:

In order that I may get a living, that Morris may get extra money, it is absolutely necessary to appeal to you from time to time on these matters of business. We could not move another step without your professional assistance, and therefore if you will not be paid the firm must come to a stop – because sponging on you is degrading.

In 1869, during another crisis, Taylor wrote:

Is everybody to be allowed to do as he likes? Ned, W.M. and Gabriel egg one another on to every kind of useless expense. How long do they intend to play boy?... What is absolutely necessary to save the firm from ruin is this: Someone must see the books weekly or fortnightly. We want vigorous, stern action, if the firm is to be saved. If you do not act no one else will. Everyone treats it as a joke.

Webb was always willing to help, but discipline was hard to maintain and the eventual reconstruction of Morris and Company in 1875 had its origin in a letter from Webb to Morris, written in December, 1873, suggesting that the firm should be re-formed on a more business-like footing.

In spite of his characteristic reserve and his refusal to publish his designs, Philip Webb was one of the most sought after and influential architects of his generation. The majority of his clients came from a fairly compact section of English society, closely linked by family ties and political interests, and in the habit of exchanging country-house hospitality. Within this circle Webb's work was well known and his services were in such demand that he could choose his clients. In a letter refusing a commission for a large country house Webb wrote: ' ... for some time past I have decided not to undertake to build for anyone who is not conversant with my work and able to judge of what would be the finished effect of that which I should agree to carry out.'

Would-be clients who failed to persuade Webb to undertake their work were forced to go to less eminent or exclusive architects, but when they did so they might well demand that their houses should be designed in the manner of one of Webb's buildings with which they were familiar. For this reason, if for no other, aspiring architects of the younger generation found it a professional necessity to keep up with Webb's house-building as well as with the latest work of fashionable town-hall and church builders. In the absence of published drawings and Academy perspectives this could only be achieved by visits to the buildings themselves and members and students of the Architectural Association were therefore delighted to take part in the visits to works-in-progress organized by Hugh Stannus, an ardent admirer of Street and Webb. These excursions must have introduced many a young architect to Webb's work at Joldwynds, Ewhurst, Standen, or Great Tangley Manor.

The same buildings made a lasting impression on Edwin Lutyens, who, many years later, wrote: 'The freshness and originality which Webb maintained in all his work I, in my ignorance attributed to youth, I did not recognize the eternal youth of genius, though it was conjoined to another attribute of genius – thoroughness.'

While Norman Shaw passed on his own ideas through the young men he trained in his office, he was himself influenced by Webb, and several of his pupils and assistants were in direct contact with Webb through the Society for the Protection of Ancient Buildings. Lethaby, Gimson and Barnsley, while working for Shaw during the day, were spending their evenings sitting at the feet of Morris and Webb in the Committee Room of the S.P.A.B., and at the suppers at Gatti's which usually followed S.P.A.B. meetings Webb expounded his views and discussed architectural problems with his juniors. In this group of S.P.A.B. supporters were not only the men from Shaw's office, but also several members of the newly-formed Architect's Department of the London County Council, notably Fleming, Winmill and Hebb, who spread the gospel among their fellows. In later years Hiorns and Minton Taylor were also active members of the S.P.A.B. and of the Art Workers Guild. Through these men Webb's teaching had an important effect upon the buildings of the L.C.C. and his ideas were developed in early housing schemes at Shoreditch and Millbank as well as in fire-stations and schools, some of them as recent as the excellent brick buildings of the Hammersmith School of Art, the St Martin's School of Art and the Eton Avenue fire-station. As Lethaby said in his biography of Gimson:

> The S.P.A.B. was itself a remarkable teaching body. Dealing as it did with the common facts of traditional building in scores and hundreds of examples, it became under the technical guidance of Philip Webb, a real school of practical building – architecture with all the whims which we usually call 'design' left out.

Of all Webb's disciples W. R. Lethaby was probably the most influential, through his writing and through his teaching at the Central School of Arts and Crafts and at the Royal College of Art he was able to hand down the ideas of Webb and Morris to innumerable students of art and architecture. His final tribute to his old master took the form of a series of biographical notes published in *The Builder* in 1925 and reprinted as a book – *Philip Webb and His Work* – in 1935. It may also have been through Lethaby that Muthesius came to realize the importance of Webb's contribution to the revival of English domestic architecture, for Webb's work was described and illustrated in *Das Englische Haus* at a time when little or nothing about him had appeared in any of the English architectural papers.

BIBLIOGRAPHICAL NOTE

W. R. LETHABY: *Philip Webb and His Work* (O.U.P., London, 1935). (Originally published as a serial in *The Builder*, 1925.)

J. BRANDON-JONES: 'The Work of Philip Webb and Norman Shaw', *Architectural Association Journal*, June and July 1955; 'Notes on the Building of Smeaton Manor', *Architectural History*, vol. I, 1958.

MARK GIROUARD: 'Red House', *Country Life*, June 16th, 1960.

WILFRED SCAWEN BLUNT: 'Clouds', *Country Life*, November 19th, 1904. (This and the following articles were written with Webb's reluctant consent under pressure from W. R. Lethaby and Sydney Cockerell.)

LAWRENCE WEAVER and other members of *Country Life* editorial staff: 'Great Tangley Manor', January 21st, 1905; 'Standen', May 7th, 1910; 'Red House', June 11th, 1910; 'New Place, Welwyn', July 23rd, 1910.

GEORGE JACK: 'An Appreciation of Philip Webb', *Architectural Review*, July 1915.

NIKOLAUS PEVSNER: 'Colonel Gillum and the Pre-Raphaelites', *Burlington Magazine*, March 1953.

C. F. A. VOYSEY

JOHN BRANDON-JONES

IN WRITING and in speaking of architecture Voysey always demanded an open mind, ready for all healthy development, prepared to accept conditions that it cannot alter such as the advent of the machine. He knew that man's habits, customs, conditions and ideas were for ever changing. 'We must shake off the fashionable convention of obedience to style,' he said, 'and be sincerely ourselves, and recognize our limitations.'

The Voysey House is white and its windows are grouped in horizontal bands. These two easily observed characteristics seem to have been enough to link Voysey with the style of architecture at present known as 'Modern', the coincidence of white walls and horizontal lines is, on the face of it, supported by the call for *fitness* that recurs so frequently in Voysey's writings on art and architecture and, as he himself has noted: 'Men are quicker to discern likeness than difference.'

Voysey himself, like Frank Lloyd Wright, had no respect for his self-appointed successors and not a little resentment at their claims. Those who have time to study his own sayings and his own buildings can judge for themselves how far it is justifiable to class him as a 'pioneer of the Modern Movement'.

Charles Francis Annesley Voysey was born in 1857, in the same year as W. R. Lethaby, and one year after Sullivan and Berlage.

Voysey's father was Vicar of Healaugh, a small and isolated parish in Yorkshire. The family was a large one and according to Voysey his two elder sisters exercised a 'salutary and humbling effect upon their brother'. Two younger sisters separated him from his three brothers, who were in consequence too young to make satisfactory companions for him in his childhood. As a result of these circumstances much of his time was spent with his father.

It is not surprising that these early years should have been of supreme importance in developing the character of the son. The Reverend Charles Voysey was himself a most remarkable man. 'He believed in a Good God instead of an Angry One', and he was eventually deprived of his living and expelled from the Church of England for denying the doctrine of everlasting Hell.

Charles was fourteen when the family migrated to London and settled in Dulwich near to the famous public school to which the boys were sent as day-scholars as they became old enough. The eldest son, however, was unable to settle down after eighteen months, was withdrawn and educated by a private tutor until the time came for him to choose a profession. His grandfather, Annesley Voysey, had been one of the old school of engineer-architects, a builder of bridges and lighthouses as well as of homes and churches. This, coupled with the fact that anyone could then call himself an architect without having to pass an examination, caused him to agree to be articled to a distinguished architect for five years.

Voysey's professional education began in 1874 in the office of J. P. Seddon, a contemporary of Brooks and Bodley, who had in hand a number of churches and vicarages as well as the University of Aberystwyth. In later years it amused him to recall that, in spite of the fact that the art master at Dulwich had reported him as 'quite unfit for an artistic profession', Seddon entrusted him, while still a pupil, with the painting of life-size figures on the walls of one of his churches. His pupilage completed, he remained with Seddon for a year and then spent a short period with Saxon Snell. In 1880 he received an invitation to join the staff of George Devey. Voysey regarded this chance as providential. The work in the office was interesting and varied and he was given several 'outside' jobs that he enjoyed and remembered.

In 1881 Devey bought some land in Northamptonshire, adjoining the estate of one of his clients, on which he decided to build a pair of small cottages. Voysey was given complete control of this work; he made all the necessary drawings, ordered the material, engaged the workmen and lived on the spot while the work was in progress. He had to send a weekly time-sheet to the office and the only limitation imposed upon him was that the total cost of the two cottages must not exceed five hundred pounds!

Devey himself was a fine water-colourist and in his youth had been a pupil of J. S. Cotman. His practice was extensive, and he specialized in the design of country houses for the nobility and gentry. Among his patrons were several members of the Rothschild family and also the Princess Louise, for whom he built a shooting lodge in Scotland. He seems to have been one of the first of the 'Gothic' architects to realize that the men of the Middle Ages had themselves built small houses as well as buildings of monumental scale, and that for the domestic architect at least there was much to be learned from farm-house, cottage and barn, and it seems likely that his experiments helped to pave the way for the greater originality of Philip Webb and Norman Shaw. It is also clear that the earliest of Voysey's published designs were very much coloured by the work that he had been doing as Devey's assistant.

There can be little doubt that the bed-rock of Voysey's life and art was the religious and ethical creed in which he was trained by his father. It was natural in such a home that he should come into contact with the teaching of John Ruskin; in fact Ruskin was a patron and frequent visitor to the school at which Voysey's sisters were pupils. It was probably Ruskin as much as anyone who turned Voysey towards the Gothic rather than the Classic in his search for architectural ideals. Pugin, too, he regarded as a master.

'Pugin', he said, 'designed to the best of his ability to meet the requirements and conditions which were presented to his mind, classifying them and anointing them with his devout spirit, allowing his moral sentiments to play like a dancing light on every detail.'

Voysey considered that no other architect of the nineteenth century could compare with Pugin for knowledge of Tudor architecture and that for all his knowledge he managed to avoid falling into the habit of copying.

'You may search the Houses of Parliament from top to bottom,' he wrote, 'and you will not find one superficial yard that is copied from any pre-existing building.'

Pugin and Ruskin were the great prophets of Voysey's generation. He was also influenced by some of his immediate predecessors and near contemporaries, especially by Norman Shaw and by Mackmurdo. He recorded the debt of architectural students of his generation to Butterfield, Brooks (Mackmurdo's former master), Bentley, and Oldrid Scott, and said that it was from the work of Bodley, Burges, Godwin, and Mackmurdo that he learned that nothing inside or outside a home was too small to deserve the consideration of the architect.

In the years immediately following his apprenticeship, the critical years during which his own architectural handwriting was formed, the principal conscious influence was Norman Shaw, partly by direct observation of his buildings and partly through the Art Workers Guild. He considered that the period, in the 'eighties, when Shaw was in full practice, was 'more Gothic than Classic' and that so long as Sedding and Mackmurdo and Morris were working for the Crafts as handmaids to architecture much good work was done, but he lamented that soon after Shaw's time the Classicism of the Georgian type became fashionable and 'corrupted even the great Lutyens'. He had a very great respect for the ability of Lutyens and regarded his desertion to the Palladian camp as a severe blow to the establishment of a real English architecture.

Although he did not put Morris on the same level as Ruskin and Pugin he very much admired his work and paid him the curious compliment of saying that having once visited the Morris shop he did not dare to go again lest his own designs should degenerate into copies of Morris! On the other hand, he was completely out of sympathy with the social and religious opinions of Morris. He wrote to a friend: 'Many thanks for the offer of Morris's book. I do not feel I want to read him. He was too much of an atheist for me.'

Writing of himself, in later years, Voysey said that he had worked upon the principle that 'good design must grow out of requirements and conditions – that fitness is the basis of beauty, and distinction in design depends more upon personal character than scholarship.' Speaking of his early days in practice he said that 'the temper of the time was revolutionary against over decoration and elaboration, and there was a revolt against scholasticism, possibly unconsciously felt at the time'. These convictions were parallel to those of Sullivan, but the particular twist that was given to them in Voysey's work seems to have had its origin in the religious tendency of his childhood training and of his heredity. His own father had left the Church to become famous as an independent preacher and further back he was proud to trace his pedigree to Susannah, the sister of John and Charles Wesley.

Voysey believed that the moral and aesthetic aspects of an architect's work were essentially interdependent. In this respect his ideas were founded upon Ruskin and Pugin. 'It is not enough', he wrote, 'to have a vague sentimental liking for artistic work, sound reason must be sought to explain one's likes and dislikes.' But, the reasons he was thinking of were not the reasons of a materialist; he explained what he meant by 'fitness' in the following terms:

Fitness is a Divine Law, and the more we investigate Nature the more we become impressed by its fitness; therefore we do wisely to work on the same lines and strive diligently after fitness. Can it then be fit to use foreign styles to express English thought and feeling? The English architect down to the Tudor period was content to learn and understand all the conditions of his own country, to understand the character of his own countrymen and to express their emotions and aspirations. He was keen to learn the possibilities and limitations of his material, and, in order that we may benefit by his experiences in this direction, we should study all the pure English examples we come across, never forgetting that it is only unalterable technical qualities which we most need to learn, and not those accidents of passing fashion, or the changing manners and customs of different periods. It is very important that we should notice, for instance, the way the stone in different districts was used, rather than the existence of battlements or moats, which tell not of the history of building so much as of the manner of life of the people.

Respect for tradition was to Voysey natural and right, but he felt that it could become a dangerous enemy to progress if it was allowed to check men's efforts towards greater fitness and improved methods of serving their own time. 'Reverence for the past is admirable when exercised by the individual for his own guidance, but mischievous when imposed upon others.'

Although Voysey said that he would speak neither for the Classic nor for the Gothic style there was never the least doubt where his sympathies lay; he did not believe that good could come from working in any style, but he considered that an Englishman had much to learn from the Gothic builders because they were his fellow countrymen and had worked under similar conditions. The great Classical architects were foreigners who had worked under completely different conditions and the results of their experience were in consequence hardly applicable to building in England.

In a paper read to the Design Club in 1911 Voysey spoke of styles, and contrasted the Renaissance and the Gothic. This paper is one of his best, and every serious student of twentieth-century architectural ideas should read the complete report published in *The British Architect* for January 27th, 1911. It is only possible to reproduce a few short extracts here.

The clamouring for style is merely a cloak to hide our want of discrimination and many think that the establishment of a national style would make it easy for them to be in the fashion; most people want to be in the fashion as to taste. The discernment of fitness needs careful consideration of many subjects, and a wise, brave judgment, which the average man finds beyond his power or inclination. The Architectural Profession has done its best to encourage the adoption of the style called English Renaissance, because it is possible for the average man to obtain a degree of proficiency in it; it is easily crammed, and is a sure crutch for the halt and lame ...

Renaissance is a process by which plans and requirements are more or less made to fit a conception of a more or less symmetrical elevation, or group of elevations. The design is conceived from the outside of the building and worked inwards. Windows are made of a size necessary to the pleasant massing of the elevation, rather than to fit the size and shape of rooms.

The Gothic process is the exact opposite; outside appearances are evolved from internal fundamental conditions; staircases and windows come where most convenient for use. All openings are proportioned to the various parts to which they apply, and the creation of a beautiful Gothic building instead of being a conception based on a temple made with hands, is based on the temple of a human soul.

It was of course the baleful influence of the Renaissance that seemed to Voysey, and also to Lethaby, to be the stumbling-block in the way of a real revival of the art of architecture. It was therefore against Classical theories of design that they levelled their heaviest artillery. Eventually the English Renaissance revival fell to their attack, but twenty years later the attackers were dismayed to find that they had demolished one style only to let in another. The neo-Georgian had gone the way of the Gothic Revival, as Norman Shaw had prophesied – but it was replaced by a new importation of Continental fashions. And the architectural students still preferred foreign travel to a serious study of the English climate. On the subject of 'Modern' architecture, Lethaby wrote to a friend: ' – my double eye! Only another kind of design humbug to pass with a shrug. Ye olde modernist style – we must have a style to copy – what funny stuff this art is?' There can be no doubt at all that Voysey would have applauded Lethaby's sentiments.

Speaking of human needs in relation to domestic architecture, Voysey noted the following qualities as essential: repose, cheerfulness, simplicity, breadth, warmth, quietness in a storm, economy of upkeep, evidence of protection, harmony with surroundings, absence of dark passages or places, evenness of temperature, and making the home the frame to its inmates. Rich and poor alike will appreciate these qualities, he said, and the effect he sought to obtain may be understood from the following quotation:

> Try the effect of a well-proportioned room, with white-washed walls, plain carpet and simple oak furniture, and nothing in it but necessary articles of use, and one pure ornament in the form of a simple vase of flowers – not a cosmopolitan crowd of all sorts, but one or two sprays of one kind – and you will then find reflections begin to dance in your brain; each object will be received on the retina and understood, classified and dismissed from the mind, and you will be as free as a bird to wander in the sunshine or storm of your own thoughts.

In 1882 Voysey set up on his own account in Broadway Chambers, Westminster. It was not for several years that his practice grew large enough to occupy his full time, but he refused his father's offer to write to friends and well-wishers on his behalf. Voysey felt that a client should choose his architect because he had a liking for the man and his work, and that the advice of an architect so chosen would be more readily accepted than the advice of an architect chosen to favour a friend, or as an act of patronage. It also is probable that his religious and moral views would have been offended by any action that might have seemed an interference with the ordained course of events. Although he would not agree to accept help, even from his father, he did what he could to help himself, he entered for a competition – the Admiralty Offices in White-hall – and in due course he heard that his scheme was unplaced.

Exhausted by the effort of preparing a complete set of competition drawings single-handed he decided to take a country holiday, and went to stay with a friend, the master of a preparatory school for boys. On the staff of the school was Mary Maria Evans, who later became Mrs Voysey. His engagement proved an added incentive to work, but the only jobs he had were surveys and small additions or alterations. Then, as luck would have it, he paid a visit to his friend Arthur Mackmurdo and found him at work on designs for wall-papers and woven fabrics. It was obvious that there were opportunities in this field and Voysey obtained from Mackmurdo the technical information necessary to make a start. Success was immediate and Voysey sold his first design to Jeffrey and Company in 1883. His talent in pattern design was soon recognized as out-standing, and the leading manufacturers of the period began to compete for his work. Ten years later, in 1893, he was able to obtain a regular contract, with the Essex Company, under which he supplied them with twenty designs a year and they undertook to accept and pay for the work without the option of refusing designs they were unable to use. While he was building up his practice Voysey found that his income from paper, textile and carpet designs was an invaluable stand-by.

Success as a decorator did not satisfy Voysey. He wanted to build, and as a start he designed a small house for himself and his future wife, hoping to per-suade a wealthy friend to finance his venture. The scheme fell through and the house was never built, but in 1888 the drawings were published in *The Architect* and caught the eye of M. H. Lakin, later Sir Michael Lakin, who gave Voysey his first important commission. This was The Cottage at Bishop's Itchington in Warwickshire, designed in the same year (Fig. 8). Gradually other commis-sions came in, most of them from strangers who had seen the architect's work. The brother and sister of the first client both had houses built by Voysey. They and other early clients were Quakers who found the characteristic severity and simplicity of his work sympathetic to their own beliefs.

Voysey married in 1885 and for the next fourteen years carried on his practice from his home. He lived for a short time in Bedford Park, then moved to Streatham Hill and then to St John's Wood, where he lived first at 11 Melina Place and afterwards at 6 Carlton Hill. In 1899 he removed with his family to Chorley Wood and established a separate office at 23 York Place, Baker Street. His own house, The Orchard, was not completed until 1900, but while it was being built he rented a house near by. The office at York Place was retained

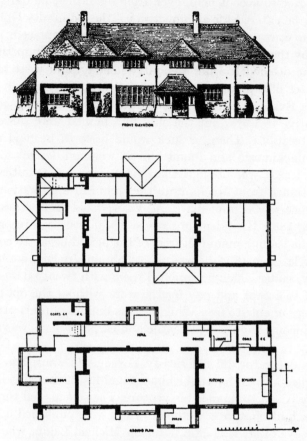

FIG. 8. *The Cottage, Bishop's Itchington*

until 1913 when the buildings were demolished. Temporary accommodation was then obtained at 25 Dover Street until Voysey was able to settle at 10 New Square, Lincoln's Inn, where he remained until 1917. In his later years he lived in a flat at 73 St James Street and once again his work was done in his home.

Even during the busy years at York Place the office retained something of its family character, for Voysey never employed a large staff of assistants. His office consisted of two rooms, one opening into the other. Both were carpeted and hung with water-colour drawings and photographs, and the folding doors to the private office were usually left open so that the pupils might overhear and learn from conversations between the principal and his client or contractors. Voysey himself worked at the drawing-board alongside his pupils and clerks, and he encouraged them to read all the inward and outward correspondence so that they should learn all that they could of architectural practice.

Punctuality and business-like habits were of the essence of Voysey's way of working. Correspondence must be attended to at once, working hours were strictly adhered to, and overtime was never found necessary. The letters were handwritten by the principal and press-copied by one of the pupils, no telephone disturbed the tranquillity of the office, yet, nevertheless, an amazing amount of work was done. Every building was meticulously detailed and in addition Voysey designed the wall-papers and fabrics, the furniture and carpets, the brass or silver lamps and fittings, the spoons and forks, the hinges and handles for doors and drawers as well as ceremonial keys and presentation caskets! Designs were made for mosaic and enamel, marble inlay and stained glass; models were made for carved work and sculpture, and in nearly every case the designer's instinctive understanding of form and colour was backed by actual experience and experiment in the craft for which he was designing. Like Webb and Street, Voysey designed every detail himself and his pupils or assistants had little to do but to make the necessary copies.

Voysey did not design in a 'style' nor did he make any conscious concessions to popular taste or to intellectual or academic theories. Changes of fashion, therefore, meant nothing to him and were never reflected in his designs. This gave to his work an amazing consistency, but both in planning and in details and mouldings a steady development can be traced. The unwary critic, however, may be confused by the fact that some of the designs were published for the first time several years after they were made. Reference to Voysey's own note-book, now preserved in the R.I.B.A. Library, is also occasionally confusing, because many of the buildings were entered several times if alternative schemes were prepared, or if the execution of the work was delayed.

The tall white house in Bedford Park (Fig. 9) so often illustrated by writers on the history of architecture, Voysey's first London house, has often been dated 1888, and one writer has placed it as early as 1882, although it was not in fact built until 1891. It is true that Voysey made drawings for a house in Bed-ford Park for J. W. Forster in 1888, but it was very different, both in plan and in elevation, from the building that later attracted the attention of the critics and historians. The drawings made in 1888 can be seen at the R.I.B.A. and they show a house with a conventional suburban plan. The front door leads into a narrow hall half filled by the stair, and the kitchen, scullery and outbuildings form the customary tail that ruins the garden behind. The elevation is also conventional with a forty-five degree tiled roof, a splayed bay running through two floors and a Tudor arch to form a porch. The upper part of the walling is

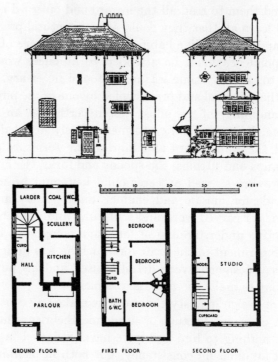

FIG. 9. *House at Bedford Park*

rough-cast and the ground floor is red brick. It might have been a good little house of its kind but there was nothing in it to mark an epoch.

A revised plan for the Forsters' house appeared in the *British Architect* in September 1891, and shows the house as it was actually built. The note accompanying the drawings gives the contract price – £494 10s. – but it indicates that the work had not in fact started at the time of publication. It is also interesting to read that the architect has had to prepare 'no less than eighteen sheets of contract drawings in order that the Contractor may *not* put in the usual thing – ovolo mouldings, stop chamfers, fillets and damnation generally!' It may seem pedantic to complain of an error of only two or three years in dating this little house, but the point assumes considerable importance when an attempt is made to assess the influences that affected Voysey's development. It is essential to place his early designs in the correct sequence, and a study of the drawings makes it clear that The Cottage, at Bishop's Itchington, and Walnut Tree Farm, at Castlemoreton, come before the executed design for the house in Bedford Park.

C. F. A. VOYSEY

During the early and middle 'eighties Voysey was mainly employed on the alteration and decoration of existing buildings. Some of these jobs were undertaken while he was still an assistant to George Devey, and the designs made at this time are very like those of Devey himself. Later in the 'eighties Voysey began to produce a series of designs for houses for imaginary clients, the drawings of which were published in the *British Architect* from 1889 onwards. Most of these schemes were reminiscent of Devey's work and of early Norman Shaw designs, but in some of the less ambitious houses that appeared late in the series Voysey discarded the Tudor mannerisms characteristic of Devey and began to show his own hand (Fig. 10). The 'House with an Octagonal Hall'

FIG. 10.   *Project for house for imaginary client, 1889, by C. F. A. Voysey*

which appeared in April, 1889, might well have been designed by Devey; the tiled roofs were decorated with dormers and Dutch gables, and the brick walls were broken up by patches of stone and half-timber. Just a year later, in April, 1890, came the design for a 'Cockney Villa minus ostentatious jimcrackery' – a square white box with a low pitched slate roof. Both in plan and in elevation the Cockney Villa seems to be the link between the first and the final designs for the house at Bedford Park.

Voysey himself said that his early work was influenced by Norman Shaw, and he was also in close contact with Mackmurdo, who, as we have seen, had helped him to find his feet as a designer of textiles and wall-papers. There is no doubt that Voysey was familiar with Mackmurdo's 'House for an Artist', the drawings of which were published in *Hobby Horse* in 1888, and Mackmurdo had already introduced, in his furniture and in the exhibition stands of the Century Guild, the lean classic profiles that became so popular a few years later.

Another factor, at least as important as the example of his older colleagues,

279

was Voysey's removal from a very ordinary semi-detached house in Streatham to an attractive Regency house in St John's Wood. The Streatham house, 45 Tierney Road, had the standard speculator's plan with the trailing out-buildings behind, the basic type to which Voysey's Bedford Park plan of 1888 belonged. The St John's Wood house, 11 Melina Place, was one of a pair. The entrance door was at the *side* of the house, opening into a square staircase hall and allowing the sitting-room to take up the full width of the front. Voysey apparently realized that the side entrance was the solution to the deep narrow plan and applied the same principle in the revised plans for Bedford Park. It is hardly necessary to add that 11 Melina Place was stuccoed and had a low pitched slate roof.

It is also interesting to notice that M. H. Lakin, for whom The Cottage, at Bishop's Itchington, had been built in 1888, again employed Voysey in 1890 – this time the design was for a new wing to The Cliff, at Warwick. The old house was stuccoed, its details were neo-Classic and its slate roof was hidden by a parapet. Voysey's new wing was also given a parapet and a slate roof; but, in contrast to the sash windows of the old building he used stone mullions and leaded panes.

Consciously, or unconsciously, Voysey seems to have responded to the severity and discipline of the Classical work with which he became acquainted at this critical point in his career. He was searching for 'truth and beauty' and, in spite of the prejudices instilled by his study of Pugin and his training under Seddon and Devey, he undoubtedly appreciated the neat and practical planning, and the simplicity of the Regency houses.

Some of Voysey's early published designs have roofs broken by innumerable gables and dormers and are planned in a way that would have made them difficult and expensive to construct, but economy was not a matter of importance in planning for imaginary clients – nor had it been very necessary in Devey's office when work was being carried out for the Rothschild family and their friends. But, as soon as he began to practise on his own account, Voysey realized that it was essential to cut down the cost of building and this necessity reinforced his instinctive preference for simplicity and led him to adopt plain rectangular plans with unbroken rooflines. His houses, large and small, were designed for easy construction, and by paying attention to details of planning he made the savings that enabled him to use first-rate materials and allow generous room sizes, while still keeping within reasonable limits of cost.

On the practical side of house-building Voysey had many unconventional ideas, some of which have recently been rediscovered! He advocated solid ground floors in order to do away with cold, damp, air spaces below; he fed his fire-places with air from the outside of the house in order to avoid draughts and cold feet; and for ventilation he provided air flues alongside the smoke flues. A low room with proper ventilation saved heating costs and was at the same time more friendly as a living place than a room of Classical proportion. Iron casements set in stone were less liable to rattling and more economical in upkeep costs than the customary wood casement, though they were comparatively costly in the first place; recent visits to one or two of Voysey's houses certainly confirm his theories on the subject of windows, the fifty-year-old casements are as sound as ever, wrought iron he used for the frames is practically rustless and requires a minimum of attention.

Voysey's concentration on the straightforward structural scheme certainly limited the variety of room shapes and restricted the possibility of experiments in contrasting spaces that was a feature of many Norman Shaw interiors. Voysey always designed the ground- and first-floor plans together, and, if possible, took the partition walls up through both floors and made them carry the roof timbers, whereas Shaw was comparatively reckless as a constructor. In Wilson Forster's house at Bedford Park, for example, Voysey placed the studio on the top floor and carried it up into the roof. His construction was therefore very cheap compared with that of Shaw's house in Netherhall Gardens (Fig 2.) in which the ceiling of the great first-floor studio had to be laced with steel joists to carry the weight of chimney-stacks and bedroom partitions on the floor above. Shaw produced a magnificent result, but his client must have paid a very long price.

Nearly all the houses designed by Voysey between 1889 and 1897 were given hipped roofs with wide eaves and elegant wrought-iron gutter brackets. The earlier houses followed the detail of Forster's house and had roofs of very low pitch, but at Perrycroft, in 1893, and most of the later houses the pitch was raised to forty-five degrees. In the smaller houses there was very little moulding, picture-rails and skirtings were reduced to battens with rounded edges, but sometimes in porches and fireplaces Voysey allowed himself a little more freedom and used cornices and columns of the attenuated Classic profile introduced by Mackmurdo, whose influence can also be seen in Voysey's earliest designs for furniture and metal-work. In the late 'nineties Voysey's work became more elaborate in detail. Norney, at Shackleford, and New Place, at Haslemere, were both designed during 1897 and are typical of the comparatively expensive houses he built just before the end of the century. The details are still distinctly Classical in spirit and the drawn-out cyma is used both in wood and in stone. There are semicircular hoods over windows and doors and decorative panels are applied to gables and chimney-stacks; other mannerisms, tried out but soon abandoned, were domical and double ogee lead roofs over bays or chimney-ingles.

In 1898 designs were made for three houses at Windermere and one at Glassonby. Their severity is perhaps a response to the harder conditions and wilder landscape in which they were set. Glassonby was to have been built of red sandstone, one of the few exceptions to Voysey's use of whitened rough-cast. The roof of 'M' section, was given top-lighting in the valley over the central corridor, and the ends of the roof were carried out to form gables. Broadleys, at Windermere, came a couple of months later – the earliest drawings, now at the R.I.B.A., are dated June, 1898 – and in this design there is a reversion to the hipped ends of earlier years (Plate XCVI). Broome Cottage would also have had a hipped roof, but the third house, Moor Crag (Fig. 11), had its

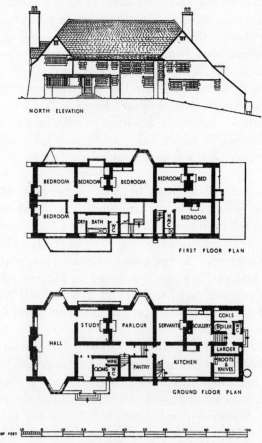

Fig. 11.   *Moor Crag, Gill Head, Windermere*

roof stopped at either end by means of cross-gables. A short ridge ran from back to front, stopping the main longitudinal ridge and showing a gable facing each way. The roof was that of an 'H' plan, but the arms did not in fact project. This device had been used a couple of years earlier over the library end of Sturgis's house on the Hog's Back.

It was from Moor Crag that the typical Voysey house of the 1900s was developed. His own house at Chorley Wood (1899), Pasture House, at North Luffenham (1901), Mr Walter's house at Pyrford Common (1902), and The Homestead, at Frinton (1905), are examples of Voysey's work at its best. In these buildings there is little trace of Mackmurdo's influence, and the elaborate detailing of Norney has been abandoned. Voysey, in his forties, was standing on his own feet, he no longer felt the urge to produce 'something different' that had at times been a weakness in his early work; he did what he liked and he could afford to turn down clients who were unwilling to give him carte blanche. His work was controlled by his love for simplicity and by his respect for materials and for the customs of the English craftsman.

While Voysey had been working out his own salvation, a new fashion had sprung up among the architects of country houses. The Gothic Revival was almost dead; but instead of attempting the approach from first principles that Voysey had advocated, the younger architects turned to look for another set of crutches and found the neo-Georgian style.

Voysey saw in this renaissance of the Renaissance the antithesis of every-thing that he had been striving for; he spoke against it and wrote against it and it was perhaps partly as a gesture of defiance that he flouted the coming fashion by once more introducing recognizably Gothic elements in his work. Pointed arches made a tentative appearance in his drawings during 1907, only to be eliminated when the time came for building, and in 1909 he had the chance to let himself go on the fascinating house he built for T. S. Cotterell at Coombe Down, near Bath. The client asked for a design reminiscent of Merton College and Voysey gave him a single-storey house built round a miniature quadrangle, elaborately detailed and decorated with sculpture and carving.

It was also in 1909 that Voysey designed Littleholme, near Kendal, one of his best small houses and one of the few to be built without a rough-cast coat. Local stone was used and it was laid according to the local tradition. Littleholme has a compact rectangular plan with a slate roof, hipped and pitched at fifty degrees.

A third design, dating from the same year, was the holiday cottage at Slindon for A. A. Voysey. The plans show one large room, twenty-four feet by twelve, on each floor. The stair rises directly from the living-room to the bedroom and at one end is an open sleeping porch above a bathroom and a diminutive kitchen. It is an attractive scheme and it must have pleased its author for it was one of the seven designs he chose to deposit at the Victoria and Albert Museum as representative of his work. It is interesting to note that the other six designs are Broadleys, Windermere (1898), Moor Crag, Windermere (1899), Dr Bowie's house at Colnebrook (1899), a house at Highams Park for Lady Henry Somerset (1904), one of the three houses designed for a site at Frinton (1908), and the design for Atkinson's shop in Old Bond Street (1911).

From 1910 onwards Voysey had a series of disappointments. Several more houses were built, all of modest scale, but during the next four years not one of Voysey's more ambitious schemes came to fruition. An interesting design was made for twin office blocks in the City for Spicer Brothers – straight cliffs of brick with unadorned openings regularly spaced. Then there was an unsuccessful competition scheme for Government buildings at Ottawa, of which only one elevation survives, and finally in 1914 drawings were made for two large houses, but building was prevented by the outbreak of war and for five years Voysey's notebook recorded nothing but minor alterations and designs for furniture, for memorial panels and the like.

Although he had no more important building work, Voysey remained alert and active to the end of his long life. He was always interested in current problems and prepared to argue for unpopular ideas and take his share in any artistic or architectural controversy. In the Academy of 1923 he was represented by a design for the elevation of an office block in which he demonstrated the possibility of introducing colour and moulded detail of Gothic type in a façade with nearly fifty per cent glass area. Later in the same year he put in a plea for the development of the Devonshire House site as a unit:

> On this site there is room for three towers of the size and majesty of Pugin's Victoria Tower at Westminster. Surely no one will deny the great beauty and design of that tower? Three such towers could be erected on the Devonshire House site, each tower would be a hundred feet away from any other building all round and would rise from a belt of trees fifty feet wide. Nobody's light and air need be interfered with in the least degree.

Voysey went on to discuss various points of detail and illustrated his idea with sketches – but once more he was out of step with the times. The practical men of the day built the buildings that we can now see and the progressives merely laughed at Voysey's design because he was perverse, or consistent, enough to clothe it from top to bottom with Gothic detail!

In this account of Voysey's architectural work the emphasis has been upon the development of his skill as a designer of country houses, for as luck would have it, the majority of executed designs were domestic buildings in rural settings. Many people must have wondered how he would have dealt with the limitations of a town site or the more complicated conditions of a large public or commercial building, and he himself regretted that he never had the opportunity to do work on a large scale.

Some indication of the work he might have done can be obtained from the drawings surviving from his unsuccessful competition schemes for the Ottawa Government Buildings, the Masonic Peace Memorial and the Croydon Town Hall. In all these buildings he came out firmly on the Gothic side and without a doubt his master was Pugin. Two earlier schemes of intermediate scale are also of distinctly Gothic cast, though the detailing is comparatively free; these are the designs for Lincoln Grammar School and for the Carnegie Library at Limerick. Very much plainer and more personal in detail is the design for offices in the City of London for Spicer Brothers. Another interesting design is the factory for Sandersons, built at Chiswick in 1902 (Plate XCV). The three lower floors have a maximum glass area between white, glazed brick piers, but the top floor is lighted through the roof, with the solid wall panels carried through to the parapet coping.

The only other examples of urban work that were actually built were the two excellent houses in Hans Road, Kensington, designed for Archibald Grove. Three houses were provided for in the original scheme of 1891, but the third was taken over by Mackmurdo. Voysey's first design provided for a rough-cast facing, but he evidently realized that such a finish would be out of place and unsatisfactory in town and the work was carried out in red brick with Ketton stone dressings – the revised elevation is dated 1892. The section of these houses is worth careful study, the ingenious use of broken floor levels and the planning of the mezzanines is sufficient proof that Voysey would have held his own if other opportunities had come his way. It is quite amazing, considering the success of these Kensington houses, that the only comparable job that came to Voysey in later years was the conversion of Garden Corner on Chelsea Embankment for E. J. Horniman. This too, was a brilliant piece of work. The interior of the house was completely gutted; the staircases, fire-places, plasterwork and panelling were all replaced; and the furniture designed by Voysey was as good as he could make it. Unfortunately the moveable furnishings have been dispersed, but the panelling and fire-places, and the unique green slate dado in the drawing-room, remain as examples of Voysey's work at its best.

Although Voysey was one of the most insular of English architects his designs made an immediate impression on his Continental contemporaries.

When illustrations of his work began to appear in the architectural papers and in *The Studio*, they were eagerly awaited and collected by architects and students all over Europe. Special articles on his work were published in *Dekorative Kunst* and other Continental periodicals and his influence, especially in Austria, in Germany and in Scandinavia, was considerable. A few years later, when a taste for 'Voysey-like' forms and details had become established, an appetite for the work of the younger architects Baillie Scott and Mackintosh followed. In the case of the two last there was to some extent an exchange of ideas with Continental designers, but Voysey retained his insularity to the end. If a foreigner chose to admire and emulate his work that was very nice for the foreigner, and in a quiet way Voysey enjoyed his flattery, but he never thought of returning the compliment, and he said that the importation of exotic architecture, though often lauded as evidence of catholicity of taste, was really the fruit of want of taste, want of sensibility to the fitness of things and a direct outcome of feeble imagination.

It has sometimes been suggested that Voysey was never appreciated in England as he was abroad. This is hardly supported by the facts. In his prime he certainly had as much on hand as he could tackle, and the work he did was described and illustrated in almost every technical journal of importance, and, of course, *The Studio* published not only architectural designs but furniture, fabrics and textiles as well as interviews and articles.

Voysey was frequently asked to address societies of architects, artists and craftsmen and his lectures were fully reported and duly discussed. In 1912 he was invited to deposit a selection of his designs at the Victoria and Albert Museum and further examples of his work were added between 1926 and 1930. In 1924 he was elected Master of the Art Workers Guild. He was one of the first to be given the distinction of Designer for Industry by the Royal Society of Arts, and in 1940 the Royal Institute of British Architects nominated him as the Royal Gold Medallist.

The basis of the legend of neglected genius is the fact that his output was small in bulk compared to that of those of his contemporaries who allowed themselves to become the general managers of design factories. Voysey did not believe that architecture could be produced by factory methods. He insisted upon being personally responsible for every detail and he would not delegate work to assistants. It is true in his later years he lived alone, working in his own flat, or spending his time quietly at the Arts Club; but his retirement from the bustle of ordinary practice was of his own choosing.

C. F. A. VOYSEY

BIBLIOGRAPHICAL NOTE

C. F. A. VOYSEY: 'Ideas in things', *The Arts connected with Building*, ed. Raffles Davison (Batsford, London, 1909); 'Patriotism in Architecture', *Architectural Association Journal*, June 1912, and discussion, July 1912; 'The English Home', *The British Architect*, January 27th, 1911; *Individuality* (Chapman and Bell, London, 1915).

Introduction to catalogue and description of exhibits for the exhibition of the work of C. F. A. Voysey at the Batsford Gallery, 1931.

Unpublished manuscripts: 'Tradition and Individuality in Art' in the R.I.B.A. Library, London, File no. 72.01 : 7.01. Also various autobiographical notes in the possession of Mr C. Cowles-Voysey.

JOHN BETJEMAN: 'Charles Francis Annesley Voysey, the Architect of Individualism', *Architectural Review*, October 1931.

J. BRANDON-JONES: 'C. F. A. Voysey', *Architectural Association Journal*, May 1957.

KAY FISKER: 'Tre Pionerer fra Aarhundredskiftet', *Byggmasteren*, 1947.

HERMANN MUTHESIUS: *Das Englische Haus* (Wasmuth, Berlin, 1904).

NIKOLAUS PEVSNER: *Pioneers of Modern Design* (Pelican Books, 1960); article in *Elseviers Maandschrift*, Holland, 1939.

VARIOUS AUTHORS: Articles and illustrations in *The Studio* from 1893 onwards.

Illustrations of designs in *The British Architect* from 1886 onwards.

The Architect (later *The Architect and Building News*) from 1885 onwards. A particularly interesting series of articles on Voysey and his work was published by an anonymous author in the spring of 1927.

Dekorative Kunst, and other German periodicals, described and illustrated the work of Voysey from 1895 onwards.

JOHN FRANCIS
BENTLEY

HALSEY RICARDO

[An obituary notice written for the *Architectural Review.*]

O<small>F THE</small> long line of 'Gothic' architects whose ancestry derives from Pugin and his contemporaries, the descendants are becoming very few, and the death of Mr J. F. Bentley removes one of the most distinguished of that race. Of the great men of fifty years ago, his particular forbear, I think, is Mr Butterfield, and in their attitude towards the work they had to do I find much in common. Scott and Pearson consciously, Pugin, Burges, and Street deliberately, attempted to put back the clock, and for an hour apparently stayed its hands. Butterfield recognized that the problems of his day had to be faced, and set himself to cope with them, using the forms of the medieval builders, because to the interest of his time in their constructions, he added his own early study and his own sympathy.

At the back of these men was the great force of cultivated opinion. The opening of the nineteenth century found the vocal part of England united – both poetry and prose were great powers in the land, and their power was widespread. On the wave of this aroused feeling rode the architects, urged and encouraged by all the genius and talent of their day. Since the days of medieval architecture, the arts of painting, sculpture, and architecture have never been of the people popular; perhaps they came most nearly so again in the early days of the Gothic Renaissance. Art, in England of the sixteenth century, was subliming itself into something that required a virtuoso to comprehend, and when the Classic Renaissance arrived in King James's time, it spoke a language that scarce anyone under the rank of noble was able to understand. But nobility was purchasable in those days; nobles were many, and, as regards architecture, unanimous. To be acquainted with the masterpieces of ancient and modern Italy was a' necessary part of a gentleman's education, as much as a familiarity with Ovid and Petrarch. The canons of taste were defined and accepted, and under this aristocratic and educated patronage advanced the architecture of the seventeenth and eighteenth centuries. Though the patronage was critical, there was not much actual interference with the architect; the minor mysteries were left in his charge for his selection, arrangement, and devising. The Romantic movement at the close of the eighteenth century found the architecture of the cultured elect growing ever stiffer, more inelastic, more rarefied; it came with a new gospel to a new audience. Gothic architecture was the indigenous architecture, the people's architecture, to be understood and appreciated by all and sundry; and for all and sundry to pronounce upon. But 'the people', long ago divorced from these arts, cared nothing about the revival. The motive power came from the book-reading class, and by this time the sluice gates of literature were well up and a flood of printed matter poured over the land. To this new tribunal the Gothic architects appealed. Old judgements were reversed, new decisions set up. Individual opinion, with an appeal to the High Court of Antiquarian Research, governed the erection of new buildings. Individual opinion at first, as became it, began modestly; but, as the area of research extended, it lost its timidity, and every student of the text-book examples of medieval buildings claimed to exercise his verdict. *Quot homines, tot sententiae.*

Living architecture was not called for. But you can't kill architecture – men must build, and to suit the conditions of their own time. The dream-palaces of Pugin and Street fulfilled no real want in the actual world; they took shape in obedience to an awakened conscience in a large section of the thoughtful public, and they owed their excellence and their impressiveness to the amount of passion and enthusiasm aroused. But these dreams had no substantial foundations; copies of medieval buildings, they came into being under quite other conditions, and they really breathed a different spirit. With Butterfield the case is different. He based himself on utility, fitness, and construction, and so far he worked side by side with the medieval builders. He had studied their work with deep analysis and sympathy, and he used from familiarity and preference their forms. The public who employed him called him a Gothic architect, and he accepted the appellation, but he really stood poles asunder from their conception of building and their processes of development. Mr Butterfield's strength lay in the great backing of popular opinion behind him; his great knowledge of medieval architecture, his keen observation of construction, that was collected and consolidated beneath him, himself and his passionate sincerity; and before him his faith and his ideal. Out of the fervour of this strength rose the ecclesiastical and collegiate buildings that call him author. Unlike his contemporaries' work, they have a quality of reality, of common sense, of directness; they breathe a passion as romantic as fervent; these buildings are not the attitude of prayer – they are prayer itself. Everything in them has been felt, has been seen; nothing eked out by formula or with padding.

And they take the world as they find it; there is no affectation, no pretence that they are the hitherto overlooked survivals of the Middle Ages. They stand on their own merits, in their own wholesome sincerity, and with a certain *gaieté de cœur* that comes from a consciousness that the work has been simply and thoroughly well done. Secure in his faith, and supported by the voices of the best in England of his time, Mr Butterfield could turn to his work and say 'It is well done'; and the shade of Christopher Wren would have hailed him as son. There have been many generations born and dead since Queen Victoria succeeded Queen Anne, but Mr Butterfield was a direct and true descendant of the architect of St Paul's.

A generation later came Mr Bentley. The wave of Romantic enthusiasm had broken, and was spending itself in multitudinous independent wavelets, spreading diffusely undirected. Its value as a power to lift one over the bar of apathy and inert resistance, and to carry one past the familiar shore to new heights and old forgotten landmarks, was gone; and a man had to reach shore with what craft and what knowledge of paddling he could command. For Mr Bentley there was no tidal wave awaiting him to mount, such as had swept Pugin on its crest; it was passing, but he followed in its wake, and was helped by the permanent impetus given to such spirits by the Church of Rome. I think one sees this loss of popular support in Mr Bentley's work – touch is not so secure, his ideals not so clearly defined. Like Mr Butterfield, he based himself on knowledge of materials and construction, but the quarter of a century that there was between them was pregnant with new methods of construction, new forms of materials, and corrosive of the old traditional processes. Early in the nineteenth century all England was covered with a multitude of medieval buildings, sadly ruined, mutilated, botched, abused, but for all that authentic so far as they went, and the traditions evolved from these early builders could authentically be discerned in the later buildings, gradually fading and stiffening as the eighteenth century drew to its close, but still unmistakably genuine. To such a repository Mr Butterfield had access in his youth, and from it he drew his knowledge. By the time Mr Bentley had directed his thoughts to the learning of architecture, much – I am afraid I say most – of this wealth of examples was gone. And worse than gone, for reconstructions stood in their place, mocking and repelling with their vacant history and their purposeless antiquarianisms the seeker after the story and purport of their existence. New facilities of construction, new materials, new adaptations, and new wants pressed upon the exponents of the verity and capability of the Gothic forms of architecture, and found most of them unprepared. A medieval builder knew his materials to the last grain of their possibilities, for he came of a long ancestry of experience, and his hand was never off them; the architect of our day, when the novelties were pressed upon him, arranged for their disposal as discreetly and intelligently as his nature would allow him, trusting to hearsay for their qualities; and there is a kind of resentfulness in such use, leading generally to a concealment of the actual services of these new agents, or else an ignorant braggadocio, still more destructive of progress.

VICTORIAN ARCHITECTURE

It was **Mr** Bentley's fortune, and possibly his choice – for fortune is more often under our grasp than we care to reflect – to enter on his life's work under favourable auspices. Almost as a boy he was put into the Clerk of Works' office when the rebuilding of Doncaster Church was in hand, and stone was passing from the quarryman, through the masons' hands, to the wrought stateliness of the present erection; and when still quite a youth he came to London and entered a builder's yard, where again he was in contact with the actual substances that go to make a building. It is this knowledge that gives the special qualities to **Mr** Bentley's work.

So far as can be done, working through other men's hands, he sets the stamp of his individuality upon every brick that is laid, every stone that is shaped, every detail that is wrought; and he does this not by torturing or straining his materials, but from sympathy with their nature, and knowledge of how to handle them. All through the mighty cathedral at Westminster, his greatest work, the dominance of **Mr** Bentley is perfect – not a thing has been done but has been done in his way, to his design, by his ordering. One mind infuses every line, every detail, and there is no escape from it. This omnipresence becomes oppressive – it is superhuman – one wants to escape into a freer element away from such tyranny. This is the despotism of architecture, and one wants an oligarchy of the aristocracy – a rule less rigid.

The church at Watford is a very complete instance of this power. Here **Mr** Bentley had full licence to do what he desired, and to carry as far as he chose his knowledge of past examples, of present possibilities, and his mastery of detail. Outwardly, and at first glance, it is a Gothic building, such a one as a pious founder might erect in the days when Edward I was stretching his long legs in England. But, on further reflection, one detects the difference between the product of one mind and the sum of many co-ordinated. The limitations of the human mind, wide and eclectic as that mind may be, still form a kind of imprisonment. In spite of **Mr** Bentley's great knowledge, in spite of his mastery over the forms that he was using, the church is a precipitate, not a growth. What is alive in it is his devotion. You have the human heart flaming itself out in sincere passion, lonely and autocratic. All that you see derives from his brain, and, in a sense, might have been executed by engines. The worker contributes his fingers, not his brains. Each craftsman was encouraged to put forth his best technical skill to carry out the design put before him, but there was to be no deviation, no thought of alteration. The design was a summary of **Mr** Bentley's knowledge and resources, and at the finish it remains purely that.

This refusal of the craftsman's invention acts injuriously on the worker; he concerns himself in consequence with perfecting his dexterity, and the sprouts of his humour and invention get frost-nipped, or wither from atrophy. Neither **Mr** **Butterfield** nor **Mr Bentley** could leave any 'school' to carry on their traditions, because neither of them permitted any growth in their work other than the growth in their own brains. All this apparatus of research, knowledge, experience and invention, together with the vast contributory contingent of labour, goes to the making of a crystal, not a plant – a crystal, brilliant, complex, many-sided it may be, but sterile; the residuum of the crucible, got by immense pains and at great heat by force of the ingredients, but without the agency, so to speak, of shaping hands. Such hands as were used might be called mechanical extensions of the official engine. This intense personality being, notwithstanding its various throwbacks into the past, a creature of its own time, passes also with the time, so far as subordinate matters are concerned. The main conceptions endure. The great architectonic qualities of size, romance, reverence, mysticism, display, touch chords that have been vibrating since man began to build – their utterance is heartfelt, perennial, universal. The dramatic interior of the Westminster Cathedral shows this (Plate XCIV). In its present unfinished state, it is full of impressive majesty – of pious sentiment. The shadow of the solid domes brooding at that great height, the tempered light from the lifted cupola over that chancel, the patient arches, the twilight recesses, these and the many other effects that impress the spectator on his entry, are architectonic ideas, indepen- dent of detail.

Here has been raised the shrine to the hopes and aspirations of the twentieth century, vast as befits our extended powers of construction, serious as befits the sense of our position in the world, and, as it at present stands, simple and impres- sive from its absence of learned details, of that invested interest laboriously col- lected, rather than foaming spontaneously out of the pent-up enthusiasm of its devisers, carrying a living cry within it.

The church at Watford exhibits Mr Bentley's powers of design unrestricted as to conditions of plan or expense; the Convent Chapel at Braintree shows them under greater limitations, both as regards the nature of the building, and the sum to be expended. But under this control, what a charming poetic effect has he achieved. At first sight, simplicity is the dominant note and a restrained quiet. On further insight, this skilled harmony is not obtained, one sees, by omission of features, vacant spaces, bald mouldings – the harmony has been obtained by vigilant thought and able concentration. The plain spaces are made contributory to the sober richness of the altar and the sense that the chancel is a shrine most carefully marked.

In the Convent of the Sacred Heart at Hammersmith – built originally for a Priests' Seminary – we have a kind of collegiate building that occurs again, with differences, in the Junior School at Beaumont College, Old Windsor (Plate XCII). The building tells its story simply and directly; the range of chimney stacks – without chimney-cans, be it noted – proclaim the nature of the rooms they serve; an air of cloistral severity pervades the place, and amid a blinding maelstrom of omnibus, electric tramcar, and every other form of horse-vehicle and man-vehicle in incessant whirl, endows it with a quiet nothing alien or superior to the seething mass of humanity at its gates.

It is strong, sturdy work, but, with the exception of the cloisters, it does not seem to have come together easily, especially as regards the garden front. This same consciousness of itself appears in even stronger form in the main front to the Junior School at Beaumont. The sides and back entrance confide their purpose with almost brusque candour, but the front is something of a frontispiece. Inside the building there is a pleasant quality of spaciousness and especially of light. The rooms smile with sunshine. For all young growing stock, sunshine is as important as food; but that is not to say that life in a greenhouse is wholesome. A room, especially a classroom, should be *riant*, but the laughter is a matter of manipulation and forethought. Ghastly sheets of undivided plate glass make a room seem desolate, sterile, inhuman – they arrest the playfulness of the sun's beams, and what they give in quantity they make pitiless from want of individuality. Quantity seems to be thought the sufficient answer. 'You have got twice or more times the area of glass one usually gets, how then can you complain!' But the light comes in from everywhere – to everywhere – there is no escape, no friendly twilight shelter, and our instincts that are within us, and our microbes that are upon us, cry out against this torture. There is a certain humorous eloquence in the treatment of this boys' building. Except in the Entrance Hall and Reception Rooms, where the boys do not go, unless on paralysing occasions, the whole building (the Chapel of course excepted) is severely simple; and, like the theory of lightning conductors, the boys' flashes of mischief are localized and drawn off to those parts of the walls and finishings where they are either innocuous or so glaring that they bring their own effacement promptly upon them.

The Entrance Hall, with its marble-stucco mantel-piece, its specially designed grate and metal-work, carefully chosen tiles and marble mosaic flooring, speaks a kind of escape from the sheer practicalities of most of the school building – an expansion from bald fact into 'style', and the quiet, nervous, tense prose is headed with a preface in the manner of Spenser, or – for there is a French flavour in the frontage – shall we say, Clément Marot? Like the critical and learned essays in the *Spectator*, we taste the flavour and charm of the cultured accomplishment, but we feel they belong to the category of the 'compositions' of the schoolboy – the real papers, that live in our memory and come home to our hearts, are those upon Addison's contemporaries, such as the Sir Roger de Coverley group. I wager that the living papers cost him less trouble and anxiety by much than the academic ones.

The Archbishop's House stands eastward of the Cathedral at Westminster, and in its dignified austerity comes rather as a surprise. The absence of scenic display or pomp gives the building at first glance a somewhat gaunt appearance; but this quickly gives way under the interest of its masses, and the able but subtle disposition of them. Conditions of site, of purpose, of accommodation, are here obviously paramount; they justify and embellish the arbitrariness of grouping. Incidents are uncalled for, and consequently they are few in number; but the few tell. The lion-headed brackets that support the balcony gape a terrifying welcome impossible to overlook. Inside, the house – though occupied – is quite unfinished, and every corner of it has as yet to shake hands and be familiarized with its inmates. The acquaintance should be both friendly and *sans gêne*, for the tone is pitched in a reasonable moderation; there is no shriek-ing, overblown *vox humana* stop apparent anywhere. Nor is there anything archaic or remote in the general management of the building; the materials are of today, and they are used to make the features of today; the distinction is in the proportion and the grouping. Moreover, it must be noted, the building is large enough, and the purposes of it clear and distinct enough, to exhibit these qualities.

The Venetian Saloon at Carlton Towers (Lord Beaumont's house in York-shire) is an example of Mr Bentley's treatment of decorative detail. The room had already been built before he appeared upon the scene, and his task was to complete it as it stood. Every item, other than structural, is from his hand; the painting, the woodwork, the fire-grate, the chandeliers, the furniture, fixed and movable. Item by item, the details are learned, forcible, and highly characteristic; but, taken as a whole, the effect is disappointing. There is a want of purpose about the decoration, the parts do not contribute to accen-tuate one another, or to lead to some prepared climax; nor have they, as in Mr Burges's work, a story to tell, which is their justification. The room is of such a size that it is neither habitable nor inhabited, but is to be used for purposes of display on occasion; the decorative treatment should be intelligible at a glance, no matter how complicated the scheme may really be when seen on further inspection, and the 'motive' of the decoration should speak to the spectator in a language of which he at least knows the leading phases and the dominant structure. The sonnet, in this case, is ingeniously and elaborately worded; but it is not poetry, for all the labour spent. In the land of advanced culture, the Muse occasionally forgets to keep her appointment, and appear.

We see, in Mr Bentley's work, the flower of 'one man' architecture; we may say, with almost untroubled confidence, that in Mr Bentley's case it has been done as well as it can be done. The Cathedral at Westminster (Plates XCIII, XCIV) has been pronounced by the voice of authority 'beyond all doubt the finest church that has been built for centuries'. What more, then, can we want? I view it as a last triumphant expression of that long line of architects who trace their ancestry back to Inigo Jones in England and the Cinquecentists (to speak broadly as to dates) in Italy. As the years sped on, we see gradually the groups of men that formed the guilds of craftsmen round the master mason deserting him. Each craft has become specialized, has an ideal of its own, and the master mason emerges, as architect, from the retreating groups, becoming more solitary, more individual, and more imperious with each decade.

Distinctions have arrived; the company has been separated into officers and privates; the officers have disbanded themselves, and the architect commands alone with scarce a lieutenant to aid him. The privates are divided off into separate functions and narrowed into mechanical excellence by special drill. The hum of wheels is heard, and soon a wreath of steam drifts across the roadway. Man's finger, that already had been extended into an arrow, a chisel, a gun, begins now to throw out a myriad of tentacles, enmeshing and enlarging upon the captives within their network. The brain is spent in organizing and directing this multiform congregation of partially absorbed entities. These are no longer individuals, with independent ideas and imaginations, but extensions of the presiding mechanism and of the brain behind it. They can originate nothing, or rather, for the statement is only partially true, it is when they come to a difficulty or a misfit, and they have to solve the problem somehow on the scaffolding, on the spot, that the chief interest of their work lies. A bit of living contrivance, living design, is generated, stimulating and freshening that part of the building where it originated. Such art is unconscious, is concerned with the actual necessities of the case, and if it happens to be beautiful, it is due to the call on the contriver's mind and temper to do something directly for the purpose according to the best that is in him. Under the conditions of today, as under the conditions of the Roman Empire, the workman is, and is desired to be, merely a mechanic. The Roman authorities impressed their soldiers, their prisoners, as well as their operatives, in the construction of their great engineering works. Today steam mortar-mills, steam cranes, the railways, and the varied batteries of machinery replace the thousands of toiling men. One man with his hand on the steam-valve represents the power of a century of men working with all their might, in accord. The splendid carcases that they produced we can reproduce; the possibilities of development that they saw and cultivated in their processes of construction we can discover. For the present we might, like them, let the matter of the veneering, the stucco, and enrichments generally go by, or else attempt a reversion to the medieval method, and form a group of artist craftsmen who shall collaborate on the spot, and with their own hands carry out their allotted portions of the building. The Imperial method we see in the great arched constructions of the engineers that carry our railways and stride across our roads and leap across our rivers, and so also in the construction of the Cathedral at Westminster. The exterior is masked, in great extent, by the polychromatic treatment and the profusion of detail; but the interior shows its kinship with the great Halls of Justice and the Baths of Imperial Roman days. Such a conception as this interior is one that can be carried out at the dictation of one man; it is what an army of builder's workman can do, thoroughly and well.

The romance and piety of those great masses of brickwork effloresce from the plain, common-sense, and direct treatment of the problem, and consecrate it apart from the usual commonplace of building, quite independent from the vastness of its scale. How in after years it may come to be encrusted is a matter of great interest, a little this side of vital; for, like the Pantheon or our St Paul's, the main conception is strong enough to override and subdue whatever may be the after-decorative treatment. Inside, the dominance of Bentley is seen at its best; we are in the presence of a great idea, conceived in terms that befit the conditions of today as regards construction; the co-operation he required was mainly mechanical – good, thoughtful brick-laying – and to this he put his constructive sense, his knowledge of what the requirements of his building would be, and ... the best of his life. The passion and the romance of the design reach us at once; the interpreter is effaced. Outside we get many things translated for us that overlay the message he had to give us; the quotations, though fresh, are almost too copious; we recognize them for quotations even when we cannot always determine their origin; and however able the insertion, however happy the translation, the downright plain prose is the real affair after all – prose so direct that it can be couched in a universal language.

For art, in the case of an architect, is an utterance that must be delivered through other men's hearts and hands. At the present day the architect stands much in the same situation as the composer of a symphony conducting an orchestra, the composition being written perforce in imitation of the old models. With such a man as Mr Bentley the score is minutely finished – the *tempi* are all indicated by metronome marks, the bowing and the fingering of

299

the strings prescribed, the phrasing and nuances described as well as words may do them. But in the composer's as in the poet's case, the music can be denoted in writing on paper, and, moreover, the composer can perform on all, or nearly all, the instruments for which he writes. The art of the symphony is quite a young art; yet it has already reached its term, and belongs to yesterday, not today. Mr Bentley, with his gifts of imagination, his stores of knowledge and critical observation, his thoroughness and whole-hearted sincerity, has been a contributor towards the progress of the art of architecture; and we, his successors, recognizing that in the main his work is done and that life long enough was granted him to achieve his work, are grateful to him for this achievement and the fresh impulse he has bequeathed us – so that we think proudly, as well as regretfully, that 'he has shook hands with Time'.

INDEX

INDEX

INDEX